CW01024002

THE BUFFOONS, A RIDICULOUS COMEDY

The Other Voice in Early Modern Europe:
The Toronto Series, 63

MEDIEVAL AND RENAISSANCE
TEXTS AND STUDIES

VOLUME 535

The Other Voice in
Early Modern Europe:
The Toronto Series

SERIES EDITORS Margaret L. King *and* Albert Rabil, Jr.
SERIES EDITOR, ENGLISH TEXTS Elizabeth H. Hageman

Previous Publications in the Series

MADRE MARÍA ROSA
Journey of Five Capuchin Nuns
Edited and translated by Sarah E. Owens
Volume 1, 2009.

GIOVAN BATTISTA ANDREINI
Love in the Mirror: A Bilingual Edition
Edited and translated by Jon R. Snyder
Volume 2, 2009

RAYMOND DE SABANAC AND SIMONE ZANACCHI
Two Women of the Great Schism: The Revelations *of Constance de Rabastens by Raymond de Sabanac and* Life of the Blessed Ursulina of Parma *by Simone Zanacchi*
Edited and translated by Renate Blumenfeld-Kosinski and Bruce L. Venarde
Volume 3, 2010

OLIVA SABUCO DE NANTES BARRERA
The True Medicine
Edited and translated by Gianna Pomata
Volume 4, 2010

LOUISE-GENEVIÈVE GILLOT DE SAINCTONGE
Dramatizing Dido, Circe, and Griselda
Edited and translated by Janet Levarie Smarr
Volume 5, 2010

PERNETTE DU GUILLET
Complete Poems: A Bilingual Edition
Edited by Karen Simroth James
Translated by Marta Rijn Finch
Volume 6, 2010

ANTONIA PULCI
Saints' Lives and Bible Stories for the Stage: A Bilingual Edition
Edited by Elissa B. Weaver
Translated by James Wyatt Cook
Volume 7, 2010

VALERIA MIANI
Celinda, A Tragedy: A Bilingual Edition
Edited by Valeria Finucci
Translated by Julia Kisacky
Annotated by Valeria Finucci and Julia Kisacky
Volume 8, 2010

Enchanted Eloquence: Fairy Tales by Seventeenth-Century French Women Writers
Edited and translated by Lewis C. Seifert and Domna C. Stanton
Volume 9, 2010

The Other Voice in
Early Modern Europe:
The Toronto Series

SERIES EDITORS Margaret L. King *and* Albert Rabil, Jr.
SERIES EDITOR, ENGLISH TEXTS Elizabeth H. Hageman

Previous Publications in the Series

GOTTFRIED WILHELM LEIBNIZ, SOPHIE, ELECTRESS OF HANOVER AND QUEEN SOPHIE CHARLOTTE OF PRUSSIA
Leibniz and the Two Sophies: The Philosophical Correspondence
Edited and translated by Lloyd Strickland
Volume 10, 2011

In Dialogue with the Other Voice in Sixteenth-Century Italy: Literary and Social Contexts for Women's Writing
Edited by Julie D. Campbell and Maria Galli Stampino
Volume 11, 2011

SISTER GIUSTINA NICCOLINI
The Chronicle of Le Murate
Edited and translated by Saundra Weddle
Volume 12, 2011

LIUBOV KRICHEVSKAYA
No Good without Reward: Selected Writings: A Bilingual Edition
Edited and translated by Brian James Baer
Volume 13, 2011

ELIZABETH COOKE HOBY RUSSELL
The Writings of an English Sappho
Edited by Patricia Phillippy
With translations by Jaime Goodrich
Volume 14, 2011

LUCREZIA MARINELLA
Exhortations to Women and to Others If They Please
Edited and translated by Laura Benedetti
Volume 15, 2012

MARGHERITA DATINI
Letters to Francesco Datini
Translated by Carolyn James and Antonio Pagliaro
Volume 16, 2012

DELARIVIER MANLEY AND MARY PIX
English Women Staging Islam, 1696–1707
Edited and introduced by Bernadette Andrea
Volume 17, 2012

CECILIA DEL NACIMIENTO
Journeys of a Mystic Soul in Poetry and Prose
Introduction and prose translations by Kevin Donnelly
Poetry translations by Sandra Sider
Volume 18, 2012

LADY MARGARET DOUGLAS AND OTHERS
The Devonshire Manuscript: A Women's Book of Courtly Poetry
Edited and introduced by Elizabeth Heale
Volume 19, 2012

The Other Voice in
Early Modern Europe:
The Toronto Series

SERIES EDITORS Margaret L. King *and* Albert Rabil, Jr.
SERIES EDITOR, ENGLISH TEXTS Elizabeth H. Hageman

Previous Publications in the Series

ARCANGELA TARABOTTI
Letters Familiar and Formal
Edited and translated by Meredith K. Ray and Lynn Lara Westwater
Volume 20, 2012

PERE TORRELLAS AND JUAN DE FLORES
Three Spanish Querelle *Texts:* Grisel and Mirabella, The Slander against Women, *and* The Defense of Ladies against Slanderers: *A Bilingual Edition and Study*
Edited and translated by Emily C. Francomano
Volume 21, 2013

BARBARA TORELLI BENEDETTI
Partenia, a Pastoral Play: A Bilingual Edition
Edited and translated by Lisa Sampson and Barbara Burgess-Van Aken
Volume 22, 2013

FRANÇOIS ROUSSET, JEAN LIEBAULT, JACQUES GUILLEMEAU, JACQUES DUVAL AND LOUIS DE SERRES
Pregnancy and Birth in Early Modern France: Treatises by Caring Physicians and Surgeons (1581–1625)
Edited and translated by Valerie Worth-Stylianou
Volume 23, 2013

MARY ASTELL
The Christian Religion, as Professed by a Daughter of the Church of England
Edited by Jacqueline Broad
Volume 24, 2013

SOPHIA OF HANOVER
Memoirs (1630–1680)
Edited and translated by Sean Ward
Volume 25, 2013

KATHERINE AUSTEN
Book M: A London Widow's Life Writings
Edited by Pamela S. Hammons
Volume 26, 2013

ANNE KILLIGREW
"My Rare Wit Killing Sin": Poems of a Restoration Courtier
Edited by Margaret J. M. Ezell
Volume 27, 2013

TULLIA D'ARAGONA AND OTHERS
The Poems and Letters of Tullia d'Aragona and Others: A Bilingual Edition
Edited and translated by Julia L. Hairston
Volume 28, 2014

LUISA DE CARVAJAL Y MENDOZA
The Life and Writings of Luisa de Carvajal y Mendoza
Edited and translated by Anne J. Cruz
Volume 29, 2014

Russian Women Poets of the Eighteenth and Early Nineteenth Centuries: A Bilingual Edition
Edited and translated by Amanda Ewington
Volume 30, 2014

The Other Voice in
Early Modern Europe:
The Toronto Series

SERIES EDITORS Margaret L. King *and* Albert Rabil, Jr.
SERIES EDITOR, ENGLISH TEXTS Elizabeth H. Hageman

Previous Publications in the Series

JACQUES DU BOSC
L'Honnête Femme: The Respectable Woman in Society *and the* New Collection of Letters and Responses by Contemporary Women
Edited and translated by Sharon Diane Nell and Aurora Wolfgang
Volume 31, 2014

LADY HESTER PULTER
Poems, Emblems, and *The Unfortunate Florinda*
Edited by Alice Eardley
Volume 32, 2014

JEANNE FLORE
Tales and Trials of Love, Concerning Venus's Punishment of Those Who Scorn True Love and Denounce Cupid's Sovereignity: A Bilingual Edition and Study
Edited and translated by Kelly Digby Peebles
Poems translated by Marta Rijn Finch
Volume 33, 2014

VERONICA GAMBARA
Complete Poems: A Bilingual Edition
Critical introduction by Molly M. Martin
Edited and translated by Molly M. Martin and Paola Ugolini
Volume 34, 2014

CATHERINE DE MÉDICIS AND OTHERS
Portraits of the Queen Mother: Polemics, Panegyrics, Letters
Translation and study by Leah L. Chang and Katherine Kong
Volume 35, 2014

FRANÇOISE PASCAL, MARIE-CATHERINE DESJARDINS, ANTOINETTE DESHOULIÈRES, AND CATHERINE DURAND
Challenges to Traditional Authority: Plays by French Women Authors, 1650–1700
Edited and translated by Perry Gethner
Volume 36, 2015

FRANCISZKA URSZULA RADZIWIŁŁOWA
Selected Drama and Verse
Edited by Patrick John Corness and Barbara Judkowiak
Translated by Patrick John Corness
Translation Editor Aldona Zwierzyńska-Coldicott
Introduction by Barbara Judkowiak
Volume 37, 2015

DIODATA MALVASIA
Writings on the Sisters of San Luca and Their Miraculous Madonna
Edited and translated by Danielle Callegari and Shannon McHugh
Volume 38, 2015

The Other Voice in
Early Modern Europe:
The Toronto Series

SERIES EDITORS Margaret L. King *and* Albert Rabil, Jr.
SERIES EDITOR, ENGLISH TEXTS Elizabeth H. Hageman

Previous Publications in the Series

MARGARET VAN NOORT
Spiritual Writings of Sister Margaret of the Mother of God (1635–1643)
Edited by Cordula van Wyhe
Translated by Susan M. Smith
Volume 39, 2015

GIOVAN FRANCESCO STRAPAROLA
The Pleasant Nights
Edited and translated by Suzanne Magnanini
Volume 40, 2015

ANGÉLIQUE DE SAINT-JEAN ARNAULD D'ANDILLY
Writings of Resistance
Edited and translated by John J. Conley, S.J.
Volume 41, 2015

FRANCESCO BARBARO
The Wealth of Wives: A Fifteenth-Century Marriage Manual
Edited and translated by Margaret L. King
Volume 42, 2015

JEANNE D'ALBRET
Letters from the Queen of Navarre with an Ample Declaration
Edited and translated by Kathleen M. Llewellyn, Emily E. Thompson, and Colette H. Winn
Volume 43, 2016

BATHSUA MAKIN AND MARY MORE WITH A REPLY TO MORE BY ROBERT WHITEHALL
Educating English Daughters: Late Seventeenth-Century Debates
Edited by Frances Teague and Margaret J. M. Ezell
Associate Editor Jessica Walker
Volume 44, 2016

ANNA STANISŁAWSKA
Orphan Girl: A Transaction, or an Account of the Entire Life of an Orphan Girl by way of Plaintful Threnodies in the Year 1685: *The Aesop Episode*
Verse translation, introduction, and commentary by Barry Keane
Volume 45, 2016

ALESSANDRA MACINGHI STROZZI
Letters to Her Sons, 1447–1470
Edited and translated by Judith Bryce
Volume 46, 2016

MOTHER JUANA DE LA CRUZ
Mother Juana de la Cruz, 1481–1534: Visionary Sermons
Edited by Jessica A. Boon and Ronald E. Surtz. Introductory material and notes by Jessica A. Boon. Translated by Ronald E. Surtz and Nora Weinerth
Volume 47, 2016

The Other Voice in
Early Modern Europe:
The Toronto Series

SERIES EDITORS Margaret L. King *and* Albert Rabil, Jr.
SERIES EDITOR, ENGLISH TEXTS Elizabeth H. Hageman

Previous Publications in the Series

CLAUDINE-ALEXANDRINE GUÉRIN DE TENCIN
Memoirs of the Count of Comminge *and* The Misfortunes of Love
Edited and translated by Jonathan Walsh
Volume 48, 2016

FELICIANA ENRÍQUEZ DE GUZMÁN, ANA CARO MALLÉN, AND SOR MARCELA DE SAN FÉLIX
Women Playwrights of Early Modern Spain
Edited by Nieves Romero-Díaz and Lisa Vollendorf
Translated and annotated by Harley Erdman
Volume 49, 2016

ANNA TRAPNEL
Anna Trapnel's Report and Plea; or, A Narrative of Her Journey from London into Cornwall
Edited by Hilary Hinds
Volume 50, 2016

MARÍA VELA Y CUETO
Autobiography and Letters of a Spanish Nun
Edited by Susan Laningham
Translated by Jane Tar
Volume 51, 2016

CHRISTINE DE PIZAN
The Book of the Mutability of Fortune
Edited and translated by Geri L. Smith
Volume 52, 2017

MARGUERITE D'AUGE, RENÉE BURLAMACCHI, AND JEANNE DU LAURENS
Sin and Salvation in Early Modern France: Three Women's Stories
Edited, and with an introduction by Colette H. Winn. Translated by Nicholas Van Handel and Colette H. Winn
Volume 53, 2017

ISABELLA D'ESTE
Selected Letters
Edited and translated by Deanna Shemek
Volume 54, 2017

IPPOLITA MARIA SFORZA
Duchess and Hostage in Renaissance Naples: Letters and Orations
Edited and translated by Diana Robin and Lynn Lara Westwater
Volume 55, 2017

LOUISE BOURGEOIS
Midwife to the Queen of France: Diverse Observations
Translated by Stephanie O'Hara
Edited by Alison Klairmont Lingo
Volume 56, 2017

The Other Voice in
Early Modern Europe:
The Toronto Series

SERIES EDITORS Margaret L. King *and* Albert Rabil, Jr.
SERIES EDITOR, ENGLISH TEXTS Elizabeth H. Hageman

Previous Publications in the Series

CHRISTINE DE PIZAN
Othea's Letter to Hector
Edited and translated by Renate Blumenfeld-Kosinski and Earl Jeffrey Richards
Volume 57, 2017

MARIE-GENEVIÈVE-CHARLOTTE THIROUX D'ARCONVILLE
Selected Philosophical, Scientific, and Autobiographical Writings
Edited and translated by Julie Candler Hayes
Volume 58, 2018

LADY MARY WROTH
Pamphilia to Amphilanthus *in Manuscript and Print*
Edited by Ilona Bell
Texts by Steven W. May and Ilona Bell
Volume 59, 2017

Witness, Warning, and Prophecy: Quaker Women's Writing, 1655–1700
Edited by Teresa Feroli and Margaret Olofson Thickstun
Volume 60, 2018

SYMPHORIEN CHAMPIER
The Ship of Virtuous Ladies
Edited by Todd W. Reeser
Volume 61, 2018

ISABELLA ANDREINI
Mirtilla, A Pastoral: A Bilingual Edition
Edited by Valeria Finucci
Translated by Julia Kisacky
Volume 62, 2018

MARGHERITA COSTA

The Buffoons, A Ridiculous Comedy

A BILINGUAL EDITION

Edited and translated by

SARA E. DÍAZ AND JESSICA GOETHALS

Iter Press
Toronto, Ontario

Arizona Center for Medieval and Renaissance Studies
Tempe, Arizona

2018

Iter Press
Tel: 416/978–7074 Email: iter@utoronto.ca
Fax: 416/978–1668 Web: www.itergateway.org

Arizona Center for Medieval and Renaissance Studies
Tel: 480/965–5900 Email: mrts@acmrs.org
Fax: 480/965–1681 Web: acmrs.org

© 2018 Iter, Inc. and the Arizona Board of Regents for Arizona State University.
All rights reserved.
Printed in Canada.

Library of Congress Cataloging-in-Publication Data

Names: Costa, Margherita, active 17th century author. | Díaz, Sara editor translator. | Goethals, Jessica editor translator. | Costa, Margherita, active 17th century. Buffoni. English. | Costa, Margherita, active 17th century. Buffoni.

Title: The buffoons : a ridiculous comedy : a bilingual edition / Margherita Costa ; edited and translated by Sara E. Díaz and Jessica Goethals.

Description: Toronto, Ontario : Iter Press ; Tempe, Arizona : Arizona Center for Medieval and Renaissance Studies, 2018. | Series: The other voice in early modern Europe: the Toronto series ; 63 | Series: Medieval and renaissance texts and studies ; volume 535 | In English and Italian. | Includes bibliographical references and index. Identifiers: LCCN 2017052904 (print) | LCCN 2017058246 (ebook) | ISBN 9780866987462 (ebook) | ISBN 9780866985925 (pbk. : alk. paper)

Classification: LCC PQ4621.C74 (ebook) | LCC PQ4621.C74 B9413 2018 (print) | DDC 852/.5--dc23

LC record available at https://lccn.loc.gov/2017058246

Cover illustration:
Portrait of Margherita Costa from Costa, *Lo stipo* (Venice, 1639). Photo credit: Charles Deering McCormick Library of Special Collections, Northwestern University Libraries.

Cover design:
Maureen Morin, Information Technology Services, University of Toronto Libraries.

Typesetting and production:
Iter Press.

Contents

Acknowledgments

This project would not have been possible without the support of Virginia Cox. Her seminal work on female authors has paved the way for a generation of exciting scholarship on long-overlooked women, including Margherita Costa, and helped set us on the path of this translation. We would like to thank Albert Rabil, Jr., for his support of the project at its earliest stages, and Margaret L. King for bringing it to fruition. Jane Tylus has lent us unfailing encouragement, as well as her eyes and expertise. A number of other colleagues have also offered assistance, feedback, and suggestions throughout this process, including Maurizio Arfaioli, Dario Brancato, Pamela Brown, Danielle Callegari, Mary Ann Carolan, Robert Epstein, Harriet Fertik, Valeria Finucci, Allen Grieco, Marco Guardo, Jerelyn Johnson, Ann Rosalind Jones, Shannon Kelley, Elisa Kollek, Tayra Lanuza-Navarro, Douglas Lightfoot, Francesco Lucioli, Carolyn MacDonald, Lia Markey, Shannon McHugh, Teresa Megale, Alessandra Montalbano, Eric Nicholson, Eugenia Paulicelli, Courtney Quaintance, Elizabeth Petrino, Meredith Ray, Eugenio Refini, Michael Roche, Sarah Gwyneth Ross, Beatrice Sica, Paola Ugolini, Mary Vaccaro, Anna Wainwright, Elissa Weaver, Yohuru Williams, and Jiwei Xiao.

Librarians and staff at the Archivio Doria Pamphilj, Archivio di Stato di Venezia, Biblioteca Apostolica Vaticana, Biblioteca Civica di Padova, Biblioteca Giovardiana (with the assistance of the Archivio Storico Diocesano di Veroli), Biblioteca Nazionale Centrale di Firenze, Biblioteca Nazionale Marciana, Biblioteca del Seminario Vescovile di Padova, Biblioteca Statale di Lucca, and the Folger Shakespeare Library facilitated research into Costa's life and times.

Sara Díaz would like to thank NYU's Faculty Resource Network's Summer in Residence Program, Fairfield University's College of Arts and Sciences for institutional funding, and Fairfield's Humanities Institute for several awards that have made this work possible. Jessica Goethals' research for this project has been supported by a grant from the Renaissance Society of America, as well as a long-term fellowship from the Folger Shakespeare Library. She also conducted a portion of the research while a fellow at Villa I Tatti—The Harvard University Center for Italian Renaissance Studies, and has received publication assistance from the University of Alabama Department of Modern Languages and Classics.

Finally, it is with deep gratitude and affection that we dedicate this book to our families, who cheerfully applaud the work of funny women.

Illustrations

Introduction

The Other Voice

Though little known to modern readers, Margherita Costa (c. 1600/1610–after 1657) was one of the most prolific secular female writers of mid-Seicento Italy. A singer, poet, dramatist, and rumored courtesan, Costa published an eclectic and expansive body of literature ranging from dramatic, historical, and devotional works to amorous, occasional, and satirical poetry.[1] She celebrated patrons such as the Barberini, the Medici, and the royal house of France in her publications, and performed before audiences in courts across Italy and Europe. As versatile in content and style as she was in genre, she did not limit herself to the high registers with which she exalted this store of elite benefactors. She also embraced a farcical and ribald approach to courtly life in a number of her works, capturing the appetites and entertainments of her age. Costa's 1641 burlesque comedy *Li buffoni,* or *The Buffoons*, is exemplary of her satirical pen.[2] Showcasing a cast of unconventional characters engaged in both erotic and bizarre occupations—a group composed of dwarfs, hunchbacks, and the titular buffoons—this "ridiculous comedy" caricatures Florence under Grand Duke Ferdinando II de' Medici.

With *The Buffoons*, the first female-authored comedy published in Italy, Costa participated in a tradition of women's dramaturgy that included such notable figures as Isabella Andreini (1562–1604), Maddalena Campiglia (1553–1595), Barbara Torelli Benedetti (1546–post-1603), and Valeria Miani (c. 1563?–post 1620). While these predecessors made bold incursions into the realm of male letters through pastoral and tragedy, Costa experimented with risqué and slapstick comedy in a period increasingly hostile to female authorship. The late Cinquecento and the first years of the Seicento had still boasted a myriad of prominent and influential women writers, but their numbers declined sharply mid-century, the very moment of Costa's activity. Aspiring female authors faced a number of obstacles in this period: male-authored polemical works increasingly

1. Costa is thus an important exception to Laura Benedetti's assertion that Lucrezia Marinella was "the only early modern Italian woman writer to move so freely among different genres"; Lucrezia Marinella, *Exhortations to Women and to Others If They Please*, ed. and trans. Laura Benedetti (Toronto: Centre for Reformation and Renaissance Studies, 2012), 2.

2. Margherita Costa, *Li buffoni, commedia ridicola* (Florence: Massi e Landi, 1641). In the introduction to her edited volume of select Costa poems, Natalia Costa-Zalessow argues that the work must have been written in 1638–39, before Stefano della Bella, the artist who executed the frontispiece, moved to Paris; Margherita Costa, *Voice of a Virtuosa and Courtesan: Selected Poems of Margherita Costa*, ed. Natalia Costa-Zalessow, trans. Joan E. Borrelli (New York: Bordighera Press, 2015), 34. However, Della Bella continued to work periodically for the Medici even when based in Rome during the 1630s, so distance did not necessarily preclude his collaboration at a later date.

targeted women; a general slump in female authority in Italy's courts, save select locations like Florence, reduced the number of patronesses; and many women were hesitant to associate themselves with the sexual suggestiveness of baroque stylistics.[3] Though Costa was not the only women writing in these years—Lucrezia Marinella published her epic *L'Enrico ovvero Bisanzio acquistato* (Enrico, or Byzantium Conquered) in 1635, for example, while the Venetian nun Arcangela Tarabotti composed a number of works in the 1640s and 1650s—she was both the most fruitful and the most unusual. Nor did her efforts go unnoticed; Costa won the support of patrons and male literary figures alike. Despite her singularity and long list of novel publications, however, this charismatic figure still remains understudied. Contemporary scholarship has largely overlooked her works as a consequence of lingering concerns over her personal sexual morality and the aesthetic value of baroque literature more broadly. The present facing-pages edition of *The Buffoons* aims to introduce readers to this *sui generis* figure and her delightful comedy, and to re-position her within seventeenth-century literary and performative culture.

The Life and Works of Margherita Costa

Like a number of Costa's biographical details, her dates are somewhat hazy. Her contemporaries place her birth in 1600 or 1610, and she last surfaces in 1657.[4] She began her singing career in her native Rome and throughout her literary engagement consistently emblazoned her cover pages with the name "Margherita Costa romana."[5] These volumes offer occasional glimpses into her life through dedicatory letters and some autobiographical poetry, though these moments should be treated with the distance and caution appropriate to the enterprise of examining

3. See especially the chapter "Backlash, 1590–1650," in Virginia Cox, *Women's Writing in Italy, 1400–1650* (Baltimore: Johns Hopkins University Press, 2008), 166–227.

4. For the main biographical studies of Costa, see Dante Bianchi's two-part "Una cortigiana rimatrice del Seicento: Margherita Costa," *Rassegna critica della letteratura italiana* 29 (1924): 1–31 and 187–203; and 30 (1925): 158–211; Natalia Costa-Zalessow, "Margherita Costa," in *Seventeenth-Century Italian Poets and Dramatists*, ed. Albert N. Mancini and Glenn Palen Pierce (Detroit: Gale Cengage Learning, 2008): 113-18; and Martino Capucci, "Costa, Margherita," in *Dizionario biografico degli italiani* (hereinafter *DBI*) 30 (Rome: Istituto della Enciclopedia italiana, 1984): 233–34; <http://www.treccani.it/enciclopedia/margherita-costa_(Dizionario-Biografico)/> .

5. For reasons that are unclear, a small number of commenters have described Costa as being from Ferrara. See, for example, Alberto Ghislanzoni, *Luigi Rossi (Aloysius de Rubeis): Biografia e analisi delle composizioni* (Milan: Fratelli Bocca, 1954), 154. Also for obscure reasons, the by-line for her final work, *Gl'amori della luna* (Venice: Giuliani, 1654), reads "Maria Margherita Costa." Assorted sources, primarily from the nineteenth and twentieth centuries, call her "Margherita Costa Ronaca," a surname that does not appear in any of her works. Costa-Zalessow hypothesizes that it may originate from an erroneous transcription of "romana"; Costa, *Voice of a Virtuosa and Courtesan*, 23.

literary works for historical facts. Medieval and early modern writers often constructed authorial personas through the revelation of ostensibly personal details, and Costa was no exception. Similarly, much of the available information about her early life originates in the satirical works of her contemporary Janus Nicius Erythraeus (the Latin pen name of Giovanni Vittorio Rossi) and must therefore be approached with prudent skepticism.[6]

By such accounts, her family was of humble social standing.[7] Costa had at least two sisters, one a fellow singer and another a nun, as well as a brother who gained an unseemly reputation due to his involvement in physical altercations and potentially to activities as a bravo in the Barberini's employ. Erythraeus suggests that Costa's father pushed her and her sister, Anna Francesca (called "La Checca"), into the role of court singer (*cantante di camera*).[8] While opera flourished in Rome during this period thanks to the talent attracted by Barberini patronage, its stages were prohibited to women.[9] Excluded from public Roman performances and replaced by castrati due to a papal ban motivated by concerns over female morality, the city's female singers performed in more private venues that lent themselves to blurred lines—both perceptual and at times actual—between being a vocalist and a courtesan.[10] As Susan McClary notes in her study of desire and seventeenth-century music, many "skilled female musicians practiced their arts as courtesans, in which case the selling of the voice attached directly to the prostitution of the body and vocal prowess operated quite literally as siren

6. For a discussion of Erythraeus, see Luisella Giachino. "Cicero libertinus: La satira della Roma barberiniana nell'*Eudemia* dell'Eritreo," *Studi secenteschi* 43 (2002): 185–215; and Luigi Gerboni, *Un umanista nel Seicento, Giano Nicio Eritreo: Studio biografico critico* (Città di Castello: S. Lapi, 1899).

7. See Bianchi, "Una cortigiana rimatrice del Seicento," 29:3.

8. Janus Nicius Erythraeus [ps. Giovanni Vittorio Rossi], *Eudemiae libri decem* (Amsterdam: Iodocum Kalcovium et socios, 1645), 84–86.

9. On Urban VIII (Maffeo Barberini) and his nephews Cardinal Francesco, Don Taddeo, and Cardinal Antonio Barberini as musical patrons, see Frederick Hammond, *Music and Spectacle in Baroque Rome: Barberini Patronage under Urban VIII* (New Haven: Yale University Press, 1994); Hammond, *The Ruined Bridge: Studies in Barberini Patronage of Music and Spectacle, 1631–1679* (Sterling Heights, MI: Harmonie Park Press, 2010); and Lois Rosow, "Power and Display: Music in Court Theater," in *The Cambridge History of Seventeenth-Century Music*, ed. Tim Carter and John Butt (Cambridge: Cambridge University Press, 2005), 223–37.

10. This ban remained in place until 1798. On female opera singers, see John Rosselli, *Singers of Italian Opera: The History of a Profession* (Cambridge: Cambridge University Press, 1992), 56–114. For a discussion of late sixteenth-century concerns over female musicianship, see Anthony Newcomb, "Courtesans, Muses or Musicians? Professional Women Musicians in Sixteenth-Century Italy," in *Women Making Music: The Western Art Tradition, 1150–1950*, ed. Jane Bowers and Judith Tick (Urbana: University of Illinois Press, 1987), 90–115.

song."[11] Virtuosity came with or at a price. Whether or not a female singer or actress engaged in amorous employment, the very act of performing before a public or semi-public audience cast her in a certain light and could signal her openness to such engagements. Accusations of courtesanship followed Costa's peers and predecessors like the prolific singer and composer Barbara Strozzi (1619–1677), while others such as the renowned actress Isabella Andreini labored to distance themselves from any hint of an unsavory reputation.[12] Despite the questions of decorousness that followed them, however, *virtuose* (accomplished female performers) could also become prized members of a court. Duke Vincenzo Gonzaga expended considerable time and energy wooing the Neapolitan singer and composer Adriana Basile (c. 1581–c. 1640) to Mantua, for example, and poetry and prose celebrated the cultural capital she brought to both cities.[13] The salty nature of much of Margherita Costa's writing lends credence to her near-contemporaries' descriptions of her as a courtesan, at least at the beginning of her career, but both she and her sister used their positions as singers to forge connections with prominent male literati and patrons that served them well in the long term. They each ultimately circulated between the courts of Italy and Paris on the basis of their talents as performers and, in the case of Margherita, as a writer.[14]

While Costa's precise movements during this early period in Rome remain elusive, Erythraeus reports one event that illustrates the social controversies that could surround female performers. In 1625 or early 1626, the composer Domenico Mazzocchi and the poet and librettist Ottavio Tronsarelli collaborated on *La catena d'Adone* (The Chain of Adonis), an operatic adaptation of Giambattista Marino's epic poem *Adone* (Adonis) of a few years prior. The staging as planned was derailed by a quarrel between the noblemen Giovanni Giorgio Aldobrandini, to whom the work was dedicated, and Giandomenico Lupi over which of two

11. Susan McClary, *Desire and Pleasure in Seventeenth-Century Music* (Berkeley: University of California Press, 2012), 81.

12. See, for example, Ellen Rosand, "Barbara Strozzi, 'virtuosissima cantatrice': The Composer's Voice," *Journal of the American Musicological Society* 31, no. 2 (1978): 241–81; Anne MacNeil, *Music and Women of the Commedia dell'Arte in the Late Sixteenth Century* (Oxford: Oxford University Press, 2003).

13. Newcomb, "Courtesans, Muses or Musicians?" 101; Jane Bowers, "The Emergence of Women Composers in Italy, 1566–1700," in *Women Making Music: The Western Art Tradition, 1150–1950*, ed. Jane Bowers and Judith Tick (Urbana: University of Illinois Press, 1987), 121–22; Bonnie Gordon, *Monteverdi's Unruly Women: The Power of Song in Early Modern Italy* (Cambridge: Cambridge University Press, 2004), 144–49, 153–55.

14. Anna Francesca Costa also played a role in the 1653 production of the musical drama *L'Ergirodo*. On the singer and her patronage network, see Teresa Megale, "Il principe e la cantante: Riflessi impresariali di una protezione," *Medioevo e Rinascimento* 6 (1992): 211–33; and Megale, "Altre novità su Anna Francesca Costa e sull'allestimento dell'*Ergirodo*," *Medioevo e Rinascimento* 7, no. 4 (1993): 137–42.

highly acclaimed female singers had the more sonorous voice and more elevated skill and thus deserved the better part: a certain "Cecca of the lagoon" or Margherita Costa.[15] While the dispute was resolved by granting both women equally significant roles in which to showcase their talents, Aldobrandini's wife intervened. When the opera debuted in February 1626 at the Palazzo Conti, both women had been replaced by castrati.[16]

Costa left Rome for Florence at some point after this debacle, most likely in 1628 or shortly thereafter.[17] The exact motivation for this move is unspecified, leading some to speculate that a scandal of some sort precipitated her expulsion from Rome or—and perhaps more likely—that an invitation to perform in the wedding ceremonies for Margherita de' Medici and Odoardo Farnese of Parma brought her to Florence in search of new opportunities.[18] The transition proved advantageous. Costa insinuated herself into the Medici court, enjoying the protection of Grand Duke Ferdinando II (1610–1670) and his brothers, and rubbed shoulders with members of the Florentine academies. She also launched her publishing career, printing an impressive nine complete works by 1641.

Costa hit the presses with her first major volume shortly after her arrival. In her first documented bid to curry favor with the Medici, she composed a hefty history of young Ferdinando II's 1627–1628 diplomatic travels to the court of his uncle, the Holy Roman Emperor (also named Ferdinand II). Days after completing this journey, the eighteen-year-old assumed the grand ducal throne from his regents.[19] The *Istoria del viaggio d'Alemagna del serenissimo Gran Duca di Toscana Ferdinando Secondo* (A History of the Voyage to Germany of Ferdinando II, Grand Duke of Tuscany) memorializes the grand duke's political coming of age through a day-by-day account of the trip's meetings and entertainments.[20] This first publication has also proven to be Costa's most problematic, however. As she acknowledges in her dedicatory letter to the Spanish ambassador to Tuscany, Costa derived her knowledge of the expedition from the notes of Ferdinando's secretary, Benedetto Guerrini. Costa's reliance on this external source led later

15. Costa-Zalessow notes that some have hypothesized that this Cecca may have been "Checca," Costa's sister Anna Francesca, but concludes that this is unlikely; Costa, *Voice of a Virtuosa and Courtesan*, 20.

16. Janus Nicius Erythraeus [ps. Giovanni Vittorio Rossi], *Pinacotheca imaginum illustrium, doctrinae vel ingenii laude virorum* (Amsterdam: Iodocum Kalcovium et socios, 1643–1648), 3:150–51.

17. On the dating of the move, see Bianchi, "Una cortigiana rimatrice," 29:8–10.

18. Bianchi, "Una cortigiana rimatrice," 29:10–11; Costa-Zalessow, "Margherita Costa," 114; Lucia Strappini, *La tragedia del buffone: Percorsi del comico e del tragico nel teatro del XVII secolo* (Rome: Bulzoni, 2003), 251.

19. On this trip and transition, see, for example, Alessandro Lazzeri, *Il principe e il diplomatico: Ferdinando II tra il destino e la storia* (Florence: Edizioni Medicea, 1996), 12–14.

20. Margherita Costa, *Istoria del viaggio d'Alemagna del serenissimo Gran Duca di Toscana Ferdinando Secondo* (Venice: n.p, n.d [after 1628]), 5.

commentators to accuse her of not having actually authored this or, by extension, any of her texts, though with no explanation as to why a work so intertwined with Ferdinando's political identity would have been attributed to a new female transplant from Rome if she truly had no hand in its composition.

Costa's arrival in Florence thus coincided with Ferdinando's assumption of power, and while the next few years witnessed trimmer offerings for musical and theatrical productions compared to those under his parents Cosimo II and Maria Maddalena, the period proved immensely fruitful for Costa as a writer.[21] After an initial gap in her print activity, by the end of 1630s she returned to the presses with a veritable torrent of works: eight full published texts in half as many years, as well as an elegant gift manuscript and individually printed poems. The first two of these works recall Costa's musical career in their titles as well as in much of their contents: *La chitarra* (The Guitar) and *Il violino* (The Violin), printed in 1638.[22] Several factors indicate that with these volumes, and especially with *La chitarra*, Costa sought to signal her belonging to elite cultural circles. First, and most prominently, she dedicated them to the grand duke himself, lauding his court for providing the kind of repose and creative leisure Rome had denied her.[23] *La chitarra* supplements this acknowledgement of Ferdinando's protection and patronage with the dedication of individual poems to members of the grand duke's household (some of whom would themselves become the dedicatees of Costa's subsequent works), as well as important personages Costa would have met in both Florence and Rome. She lent further legitimacy to her publishing enterprise in both volumes by including male-authored celebratory poetry composed on her behalf by academicians, poets, and librettists from Florence and beyond (including Ottavio Tronsarelli), as she would also do for her collections of poetry and letters of the following year.[24] Finally, *La chitarra* features a portrait of Costa, one fashioned by the most renowned Florentine draftsman and etcher of the day,

21. On the drop in Medici-sponsored musical theater and festivities after 1628/1629, see Kelley Harness, *Echoes of Women's Voices: Music, Art, and Female Patronage in Early Modern Florence* (Chicago: University of Chicago Press, 2006), 195.

22. Margherita Costa, *La chitarra, canzoniere amoroso* ([Frankfurt: Daniel Wastch], 1638); *Il violino* ([Frankfurt: Daniel Wastch], 1638). Both the publisher and place are likely false. The only other work published by Wastch the editors could locate is Girolamo Fantini's *Modo per imparare a sonare di tromba*, also dedicated to Ferdinando II in 1638.

23. See the dedicatory letter in Costa, *La chitarra.*

24. These men were: Alessandro Adimari, Andrea Barbazza, Bernardino Biscia, Oviedo Spinosa, Tronsarelli, Ferdinando Saracinelli, and the prince of Gallicano (typically identified as Pompeo Colonna), as well as anonymous (but assumedly male) poets. In addition to some of these same figures represented in *La chitarra* and *Il violino*, the *Stipo* includes two poems in Spanish by Juan Silvestro Gomez and Miguel de Silveira. The *Lettere amorose* contain poems by several of these same figures, as well as Francesco Roncone, and unattributed poems in Spanish and, interestingly, Portuguese.

Stefano della Bella (1610–1664), who contributed to many of Costa's works published during her time in Florence.[25]

This portrait (Fig. 1) fuses Costa's musical and emerging poetic identities. Set within an ennobling cartouche whose inscription heralds her as a "most excellent lady" (*ad efigiem* [sic] *ex[cellentissi]mae Dominae Margheritae Costae*), Costa rests her crossed hands across what is likely a book.[26] An elegiac couplet by Alfonso de Oviedo Spinosa (who also contributed two celebratory poems to the volume) likens her to a tenth muse who, to the objections of her readers, is pictured without the laurel wreath she so merits (*Cernere laurigero quereris sine crine poetam factum quod decima haec visa camena foret*). The epithet "tenth muse" was a common means of praising early modern women writers, but it also bore longstanding associations with Sappho, famous as both a poet and a lover.[27] This ambiguity between the lofty and the lowly is reflected in the inclusion below Costa's bust of musical part books and, in harmony with the volume's title, baroque guitars. As Costa underscores in her letter to Ferdinando, the guitar's ignoble origins did not impede it from becoming immensely popular in this period.[28]

A versatile though at times criticized instrument, the guitar's repertoire could oscillate from "boisterous street music to the elegance of courtly performance"—much like Costa herself.[29] A protean writer, Costa often defies in both circumstance and content the standard classifications of women's literary engagement. As would be the case in many of her works, in *La chitarra* and *Il violino* she simultaneously elevates her status in a manner akin to predecessors like Isabella Andreini and rejects such pretenses by incorporating genres, language, and

25. On Stefano della Bella, see Phyllis Dearborn Massar, "Presenting Stefano della Bella," *The Metropolitan Museum of Art Bulletin* 27, no. 3 (1968): 159–76; Massar, *Presenting Stefano della Bella: Seventeenth-Century Printmaker* (New York: Metropolitan Museum of Art, 1971); Alexandre Baudi de Vesme and Phyllis Dearborn Massar, eds., *Stefano della Bella: Catalogue raisonné*, 2 vols. (New York: Coll. Edition, 1906, 1971); and Charles Johnson, *Stefano della Bella, Baroque Printmaker: The I. Webb Surratt, Jr. Print Collection* (Richmond, VA: Marsh Art Gallery, University of Richmond Museums, 2001). Della Bella's contemporary biographer, Filippo Baldinucci, describes the portrait as a "ritratto al naturale di Margherita Costa." Her name appears directly above that of Emperor Ferdinand II in his list of Della Bella's most notable works; Filippo Baldinucci, *Notizie de' professori del disegno da Cimabue in qua* (Florence: Santi Franchi, 1681), 1:231.

26. All translations are the editors' own unless otherwise indicated.

27. On the portrait, and its Sapphic undertones, see Amy Brosius, "'Il suon, lo sguardo, il canto': The Function of Portraits of Mid-Seventeenth-Century *Virtuose* in Rome," *Italian Studies* 63, no. 1 (2008): 29–32. Brosius argues that both this and a later 1639 portrait of Costa were based on painted portraits. This supposition is derived from conclusions about common practices, though there is no evidence that such a painting (or paintings) existed.

28. Costa, *La chitarra*, dedicatory letter.

29. Victor Coelho, "The Baroque Guitar: Players, Paintings, Patrons, and the Public," in *The World of Baroque Music: New Perspectives*, ed. George B. Stauffer (Bloomington: Indiana University Press, 2006), 169.

Figure 1. Stefano della Bella, portrait of Margherita Costa.
From *La chitarra* (Frankfurt, 1638).

themes generally deemed unsuitable for female audiences or authors in a manner that at moments recalls Veronica Franco.[30] Following the *Chitarra*'s dedicatory letter to the grand duke, portrait by a court artist, and celebratory poetry by culturally elite men—all of which would typically signal the high status of the work—are over two hundred sonnets, idylls, *canzonette* (playful songs), and octaves centered on almost exclusively amorous themes. Of these, nearly all are written from the perspective of a beautiful woman (*bella donna*) who addresses her lover. While the most prevalent theme is the separation of the lovers by distance, in other poems the *bella donna* targets, for example, a "lover who tries to procure her love through money and through one of her former lovers that she had already chased off" and "her lover who in his sleep would seem to love another woman."[31] In other poems, the *bella donna*'s audience is women; her advice ranges from warning them to abandon lovemaking for the spindle to encouraging them to let any desiring man kiss them lest he harm them.[32] In many of the love laments, as in several of Costa's later publications, the lady addresses her cruel beloved as Tirsi, a shepherd common to the pastoral tradition who wrangles with issues of love.[33] Allusions to music abound, both in Costa's poems and those of her male commentators, as do references to the craft of poetry. These range from a sonnet in which the *bella donna* speaks to "her lover who is jealous that two men praise her poetry"[34] to a poetic acknowledgement that Costa's volume may face criticism, either for being of such good quality as to raise questions about its authenticity or for being inappropriate in language and style.[35] Costa would later redeploy extended passages from *La chitarra* in a manuscript that bills itself as a

30. On this poet and "honest courtesan," see Veronica Franco, *Poems and Selected Letters*, ed. and trans. Ann Rosalind Jones and Margaret F. Rosenthal (Chicago: University of Chicago Press, 1998).

31. "Bella donna ad uno amante che procura ottenere l'amor suo per prezzo di danari e per via d'uno amante di lei già da lei discacciato"; "bella donna al suo amante mentre dormendo nel sogno li pare ch' egl'ami altra donna." Costa, *La chitarra*, 280–84, 328–30.

32. Costa, *La chitarra*, 273–74, 544–45.

33. One of Costa's twentieth-century biographers expended a fair deal of ink trying to determine the historical identity of this "Tirsi" as one of Costa's lovers, but it is less likely to be an alias than an adaptation of the pastoral tradition. There are a variety of Tirsi-related works from the sixteenth and seventeenth centuries, with notable examples including Castiglione's 1506 *Tirsi*, Tasso's 1573 *Aminta*, and Monteverdi's 1616 musical dance *Tirsi e Clori*. To give another example from Costa's oeuvre, *Il violino* contains a poetic exchange between Tirsi and Filli, figures who appear in Isabella Andreini's pastoral comedy *La Mirtilla* (which enjoyed multiple publications between 1588 and 1620) and Marino's *Egloghe boscherecce*. See Isabella Andreini, *La Mirtilla*, ed. Maria Luisa Doglio (Lucca: Pacini Fazzi, 1995); and Giambattista Marino, *Egloghe boscherecce del cavalier Marino, cioè, Tirsi, Aminta, Dafne, Siringa, Pan, Elcippo, et i Sospiri d'Ergasto, con cinque canzoni … et il Camerone d'istesso* (Milan: G. B. Cerri, 1627).

34. "Bella donna al suo amante ingelosito da dui signori che lodano le poesie di lei." Costa, *La chitarra*, 485.

35. See the volume's first and final poems; Costa, *La chitarra*, 1–5, 567–73.

conversion narrative but that nonetheless offers a humorous take on early modern forms of divertissement.[36]

Counterbalancing nods to her own talents and audacity are declarations of her humility as both a woman and a writer. While self-effacement was a pervasive rhetorical strategy, Costa blends gendered and grotesque images in verse and in dedicatory letters throughout her career. With *La chitarra*, for example, she professes to have "birthed an obscene and reprehensible monster," a "crippled and malformed dwarf," language she would later echo for her cast of misfit characters in *The Buffoons.*[37] In *Il violino*, as in *La chitarra*, Costa presents herself as prostrate before the feet of her benefactor and excuses herself for "staining paper with [her pen's] crude and clunky scribbles."[38] She pleads in verse for Ferdinando to "protect these *parti* [births/ labors] of mine and my stylus naked of all style."[39] In the poem *La mia musa è svegliata* (My Muse Has Awakened), however, Costa also dramatizes her rough-and-tumble relationship with an almost savage muse. She emphatically rejects the artificiality and constraints of classicizing poetry and embraces her own original and brutally honest verse.[40]

While *La chitarra* primarily features a female voice that speaks longingly or disdainfully of a male lover, in *Il violino* Costa primarily adopts a ventriloquized male voice that she would redeploy again in her *Lettere amorose* (Love Letters) the following year, though many of the volume's most compelling poems feature women. This collection of amorous verse frequently assumes a light and at times satirical air, demonstrates Costa's familiarity with predecessors like Tasso and Marino, and incorporates familiar pastoral characters such as Aminta, Tirsi, Filli, and Eurilla. The male, and occasional female, speakers explore themes of heartsickness, jealousy, and death. While several poems present women in the clutches of sexual possessiveness, for instance, another presents a man who relishes in the sight of his beloved with other paramours, asking "what's a beautiful woman worth if she doesn't have a host of lovers before her?"[41] One woman opts for suicide rather than lead a "servile life of proper obedience, docile and demure" after being

36. The work, *Le sette giornate o vero Il Viaggio di Loreto* (Seven Days, or The Journey to Loreto), held in the Doria Pamphilj Archive, is undated but was likely composed (or at least finished) around 1644, when Costa was back in Rome. Its dedicatee, called simply "Sir Count," was probably Camillo Pamphilj. *Le sette giornate, o vero Il viaggio di Loreto della Signora Margarita Costa al S[ignor] C[onte].* Fondo Archiviolo, XX, busta 122, fols. 268r–297v. For a discussion of this work, see Jessica Goethals, "The Bizarre Muse: The Literary Persona of Margherita Costa," *Early Modern Women: An Interdisciplinary Journal*, 12, no. 1 (2017): 48–72.

37. "partorito un sconcio e biasimevole mostro … uno storpio e malformato nano." Costa, *La chitarra*, dedicatory letter.

38. "machiar le carte degli suoi rozzi e mal correnti inchiostri." Costa, *Il violino*, dedicatory letter.

39. Costa, *Il violino*, 7.

40. Costa, *La chitarra*, 1–5.

41. "Che pregio ha donna bella | se non vedersi avanti | le schiere degli amanti." Costa, *Il violino*, 116.

scorned by her lover, while another in a male-voiced idyll parodying a Marino rape poem upbraids her assailant for ruining her purity before swiftly and "cruelly" taking up with a new lover.[42] Costa interweaves male and female perspectives in a poem about a baby girl who transforms into a boy; rather than recoiling in surprise or horror, his mother envisions the happiness that adulthood can now afford him.

While in these first two poetic volumes Costa incorporates the voices of beautiful women, male lovers, and the occasional mother, in her next major publications she sharpens her comedic edge by showcasing a vast cast of satirical and grotesque characters. The *Lettere amorose*, dedicated to Giovan Carlo de' Medici, Ferdinando's brother, fall within a long tradition of the early modern Italian letterbook, which enjoyed such notable recent contributors as Isabella Andreini and Marino.[43] Costa's text—introduced by the Della Bella portrait (though now without the original Spinosa epithet) and celebratory poems in Italian, Spanish, and Portuguese by her usual circle of male literary contacts—imitates the theatrical and "hermaphroditic" style of an Andreini in its impassioned debates between male and female lovers. Costa ultimately moves beyond the more traditional love concerns of her predecessor's repertoire, however, transitioning from questions of fidelity and separation to an exploration of the burlesque underworld of lovemaking. With a fusion of prose and poetry, Costa pairs a beautiful lady and a dwarf, a hunchback and a cross-eyed lady, a sorceress and her bald lover, a chatterbox and his slovenly woman, and a syphilitic man and his scabies-ridden paramour, to give but a few examples. The publication won enough acclaim that it was published twice more, in 1643 and posthumously in 1674, and was sampled in a letter anthology first published in 1656.[44]

At first glance, *Lo stipo* (The Cabinet) might appear to be a more typical case of panegyric, but this work too soon veers toward jocosity. Taking her title from the ornately decorated cabinets popular at the time, Costa structures her volume as a series of seven *cassettini* (drawers) of jewels, each associated with a certain

42. Costa, *Il violino*, 26 and 49. On Costa's parody of Marino's "I trastulli estivi" in the rape-fantasy poem, see Costa-Zalessow, "Margherita Costa," 116; and Cox, *Women's Writing in Italy*, 214–15.

43. Margherita Costa, *Lettere amorose* (Venice: n.p., 1639). The *Lettere di Isabella Andreini padovana, comica gelosa e academica intenta nominata l'Accesa* (Venice: Marc' Antonio Zaltieri) were published posthumously in 1607 by Andreini's husband Francesco, but she had begun assembling them a few years prior. On Andreini's letters and influence on Costa, see Meredith K. Ray, *Writing Gender in Women's Letter Collections of the Italian Renaissance* (Toronto: University of Toronto Press, 2009), 156–83.

44. Margherita Costa, *Lettere amorose* (Venice: Li Turini, 1643); *Lettere amorose della Signora Margherita Costa Romana, con tutte l'aggiunte* (Venice: Giacomo Turini, 1674); *Scielta di lettere amorose di Ferrante Pallavicino, Luca Asserino, Margarita Costa Romana, Gerolamo Parabosco* (Venice: Giacomo Bortoli, 1656). The anthology was reprinted by multiple editors several times later that century. In *Voice of a Virtuosa*, her selection of Costa's verse, Costa-Zalessow lists three editions of the *Lettere*; however, we have yet to independently verify the existence of the listed 1652 edition.

class of poetic object. The first of these include laudatory and occasional poetry honoring the extended Medici family and their happenings, but later drawers feature more risqué personalities such as an aging dandy, a syphilitic astrologer, and a procuress who lost her nose "in the service of love."[45] In other words, while the volume has all the trappings of an endeavor aimed at its author's social ennoblement—a dedication to Ferdinando's uncle Lorenzo de' Medici, as well as male-authored celebratory poetry and a new refined portrait (see Fig. 2)—in the final pages Costa embraces the ribald. She also dedicates a series of poems to the various Florentine academies, including the prominent and powerful Accademia della Crusca and Accademia del Disegno.[46] In the volume's captivating and autobiographical final poem, Costa grieves as some of her verses are burned and swears herself to a silence that, prolific writer that she is, she soon breaks.[47]

The following year was not only the most productive of Costa's literary career but also the start of her partnership with the prominent Florentine publishing team of Amadore Massi and Lorenzo Landi.[48] With an elegy collection, a drama, a multi-canto poem, and a manuscript libretto for an equestrian ballet, 1640 was also the year in which Costa best displayed her versatility with respect to genre. Curiously, in her writing from this period she set aside the burlesque and amorous tropes so prevalent in her other poetry and letters and returned instead to the political and dynastic concerns that had motivated the *Istoria*.

La selva dei cipressi (The Cypress Forest) is a volume of lamentation poetry occasioned by the premature demise of two sons of Charles de Lorraine, duke of Guise, who would himself die a French exile in Florence later that year.[49] Introduced by a possible Stefano della Bella frontispiece depicting the eponymous cypress forest, a symbol of death, the volume bewails the loss of prominent Italian and European figures.[50] In addition to the Lorraine men, these include members

45. "ne' servigi amorosi." Margherita Costa, *Lo stipo* (Venice: n.p, 1639), 194–221.

46. Costa, *Lo stipo*, 86–116. The volume also reproduces a poem on a fire in Palazzo Pitti that Costa had published separately the previous year. See Margherita Costa, *Per l'incendio di Pitti* (Florence: Stamperia nuova, 1638). Costa published a handful of poems individually; known extant cases are *Al Serenissimo Ferdinando II, Gran Duca di Toscana, per la Festa di San Gio. Batista* (Venice: n.p., n.d.); *Alla Serenissima Vittoria della Rovere, Gran Duchessa di Toscana, per la Festa di San Gio. Batista* (Venice: n.p., n.d); *Alla Serenissima Margherita de Medici, Duchessa di Parma, per l'arrivo in Fiorenza* (Venice: n.p., n.d); and *Al Serenissimo Principe Gio. Carlo di Toscana, per la carica di generaliss. del mare conferitagli dalla M. Cattolica* (Florence: Massi e Landi, n.d.); *All'Altezza Serenissima di Ferdinando Secondo Gran Duca di Toscana nel giorno della sua nascita* (Florence: Nella Stamperia de Landi, 1655).

47. Costa, *Lo stipo*, 288–304.

48. Roberto Bruni, "Editori e tipografi a Firenze nel Seicento," *Studi secenteschi* 45 (2004): 325–419. At 386, Bruni presents Costa as a representative example of Massi and Landi's activity.

49. Margherita Costa, *La selva di cipressi, opera lugubre* (Florence: Massi e Landi, 1640).

50. The two most prominent Della Bella scholars disagreed on the *Selva di cipressi* attribution; see Baudi de Vesme and Massar, *Stefano della Bella*, 1:146.

Figure 2. Portrait of Margherita Costa, from *Lo stipo* (Venice, 1639).

of Ferdinando's and Vittoria della Rovere's families (Ferdinando I, Cosimo II, and Francesco I de' Medici, and Francesco Maria della Rovere), the Florentine court (the librettist Ferdinando Saracinelli), and prominent generals in the Thirty Years' War (Ambrogio Spinola, Albrecht von Wallenstein).[51] In addition to a *lamento storico* in which a personified Italy deplores her loss of peace, the publication also revisits pastoral themes, such as a poem in which the aforementioned Tirsi has been stabbed in the neck, and concludes with a poem on Costa's own professional hardships.

Costa's biographers have traditionally associated her operatic equestrian ballet, the *Festa reale per balletto a cavallo* (Royal Celebration for a Horse Ballet), primarily with her 1647 Parisian period. While Costa did bring the work to press while performing in France, it is definitively the product of her time in Florence

51. Costa also alludes to a member of the Spinola family, surely Ambrogio, in *The Buffoons*. See I.vii.97.

and first appears in a handsome gift manuscript dedicated to Ferdinando.[52] A performative genre popular from the late sixteenth through the seventeenth century, equestrian ballet had particularly strong roots in Florence and dazzled audiences at key socio-political court events such as Medici weddings. The first female-authored libretto of its kind, the *Festa reale* is a spectacular pageant of two golden chariots and sixty colorfully attired horsemen, accompanied by splendidly liveried attendants, who together perform dressage movements to instrumental and vocal music before being lifted by theater machinery into the heavens to become constellations.[53] Classical deities (Jove, Mars, and Apollo) simultaneously transform into planets that form the shape of the Medici coat of arms, which Costa—alluding to Galileo's nomenclature for his 1610 discovery of Jupiter's moons—calls the "Medicean stars."[54] While throughout this lofty work Costa buttresses her patron family's claims to influence and authority, she would demonstrate her protean range in *The Buffoons* of the following year by satirizing many of the *Festa reale*'s themes, from dressage to astronomy.

In the ballet's dedicatory letter to Ferdinando, Costa states that she presents him the manuscript alongside her *Flora feconda* (Fertile Flora).[55] This poem celebrates the birth of Ferdinando's and Vittoria della Rovere's first son. Originally organized into nine cantos, one dedicated to each month of the grand duchess's pregnancy, this mythological tale adapted from Ovid depicts Zephyr's and Flora's journey to the oracle of Jove in order to conceive a male heir. In addition to shrewdly selecting a conceit already popular with Ferdinando and associated with his reign, Costa packs the work with dynastic imagery associated with both the Medici and the Della Rovere family lines.[56] Because the child died after three short days, however, Costa found herself needing to amend the poem. She did

52. Biblioteca Nazionale Centrale di Firenze (BNCF), Florence. MS II II 371: Margherita Costa, *Festa reale per ballo de' cavalli* (1640). The work is later published under the title *Festa reale per balletto a cavallo* (Paris: Cramoisy, 1647). On the transition from manuscript to print, as well as the centrality of equestrian themes to Costa more broadly, see Jessica Goethals, "The Patronage Politics of Equestrian Ballet: Allegory, Allusion, and Satire in the Courts of Seventeenth Century Italy and France," *Renaissance Quarterly* 70, no. 4 (Winter 2017): 1397–448.

53. The Florentine composer Francesca Caccini (1587–after 1641) wrote the first female-authored musical score for an equestrian ballet with her 1625 *La liberazione di Ruggiero*. See Suzanne Cusick, *Francesca Caccini at the Medici Court: Music and the Circulation of Power* (Chicago: University of Chicago Press, 2009), 191–246.

54. "stelle medicee." Galileo Galilei, *Sidereus nuncius, magna longeque admirabilia spectacula pandens* (Venice: Baglioni, 1610).

55. Margherita Costa, *Flora feconda, poema* (Florence: Massi e Landi, 1640).

56. A poem entitled *La celeste Flora* (Francesco Campani, 1610) was composed on the occasion of Ferdinando's own birth, and the first organized festivities of his grand dukedom, celebrating his sister Margherita's 1628 marriage to Odoardo Farnese of Parma, included the opera *La flora, overo Il natal de' flori* (Florence: Pietro Cecconcelli, 1628), libretto by Andrea Salvadori, music composed by Marco

so by appending a tenth canto in which Jove claims the infant boy for the stars, and, later that year, by refashioning the work as a drama entitled *La flora feconda*, which she dedicated to Vittoria.[57]

If in these four works Costa concentrated her energies on the serious stuff of courtly message making, she pivoted drastically with *Li buffoni* the following year. As shall be discussed at greater length below, this irreverent drama takes satirical aim at the pastimes and personages of Medicean Florence. Hers is a comedy of misfits and base occupations, one peppered with *double entrendres*, slapstick, and caricature. With this court parody, Costa fully embraced the vulgar burlesque with which she had already been experimenting in works like *La chitarra*, *Lo stipo*, and especially the *Lettere amorose*. Importantly, this penchant for the grotesque is particular to Costa's Florentine period. While in subsequent years spent in other cities she would continue to experiment with genre, as well as explore amorous and gender themes, Costa seems to have found in Florence the liberty to pursue racier subjects alongside the panegyric texts she composed throughout her career.

At some point around 1644, and for unspecified reasons, Costa returned to Rome.[58] After an approximately sixteen-year hiatus from the Eternal City, she renewed her relationship to the Barberini family. Her overtures to these important patrons are exemplified by the dedication of her first and only major Roman publication, *Cecilia martire* (St. Cecilia, Martyr), to Cardinal Francesco Barberini, the pope's nephew.[59] This four-canto hagiographic poem, also available in a manuscript version, focuses on the life, death, and legacy of this second-century Roman martyr and patron saint of music.[60] Cecilia's piety and the Barberini's power are

---

da Gagliano and Jacopo Peri. Though the singers' names were not recorded, it is conceivable that Costa herself could have been part of this production, as she likely arrived in Florence that year.

57. Margherita Costa, *La Flora feconda, drama* (Florence: Massi e Landi, 1640).

58. Costa-Zalessow hypothesizes in *Voice of a Virtuosa and Courtesan*, 22, that Costa was run out of town on account of a scandal caused by the *Buffoni*. This seems inconsistent with both the existence of multiple versions of the text and with the assistance the Medici continued to offer her, both discussed below. It had been previously hypothesized that Costa left after the death of the buffoon Bernardino Ricci, dedicatee of the *Buffoni* and once imagined to be Costa's husband, but since Ricci actually died more than a decade later, this could not have been the case. For more on their relationship, see below.

59. Margherita Costa, *Cecilia martire, poema sacro* (Rome: Mascardi, 1644). An edition of the poem held at the Biblioteca Giovardiana di Veroli bears the slightly modified title *La Santa Cecilia, poema sacro* and—though the publisher and city remain the same—a publication date of 1630. However, both these cover page details are written by hand on a seemingly pasted-in title page. This fact, and the uniformity of the texts themselves, indicate that the Giovardiana version likely originated with the 1644 printing and that the cover page was subsequently replaced or concealed, though the reason for the anticipated publication date is unclear.

60. Though not as fine as the *Festa reale* manuscript, the *Cecilia martire* manuscript (BAV Barb. lat. 4069) is a good copy meant for circulation. It does not contain the print edition's *Allegoria* section, and it diverges in twenty consecutive stanzas, though it includes the alternative text at the end.

highlighted in a pair of elaborate etchings: one showing the saint's grace as the executioner's blade swings toward her unguarded nape, the other a heroic Minerva upon whose shield fly the Barberini bees.

Any progress Costa made with the cardinal and his kin was cut short by the pope's death in July. The family's power quickly dissipated, and Francesco and his brothers fled to France in 1645 and 1646 after having made crucial miscalculations in the new papal politics. Surely on the hunt for more stable benefactors, Costa spent the first part of 1645 performing for Marie Christine of France, the duchess and regent of Savoy. While Costa's twentieth-century biographer Dante Bianchi presumes that her arrival at the northern court was for a carnival production, it would seem just as likely that Costa was called into service for the special sequence of festivities sponsored by the duchess during that winter and spring.[61] After the resolution of the 1639–1640 Spanish-French siege that had torn Turin apart a mere two years after her assumption of power, Marie Christine set about restoring the city and signaling her legitimacy through patronage projects.[62] In the first months of 1645, she organized a series of celebrations, ballets, and other spectacles with an enthusiasm certainly heightened by the departure of the last of the French troops in March and the triumphal re-entry of her son, Charles Emmanuel II, in April. It is conceivable, even likely, that the duchess or her agents extended an invitation to Costa for the purpose of these festivities so crucial to the dynastic messaging of the court. Costa remained in Turin for a relatively brief period, despite being generously remunerated for the performance of chamber operas.[63] The relationship seems not to have soured, however, as three years later Costa continued to court the duchess's favor with a volume of verse, *La selva di Diana* (The Forest of Diana). This publication flatteringly fashions Marie Christine as the titular goddess and opens with a thirty-eight-octave poem lauding her former patroness with the very terms and themes predominant in the 1645 celebrations, including representations of her as the ruler of the Alps.[64]

61. Bianchi, "Una cortigiana rimatrice," 29:188–89.

62. See Martha D. Pollak, *Turin, 1564–1680: Urban Design, Military Culture, and the Creation of the Absolutist Capital* (Chicago: University of Chicago Press, 1991), esp. the chapter "The Regency of Cristina: Dynastic War and the Creation of Piazza Reale," 108–50.

63. A court document licenses the annual payment of one thousand lira to Costa "as our chamber musician from the start of this year and for the duration of our pleasing." For this contract in the context of court musicians, see Gaudenzio Claretta, *Storia della reggenza di Cristina di Francia, Duchessa di Savoia: Con annotazioni e documenti inediti*, 3 vols. (Turin: Civelli, 1868–1869), 2:536. For a fuller citation of the document, see Alessandro Ademollo, *I primi fasti della musica italiana a Parigi, 1645–1662* (Milan: Ricordi, 1884), 38. The *avvisi* of Rome suggest that Costa may have been back in town by August 1645; see Bianchi, "Una cortigiana rimatrice," 29:188.

64. Margherita Costa, *La selva di Diana* (Paris: Cramoisy, 1647). On 1645 representations of the duchess, see Pollak, *Turin, 1564–1680*, 134–36.

In 1647, Costa left Italian shores in pursuit of opportunities and accolades in France. The Parisian court had opened its stages to Italian performers, composers, and theater designers a few years prior when the death of Louis XIII and the youth of his son created a vacuum of power into which stepped Cardinal Jules Mazarin (Giulio Mazzarino), the Italian-born chief minister. The cardinal, who had come of political age in Barberini Rome, had a taste for Italian music and theater that he increasingly sought to import to France.[65] With the approval of the regent, Queen Anne of Austria, whose ear he held, he put his agents in Rome, Florence, and Venice to the task of attracting the appropriate talent. In 1645 an Italian opera opened in France, and two years later the first Italian production composed specifically for a French audience debuted. It was to join the cast of this work, Luigi Rossi's *L'Orfeo* (Orpheus), that Costa, together with her sister Anna Francesca, traveled abroad.[66]

While Mazarin's scouts (Giovanni Bentivoglio in France, Cornelio Bentivoglio in Florence, and Elpidio Benedetti in Rome) recruited both sisters specifically to satisfy the queen's tastes in chamber and theater music, the successful enlistment of Margherita does not appear to have been a sure thing.[67] Although the initial invitation arrived in September, she seems to have accepted only in December.[68] During the intervening months, Benedetti wrote concerned updates to Cornelio Bentivoglio about whether Costa would agree to join the cast or if they would need to replace her with one Signora Felice who, he noted with optimism, was not only available but also had the added benefit of being thirty years Costa's junior.[69] When the *Orfeo* premiered to great applause in March,

65. On Mazarin's Italian-centered cultural policy, see Hammond, *The Ruined Bridge*, 153–89. On his life and influence, as well as backlashes against his sponsorship of extravagant Italian performances, see Geoffrey Treasure, *Mazarin: The Crisis of Absolutism in France* (London: Routledge, 1995); as well as Jeffrey Merrick, "The Cardinal and the Queen: Sexual and Political Disorders in the *Mazarinades*," *French Historical Studies* 18, no. 3 (1994): 667–99.

66. Anna Francesca had already sung in Paris two years prior as part of the cast of *La finta pazza*, followed by a performance in the 1646 opera *Egisto*. On the sisters', and especially Anna Francesca's experience in Paris, see Megale, "Il principe e la cantante."

67. "Since the Queen has resolved to have a good number of musicians for both the chamber and the theater in Paris this winter, write to Signora Francesca Costa and her sister Signora Margherita Costa" (Havendo la Maestà della Regina risoluto di volere havere in Parigi quest'inverno una buona mano de musici tanto per la camera quanto per il theatro, si scrive alla S.ra Francesca Costa et alla Sig.ra Margherita sua sorella); September 28, 1626, letter from Giovanni Bentivoglio in Fontainebleau to Cornelio Bentivoglio in Sergio Monaldini, *L'orto dell'Esperidi: Musici, attori e artisti nel patrocinio della famiglia Bentivoglio, 1646–1685* (Lucca: Libreria Musicale Italiana, 2000), 5.

68. December 1, 1646, letter from Elpidio Benedetti to Cornelio Bentivoglio, in Monaldini, *L'orto dell'Esperidi*, 11.

69. "[Felice's] advantage is as great as the difference between the ages of 17 and 47" (*tanto avantaggio quanto grande è la differenza dall'età di 17 a quella di 47*); October 29, 1646, letter from Benedetti, in Monaldini, *L'orto dell'Esperidi*, 9.

however, the all-star cast included both Costa sisters, with Anna Francesca playing the part of Eurydice and Margherita that of Juno.[70]

Costa's success as a performer in the *Orfeo* came at the expense of her achievements as a dramatist, however. Plans were initially at hand to stage another Italian work following Rossi's production. Giovan Battista Andreini's musical comedy *La Ferinda* was a contender, as was Costa's *Festa reale*, which she reworked to better fit its new French context. Mazarin ultimately deemed the equestrian ballet too technologically difficult for production and, still charmed by the *Orfeo*, he opted to extend Rossi's production schedule to include an additional six performances through May. Never able to see her grandiose ballet on the stage, Costa settled for seeing it in print with a 1647 Parisian edition dedicated to the cardinal himself. While later commentators such as Henry Prunières have looked upon this as a failure on Costa's part, the seventeenth-century music and dance theorist Claude-François Ménestrier instead commended her "genius and talent for poetry."[71]

No neophyte to courtly politics and the stratagems of securing patronage, Costa coupled her entrée into Parisian theater circles with an additional pair of 1647 publications honoring her new hosts. Though the aforementioned poetic volume *La selva di Diana* bears a dedication to the duchess of Savoy, its focus on the largesse and virtues of Costa's assorted benefactresses makes it an appropriate forum for a poem thanking Queen Anne for her favor and generosity. In this nineteen-octave homage to the regent, Costa professes that in France "the Golden Age has been reborn."[72] Another publication dedicated to Anne herself, *La tromba di Parnaso* (The Trumpet of Parnassus), centers on the Parisian court. Setting aside the comedic and amorous themes that had peppered some of her other poetry publications, she concentrates her energies on extolling "the glories of such a great queen," the munificence of Mazarin (the "patron to the world"), and the cultural wealth of their court.[73] The volume highlights the constellation of desirable personages associated with the royal family, from Henrietta Maria, Anne's sister-in-law and the queen of England, down to her ladies-in-waiting. Several poems recall the memory of Pope Urban VIII and laud the Barberini, benefactors to whom Costa and Cardinal Mazarin shared a longstanding connection.

70. One of the two manuscript copies of *Orfeo's* scenario held at the Vatican Library (Barb. lat. 4059, fol. 131v–137v) includes a full cast list, on which both sisters' names appear. The manuscript is transcribed in Hammond, *The Ruined Bridge*, 182–89.

71. Henry Prunières, *L'opéra italien en France avant Lulli* (Paris: E. Champion, 1913), 130; Claude-François Menestrier, *Des représentations en musique anciennes et modernes* (Paris: Rene Guignard, 1681), 232.

72. "Qui vi rinasce il secol d'oro." Costa, *La selva di Diana*, 81.

73. "le glorie di sì gran regina"; "mecenante al mondo." Margherita Costa, *La tromba di Parnaso* (Paris: Cramoisy, 1647), dedicatory letter and 30. The volume was later transcribed in full in two nineteenth-century manuscript volumes: BAV, Codices Ferrajoli 125, cc. 53–118; Codices Ferrajoli 128, cc. 247–431.

Concluding the volume are poems celebrating the court's most recent triumph, the *Orfeo* opera. Within a publication devoted to eulogizing the royal French court, these poems addressed to Rossi, the singer-actor Marc'Antonio Pasqualini, and the librettist Francesco Buti effectively attribute that eminence in no little part to the talents of Italian artists and authors.[74]

While Costa's modern biographers have suggested that little can be known about her movements after 1647, it would seem that by at least 1650 she had moved to Venice with recommendations from her former Medici patrons in hand. In an August letter, the Florentine ambassador Francesco Maria Zati assured Giovan Carlo de' Medici that he would provide her all necessary assistance in that city.[75] Shortly thereafter Costa's name appears in the account books of the librettist and impresario Giovanni Faustini.[76] Detailing her hire dates and pay, these records indicate that Costa sang as a leading lady in two operas composed by Francesco Cavalli and performed at the Teatro Sant'Apollinare in 1651–1652: *La Calisto* and *L'Eritrea*, which Faustini called his "twin princesses."[77] It appears from her comparatively high salary and bonuses that Costa may have performed the titular roles in both of the Sant'Apollinare operas: the nymph Calisto who happily lets herself be seduced by a Jove disguised as Diana (who meanwhile is off saving her beloved, the shepherd Endymion, from danger) and the princess Eritrea who rules Assyria in the guise of her dead brother and who "marries" the princess for whom her former lover had scorned her.[78] In addition to the financial support they provided, it is easy to see why works so characterized by "rapid shifts

74. On these poems, see Ademollo, *I primi fasti*, 36–39. Apparently motivated primarily by a moralizing objection to Costa's sexual activities, Ademollo writes dismissively that in the *Tromba di Parnaso* Costa "celebrated in ugly Italian verse the entire French kingdom and court," works that "today, without any merit, receive the honor of being remembered as historical documents."

75. Sara Mamone, *Serenissimi fratelli principi impresari: Notizie di spettacolo nei carteggi medicei: Carteggi di Giovan Carlo de' Medici e di Desiderio Montemagni suo segretario, 1628–1664* (Florence: Le Lettere, 2003), #919 (442).

76. Faustini papers, Archivio di Stato di Venezia, Scuola Grande San Marco, b. 112.

77. These accounts, made by Faustini's brother Marco, were recently discovered and analyzed by Beth L. Glixon and Jonathan E. Glixon, *Inventing the Business of Opera: The Impresario and His World in Seventeenth-Century Venice* (Oxford: Oxford University Press, 2006), 198, 203, 345, 347. For the citation and a discussion of these works, and especially *La Calisto*, see Francesco Cavalli, *La Calisto*, ed. Jennifer Williams Brown (Middleton, WI: A-R Editions, 2007), xiii–xliii, citation at l; Wendy Heller, *Emblems of Eloquence: Opera and Women's Voices in Seventeenth-Century Venice* (Berkeley; Los Angeles: University of California Press, 2003), 178–219; and Herbert Lindenberger, *Situating Opera: Period, Genre, Reception* (Cambridge: Cambridge University Press, 2010), 223–28.

78. Glixon and Glixon, in *Inventing the Business of Opera*, 203, suggest that "Margarita da Costa" was the *seconda donna* in these operas, but they also show that she and the other soprano (Caterina Giani) received equal salaries. In contrast, Jennifer Williams Brown argues that Costa was the *prima donna* on the basis of a handsome set of gifts she received as a bonus. See Cavalli, *La Calisto*, xxiv.

from serious to comic, from sensual to frenetic, from divine to earthly" would have caught the eye of a figure like Costa.[79]

A poem by the Vicentine poet Paolo Abriani celebrates Costa's performance in another Cavalli-Faustini collaboration held in the same venue, the 1651 *La Rosinda.* Hailing the soprano's captivating voice, he describes her as the "ethereal siren … from the Tiber."[80] Though there have been initial hesitations over whether the soprano listed as "Margarita da Costa" in the Faustini account books and our singer-author were really one and the same, Abriani's allusion to her Roman origins, as well as her Florentine period, clears away all doubt.[81] Costa likely met or already knew Cavalli and Faustini through her Medici contacts or her sister, Anna Francesca, who had starred in the 1646 Parisian staging of their opera *L'Egisto.*[82] Moreover, this may not have been Costa's first visit to the Serenissima. When Mazarin's agents were coordinating her journey to France in the fall of 1646, they described her as then being stationed in Venice.[83] On the basis of this letter, Ellen Rosand has hypothesized that Costa may have been performing in one of the Venetian operas of that season, such as Monteverdi's *Incoronazione di Poppea.*[84] Costa's collaboration with Cavalli likely began before 1651. The Lucchese poet Isabetta Coreglia, an admirer and something of an imitator of Costa, wrote in praise of her performance as Queen Isifile in a production of *Giasone.*[85] The renowned opera, composed by Cavalli in collaboration with the Florentine librettist Giacinto Andrea Cicognini, premiered in 1649 at Venice's Teatro San Cassiano before traveling to Florence and to Lucca in 1650, perhaps the city in which Coreglia saw Costa sing. A December 1652 letter to Giovan Carlo de' Medici's secretary similarly places Costa in Venice during this period; it is a request, sent to Florence from Venice by one Giovanna Vittoria Costa, that

79. Heller, *Emblems of Eloquence*, 190.

80. "Dal Tebro, o Costa … Sorgi eterea sirena." In "Alla Signora Margarita Costa, nel Teatro S. Apollinare, Nerea la maga." Paolo Abriani, *Poesie* (Venice: Francesco Valvasense, 1663), 20.

81. Glixon and Glixon expressed this doubt in *Inventing the Business of Opera*, 195n2, but they rely on Capucci's and Carter's biographies, neither of which link our Costa to Venice, and apparently had not yet encountered the other documentation placing Costa in the city.

82. Anna Francesca received the part thanks to the recommendations of Leopoldo and Giovan Carlo de' Medici; see Megale, "Il principe e la cantante," 215.

83. "Si scrive alla S.ra Francesca Costa et alla Sig.ra Margherita sua sorella, che si ritrova in Venetia." Monaldini, *L'orto dell'Esperidi*, 5. Costa's biographers tend to place her exclusively in Rome during this time (in part due to Costa's poem in the *Selva di Diana* about her 1647 departure from the Eternal City), but this letter—together with others from Elpidio Benedetti who wrote from Rome itself about awaiting a response letter from Costa—suggest that she may have spent part of that year in the Veneto.

84. Ellen Rosand, *Monteverdi's Last Operas: A Venetian Trilogy* (Berkeley: University of California Press, 2007), 126.

85. "Raccolta di varie composizioni della signora Isabetta Coreglia," Biblioteca Statale di Lucca, MS 205 c. 21v. On the relationship between the two women, see Cox, *Women's Writing in Italy*, 215.

the other Medici-backed singer Anna Maria Sardelli ("la Campaspe") be made to stop diverting male opera patrons away from "my lady mother."[86]

Maintaining such relationship with influential audience members was of the utmost importance. Performances like those for Cavalli (or her work in Venice more broadly) would have helped Costa catch the attention of her final dedicatees and likely patrons: the Brunswick-Lüneburg dukes Georg Wilhelm, Ernst Augustus, and Johann Friedrich. These German brothers shared a passion for Venetian opera, of which they became lifelong supporters and which they sought to import and imitate back home, competing with one another to establish the premier center for northern performance.[87] Italian librettists and artists did not overlook this important source of financial support; at least thirty libretti were dedicated to the dukes in as many years, from 1654 to 1688.[88] With the 1654 publication of her own libretto, *Gl'amori della luna* (The Loves of the Moon), Costa numbered among the first to approach them as benefactors.

In the *apologia* to the reader that introduces this libretto, Costa defends her "lowly style" by professing that she composed the work in a mere fifteen days after a four-year period of literary inactivity.[89] She further states that she now finds herself under "foreign skies," suggesting that she may have been one of the singers that moved between Venice and the brothers' German courts, though it also is conceivable that she may have meant Venice itself.[90] When choosing a conceit for her three-act pastoral opera, Costa settled on an adaptation of the story of Diana (goddess of the moon) and Endymion, two of the figures recently portrayed in *La Calisto*. For the publication itself, she turned to Andrea Giuliani, who printed

86. Mamone, *Serenissimi fratelli principi impresari*, #971 (464). The letter also mentions the author's sister, Vittoria Maria Costa. In a 1657 letter discussed below, Costa discusses her two daughters, albeit not by name. Costa-Zalessow has instead identified the subject of the letter as Anna Francesca, and Giovanna Vittoria and Vittoria Maria as Anna Francesca and Margherita's sisters; however, the former would require evidence of Anna Francesca's activity in Venice, and the latter is contradicted by the several mentions of their mother. Costa, *Voice of a Virtuosa and Courtesan*, 20n5. On the Medici's role in bringing Sordelli to Venice, see Sara Mamone, "Most Serene Brothers-Princes-Impresarios," Theater in Florence under the Management and Protection of Mattias, Giovan Carlo, and Leopoldo de' Medici," *Journal of Seventeenth-Century Music* 9, no. 1 (2003); <http://sscm-jscm.org/v9/no1/mamone.html)>.

87. On the connection of the Duchy of Brunswick-Lüneburg to Venetian opera, see Ellen Rosand, *Opera in Seventeenth-Century Venice: The Creation of a Genre* (Berkeley: University of California Press, 1991), passim; Lorenzo Bianconi and Thomas Walker, "Production, Consumption, and Political Function of Seventeenth-Century Opera," *Early Music History* 4 (1984): 267–70; and Louise K. Stein, "How Opera Traveled," in *The Oxford Handbook of Opera*, ed. Helen M. Greenwald (Oxford: Oxford University Press, 2014), 850–51. On their efforts back home in Germany, see John Warrack, *German Opera: From the Beginnings to Wagner* (Cambridge: Cambridge University Press, 2001), 29–30.

88. Stein, "How Opera Traveled," 851.

89. "[il] mio rozzo stile." Costa, *Gl'amori della luna.*

90. "Sotto cielo straniero." Costa, *Gl'amori della luna.*

the majority of Venetian libretti in the 1650s, including *La Calisto* and *L'Eritrea*.[91] Though free from the risqué language and imagery of *Li buffoni, Gl'amori della luna* recalls Costa's early comedy through its incorporation of music, dance, and games, as well as its thematic focus on a woman's unrequited affections. Here an enamored Diana despairs that Endymion does not return her ardour, so overcome is he with the continual lethargy of sleep, until finally Cupid intervenes, Slumber is overcome, and love prevails.

Though this libretto was Costa's final full-length work, she continued to circulate her verse. In 1655 she renewed her ties with the Florentine publisher Landi in order to print a twelve-stanza poem in honor of Ferdinando II's birthday. This *foglio volante* allots equal space to aggrandizing the grand duke and explicitly petitioning for his favor. While she had found happiness in Florence, Costa writes, she deleteriously followed another path that ultimately led her astray. Now she runs back to Ferdinando's feet, entreating him to accept her and to "nourish [her] work."[92] It is unclear whether Costa's supplication met with any renewed patronage, but it appears that by early the following year she was back in Rome. The city was abuzz with the arrival of Queen Christina of Sweden, a generous patron of the arts who had publicly converted to Catholicism and abdicated her throne before establishing a new residence in the Eternal City. The city's elite staged elaborate spectacles on her behalf, including three operas and an operatic equestrian tournament put on by the Barberini.[93] Costa contributed to the commemorative literature on these events, dedicating a broadsheet sonnet to the sponsor and star performer of the tournament, Maffeo Barberini.[94]

Costa's last known appearance is in a 1657 letter in which she solicited the assistance of Mario Chigi, referring to herself as a "widow and poor *virtuosa*" struggling to support two daughters."[95] Of Costa's family circumstances we have scant details—this letter is a departure from her general reticence about her role as mother or spouse—but she was was married at least once before finding herself a widow by 1645, when the documents for her contract in Turin refer to her as

91. Rosand, *Opera in Seventeenth-Century Venice*, 120.

92. "Nudrire il mio lavoro." Costa, *A Ferdinando Secondo nel giorno della sua nascita*, unnumbered pages, stanza vii.

93. Hammond offers a detailed analysis of all four Barberini works; *The Ruined Bridge*, 207–43.

94. "Sonetto stampato di Margherita Costa all'ecc. principe di Palestrina per la festa a cavallo fatta da S. E. alla maestà di Cristina Regina di Svezia," BAV, Archivio Barberini Indice 1 1088. The Barberini Archive possesses three identical copies of this printing. A transcription (though with an error in line breaks) is available on the website *Scritture di donne (secc. XVI–XX): Censimento degli archivi romani maintained by the Università di Roma "La Sapienza"* <http://212.189.172.98:8080/scrittutedidonne/Vaticana_ArchBarberini/scritturedidonne.jsp>.

95. BAV, Chigi I.VII.273, fol. 125r, letter dated May 4, 1657. Also see Capucci, "Costa, Margherita"; Costa, *Voice of a Virtuosa and Courtesan*, 24.

"vedova Margherita Costa."[96] The identity of her husband is not yet known; until Teresa Megale demonstrated that the dates did not align, some had even suggested that the Florentine court buffoon Bernardino Ricci—the dedicatee of *The Buffoons*—had been her spouse.[97] In her letter to Chigi written after at least a decade of widowhood, Costa endeavored to not only rouse his sympathy with her plaintive message but also to catch his eye with a sample of her poetry.[98] While Costa may very well have faced financial and even social hardship, particularly in her later years, it is difficult to ascertain how much of her plea speaks to real need and how much reveals a strategic tug on the patronage network, as her recipient's brother had recently been elected pope and he himself had just come to Rome as the new commander of the papal army.

It is not yet known how or when Costa died. Although the biographical trail at times runs cold, Costa's literary and dramatic legacy is readily apparent. With fourteen full-length printed works across a spectrum of genres, as well as an assortment of single-poem publications and an elegant gift manuscript, she proved herself a prolific author, poet, playwright, and librettist.[99] While she may not have seen many of her dramatic works realized on the stage, at least one of her poems was set to music and presumably performed before audiences.[100] Just as impressive as the expansiveness of Costa's publishing activity is her versatility in genre,

96. Ademollo, *I primi fasti*, 38.

97. This rumor seems to have entered into circulation with Antonfrancesco Marmi, who reports being told that Costa refers to Ricci as her husband in *The Buffoons*, which she does not. A second hand pens in a doubt about the authenticity of this claim. See BNCF, MS Magl. VIII 15, Antonfrancesco Marmi, *Miscellanea di diverse notizie letterarie e storiche, raccolte per lo più dagli eruditissimi discorsi del Signor Antonio Magliabechi tenuti col Cavalier Antonfrancesco Marmi*, fol. 39r. Ricci died in 1653, nearly a decade after Costa is described as a widow.

98. *Gran prence, a te, che di Quirino al trono*, BAV, Chigi I.VII.273, fol. 126r. For a transcription and a brief discussion of Costa's relationship to Chigi, see Giovanni Mario Crescimbeni, *Comentari intorno alla sua istoria della volgar poesia* (Rome: Lorenzo Basegio, 1730–1731), 3:323. Costa-Zalessow remarks on the poem's thematic similarities to the letter in *Voice of a Virtuosa and Courtesan*, 40–41, but does not note that they were sent together.

99. Costa-Zalessow has attributed an additional text to Costa, an anonymous poem entitled *Doralinda amazzone ai detrattori del valor delle dame disfida.* However, the current editors find the evidence for this attribution (including hypotheses about the posthumous publication) too conjectural to include the poem among Costa's works at this time. See Natalia Costa-Zalessow, "Una poesia femminista del 1672 anonima e dimenticata, da attribuire a Margherita Costa," *Esperienze letterarie* 35, no. 4 (2010): 79–85.

100. The poem "della Signora Costa," *Oh Dio, voi che mi dite*, was set to music by the Roman composer Marco Marazzoli. For the original score, see BAV, Chigi Q.VIII.177.9 fols. 15v–18r. For a reproduction and a transcription of the text, see *Cantatas by Marco Marazzoli*, ed. Wolfgang Witzenmann, in *The Italian Cantata in the Seventeenth Century*, vol. 4 (New York: Garland, 1986), 138–43, 280. Christine Jeanneret discusses this work, and an earlier hypothesis that Anna Francesca Costa had authored the poem, in "Gender Ambivalence and The Expression of Passions in the Performances of Early Roman Cantatas by Castrati and Female Singers," in *The Emotional Power of Music: Multidisciplinary*

style, and content and her ability to maneuver within the patronage networks of early modern Europe.

Cultural Context

Baroque Aesthetics

The Seicento was the century of the theatrical and the marvelous. Theater in this period "allied art and technology to create a medium that vanquished all competitors."[101] From the emerging art forms of opera and ballet to the machines that propelled objects and actors across elaborate stages, performative culture honed an aesthetic of spectacularity. Art and literature shared in its expressive vocabulary of ornamentation, exuberance, and artificiality. The congruity of this aesthetic across creative fields is exemplified by figures such as Gian Lorenzo Bernini (1598–1680), who brought a similar eye to his work in sculpture, architecture, and theater. Within literary circles, poets and writers—following especially the lead of Giambattista Marino—distanced themselves from the measured and decorous Petrarchism dominant in the previous century. They instead endeavored to astonish their readers through novel or witty conceits, hyperbole, and sensory stimulation.[102] Rather than adhering to the classicizing precepts set forth by figures like Pietro Bembo, Marino insisted that poetic enterprise should rely on rule-breaking—though, he stressed, one should know how and where to do so in a manner befitting the tastes of the age.[103]

This new aesthetic landscape impacted women's relationship to literature as both subjects and authors. The Petrarchists had largely crafted their verse around the image of an idealized lady, superlative in both beauty and virtue. This affirming attitude toward women and their ennobling influence, coupled with the Cinquecento emphasis on courtly urbanity, extended into their increasingly visible role as patronesses, dedicatees, and writers in their own right. As Virginia

---

Perspectives on Musical Arousal, Expression, and Social Control, ed. Tom Cochrane, Bernardino Fantini, and Klaus R Scherer, 85–102 (Oxford: Oxford University Press, 2013), 93–94, 98.

101. Larry F. Norman, ed., *The Theatrical Baroque* (Chicago: David and Alfred Smart Museum of Art, University of Chicago, 2001), 1.

102. On baroque literature and its broader cultural contexts, see Franco Croce et al. eds., *I capricci di Proteo: Percorsi e linguaggi del Barocco; Atti del convegno di Lecce, 23–26 ottobre 2000* (Rome: Salerno, 2002); Lucia Strappini, ed., *I luoghi dell'immaginario barocco: Atti del convegno di Siena, 21–23 ottobre 1999* (Naples: Liguori, 2001); Andrea Battistini, *Il barocco: Cultura, miti, immagini* (Rome: Salerno, 2000); Christopher D. Johnson, *Hyperboles: The Rhetoric of Excess in Baroque Literature and Thought* (Cambridge, MA: Harvard University Press, 2010).

103. "Io pretendo di saper le regole più che non sanno tutti i pedanti insieme, ma la vera regola (cor mio bello) è saper rompere le regole a tempo e luogo, accomodandosi al costume corrente et al gusto del secolo." Giambattista Marino, *Lettere*, ed. Marziano Guglielminetti (Turin: Einaudi, 1966), 366.

Cox has outlined, the Seicento's transgressive approach to literary norms largely triggered a reversal of that model, exemplified by an uptick in misogynist literature and the substitution of Laura-like beloveds with "the 'tainted' ladies of the baroque [who] manifested their carnality precisely by virtue of their flaws."[104] Elite female would-be authors and poets confronting this more hostile terrain also had to grapple with the sensuality of baroque literature, much in vogue but poorly suited to maintaining a public persona of respectability. As a consequence, by mid-century the number of women entering the world of print declined sharply in comparison with previous generations.[105] Notable exceptions included Lucrezia Marinella (1571–1653), the nun Arcangela Tarabotti (1604–1652), the Jewish author Sarra Copia Sulam (c. 1592–1641), and Costa herself.[106]

Perhaps more than any other woman of her age, Costa advertised her comfort with baroque aesthetics. In the first line of *The Buffoons'* dedication, she advocates breaking with traditional themes and styles: "The usual is always the same, but the unusual is far more novel." Much like Marino and the *marinisti*, Costa strove to inspire awe and wonder, or *meraviglia*, in her readers with an array of surprising metaphors, novel word plays, and unexpected conceits. Her language is often bizarre, contradictory, and hyperbolic, and embraces monstrous forms that purposefully subvert Petrarchan canons of female beauty. The rhetorical paradox is a returning trope in her epistolary and lyric collections, and shows a close affinity with the poetry of contemporaries such as Alessandro Adimari. His *Tersicore*, also published in Florence by Massi and Landi, consists of a series of fifty *contreblasons* (paradoxical characterizations) in praise of women with a host of physical defects.[107] Here, the laudatory erotic lyric is turned on its head and addressed to comic inversions of the Cinquecento beloved. Instead of Petrarch's golden-haired Laura, Adimari dedicates his poems to old, lame, and mangy women.[108] But Costa, as we have seen, takes the conceit one step further. She celebrates malformed paramours of both genders, and even aligns the grotesque and the bizarre with her own authorial identity in her dedications.[109] The deformed body

104. Cox, *Women's Writing in Italy*, 177–79, citation on 179.

105. For an overview of this transition, see Cox, *Women's Writing in Italy*, 166–227.

106. For a comparison of Marinella, Tarabotti, and Sulam, particularly in light of growing misogyny, see Lynn Westwater, *The Disquieting Voice: Women's Writing and Antifeminism in Seventeenth-Century Venice*. PhD diss., University of Chicago, 2003.

107. Alessandro Adimari, *La Tersicore, o vero scherzi, e paradossi poetici sopra la beltà delle donne fra' difetti ancora ammirabili, e vaghe* (Florence: Massi e Landi, 1637). For more on Adimari's *Tersicore* and its poetry of transgressive beauty, see Patrizia Bettella, *The Ugly Woman: Transgressive Aesthetic Models in Italian Poetry from the Middle Ages to the Baroque* (Toronto: University of Toronto Press, 2005), 129–32.

108. "vecchia," "zoppa," "rognosa"; Adimari, *Tersicore*, 111, 27, 39.

109. Costa associates herself with *bizzarria*, bizarreness or capriciousness, in the autobiographical poem *Ardano i parti miei, e co' i miei parti* in *Lo stipo*, 292, as well as the first and final poems of *La*

thus simultaneously signals her own creative innovation as well as her debt to the anti-classicizing and farcical poetics of her baroque era.

As tastes shifted towards the end of the century, baroque style drew the disdain of writers and theorists looking to define themselves against its extravagance. Prompted especially by the foundation of the Arcadian Academy in 1690, they uprooted the pomp of earlier generations in preference for a more pastoral aesthetic grounded in verisimilitude and harmony. Their disparagement of the Seicento as an era of "bad taste" remained a fixture in criticism until recently.[110] A mid-twentieth-century poetic dictionary, for example, defined the entire century as "The Drought" of Italian literature, observing that "*marinismo* is generally deplored as a disease."[111] Of late, however, critics have begun to reevaluate this view of the baroque as being somehow parenthetical to Italy's literary history. One recent volume, for example, considers authors, genres, and texts from forty-six perspectives, plunging deep into what its editor calls the "forest" of a newly rediscovered cultural imagination stretching across literary, artistic, and theatrical disciplines.[112]

Medici Rule, Patronage, and Entertainments

Margherita Costa came into her own as an author amidst the baroque pomp and ephemeral splendor of Florence's languishing dynasty. As noted above, her arrival in Florence coincided with crown prince Ferdinando II's ascent to the Medici throne.[113] Son of Grand Duke Cosimo II de' Medici (1590–1621) and Archduchess Maria Maddalena of Austria (1589–1631), a then ten-year-old Ferdinando inherited the Tuscan Grand Duchy upon his father's premature death in 1621. Governance of the Medici state passed on to his mother and his grandmother, Christine of

---

chitarra, 1–5 and 567–73. Also see I.viii.138 and note. For a discussion of this facet of her persona, see Goethals, "The Bizarre Muse."

110. For an analysis of this history, see Vernon Hyde Minor, *The Death of the Baroque and the Rhetoric of Good Taste* (Cambridge: University of Cambridge Press, 2006).

111. *The Princeton Encyclopedia of Poetry and Poetics*, ed. Alex Preminger (Princeton: Princeton University Press, 1965), 67 and 414.

112. Strappini, *I luoghi dell'immaginario barocco*, citation on 3. Also see, for example, Paolo Cherchi, *La metamorfosi dell'*Adone (Ravenna: Longo, 1996); Cherchi, "Marino and the Meraviglia," in *Culture and Authority in the Baroque*, ed. Massimo Ciavolella and Patrick Coleman (Toronto: University of Toronto Press, 2005), 63–72; Johnson, *Hyperboles*; Lucinda Spera, ed., *Verso il moderno: Pubblico e immaginario nel Seicento italiano* (Rome: Carocci, 2008).

113. The bibliography on Ferdinando II is slim. See Lazzeri, *Il principe e il diplomatico*; and Irene Cotta Stumpo, "Ferdinando II de' Medici, granduca di Toscana," *DBI* 46 (1996), 278–83; <http://www.treccani.it/enciclopedia/ferdinando-ii-de-medici-granduca-di-toscana_(Dizionario-Biografico)/>. Harold Acton carves out some space for him in the now classic *The Last Medici* (New York: Thames and Hudson, 1980); as does John Rigby Hale in his *Florence and the Medici: The Pattern of Control* (London: Thames and Hudson, 1977).

Lorraine (1565–1637), who served as co-regents until Ferdinando came of age in 1628. Together, the *tutrici* (protectors) exercised considerable influence over the young grand duke, shaping patronage and policy well past his minority. Florence stagnated under their regency: the administrative offices at the Uffizi were overrun by parasites and prelates seeking benefices, the treasuries were depleted, and the merchant trades—traditionally the backbone of Tuscany's economy—suffered from neglect. Even their efforts to increase the Medici's dynastic capital by securing a favorable marriage alliance for Ferdinando with one of Europe's great houses fell woefully short of the mark. Locked in a tug of war over their contrasting loyalties—Christine supported her native France while Maria Maddalena advanced the Austrian Habsburg agenda—the *tutrici* finally settled on a relatively inferior union with Vittoria della Rovere (1622–1694), the last heir to the failing Duchy of Urbino.[114] By all accounts, their union was far from happy, or even fruitful.

Vittoria was the daughter of Federico Ubaldo della Rovere and Claudia de' Medici, Ferdinando's aunt, and was therefore Ferdinando's first cousin. Betrothed before she was even two, she spent her youth surrounded by the women of the Medici family in the convent of Santa Croce, La Crocetta, where she received a religious education in keeping with the wishes of the dowagers.[115] Vittoria was married to Ferdinando in a private ceremony in 1634 but remained at La Crocetta until 1637, when the union could finally be consummated and publicly celebrated. Soon after they officially wed, the couple conceived a son who, as already noted, tragically died shortly after birth. A second stillbirth followed, this time a girl. They would have to wait until 1642 to welcome a healthy heir into the world, the future Grand Duke Cosimo III (1642–1723), and a full eighteen years more for the arrival of their second child, Francesco Maria (1660–1711). The years in between were marked by marital discord and estrangement, rumored to have been caused by Vittoria's discovery of Ferdinando in flagrante with a court page. They lived separate lives, Vittoria preferring the Medici villas of Artimino, Pisa, and Poggio Imperiale, leaving Ferdinando free to enjoy the sprawling Palazzo Pitti or to hunt in any one of his many well-stocked game preserves.

The dwindling fortunes of the Medici principate dampened but did not extinguish artistic patronage under the rule of Ferdinando II. In many ways, it was business as usual. The palace workshops at the Uffizi continued to keep a small army of local artisans busy, occupied by large-scale projects set into motion by previous grand dukes. With a well-oiled artistic mechanism in place, work on the opulent Cappella dei Principi at San Lorenzo moved forward, as did the expansion of

114. Cotta Stumpo, "Ferdinando II de' Medici."

115. For more on Vittoria's circle of female intimates, including her aunts, cousins, friends, and artists, see Giovanna Benadusi, "The Gender Politics of Vittoria della Rovere" in *Medici Women: The Making of a Dynasty in Grand Ducal Tuscany*, ed. Giovanna Benadusi and Judith C. Brown (Toronto: Centre for Reformation and Renaissance Studies, 2015), 265–301.

Palazzo Pitti and the Boboli Gardens.[116] The Flemish portraitist Justus Sustermans (1597–1681) enjoyed a long career at the grand ducal court chronicling more than sixty years of the Medici with their buffoons, pets, and associates. Three generations of Medici extending from Archduchess Maria Maddalena to Cosimo III posed for his canvases, proudly displaying their lavish costumes, vanities, and conceits for posterity to admire. A double portrait of Ferdinando II and Vittoria della Rovere from circa 1660 (Fig. 3), for example, advertises the individual trappings of the mature couple's grand ducal power: Vittoria's milky-white flesh, complimented by the strands of large pearls that conspicuously adorn her dress, neck, and hair, shines against her sober black attire; Ferdinando, clad in fancifully baroque armor and bearing the insignia of the military Order of Saint Stephen, meets the viewer's gaze with an almost cavalier authority.[117] Just as they were for Ferdinando's mother before him and later his son Cosimo III, Sustermans' talents were at the service of the Medici's dynastic message-making. But as Ferdinando came into his own as a ruler and a patron, he also ventured away from the cadre of local artists passed down to him by the *tutrici*. He recruited outside talent, most famously luring the renowned master Pietro della Cortona (1596–1669) away from his Barberini patrons, and as a consequence filled the palace with a new creative energy that ushered in a shift away from Florentine Mannerism towards the dynamic baroque style of Rome.[118]

Artistic patronage was in truth a responsibility shared among members of the Medici family. Ferdinando acted in concert with his younger brothers Giovan Carlo, Mattias, and Leopoldo, the latter being an exceptionally energetic steward of the Medici's cultural patrimony.[119] Grand Duchess Vittoria was also an active patron of art, music, and literature, lending her support to the first all-female literary academy, the Sienese Le Assicurate (The Academy of the Self-Assured), and

116. For more on the workshops and self-perpetuating system of artistic obligations which Ferdinando inherited when he assumed power, see Edward L. Goldberg, *Patterns in Late Medici Art Patronage* (Princeton, NJ: Princeton University Press, 1983), 9.

117. The commander's sash, baton, and cross featured in Susterman's portrait point to Ferdinando's command over the Order of Saint Stephen—a dynastic military order founded by his great-grandfather, Cosimo I, and charged with defending the Mediterranean from marauding pirates and Ottoman Turks. For more on Ferdinando II and the Order, particularly on his reduction of his naval forces, see Niccolò Capponi, "Le Palle di Marte: Military Strategy and Diplomacy in the Grand Duchy of Tuscany under Ferdinand II de' Medici (1621–1670)," *The Journal of Military History* 68, no. 4 (2004): 1108–31.

118. Malcolm Campbell discusses Ferdinando's apparent shift away from local masters in favor of non-Tuscan painters in "Medici Patronage and the Baroque: A Reappraisal," in *Art Bulletin* 48, no. 2 (1966): 133–46. For more on Cortona's Medici commissions, also see his *Pietro da Cortona at the Pitti Palace: A Study of the Planetary Rooms and Related Projects* (Princeton, NJ: Princeton University Press, 1977).

119. Goldberg dedicates considerable space to Cardinal Leopoldo's engagement with the arts in *Patterns in Late Medici Art Patronage*, 21–78.

Figure 3. Justus Sustermans, *Grand Duke Ferdinando II de' Medici and his Wife Vittoria della Rovere*. c. 1660s.

corresponding with several women authors including Arcangela Tarabotti and Maria Selvaggia Borghini (1656–1731).[120] Scientific patronage under the Medici

120. In her 2008 *Women's Writing in Italy*, 361n162, Virginia Cox lamented the fact that Vittoria's efforts as a literary patron had as of then received insufficient attention. Two years later, Eve Straussman-Pflanzer answered the call with an in-depth dissertation on Vittoria's capacity as a patroness, including her support of female literary academies and individual poets: Eve Straussman-Pflanzer, *Court Culture in Seventeenth-Century Florence: The Art Patronage of Medici Grand Duchess Vittoria della Rovere, 1622–1694*, Ph.D. diss., New York University, Institute of Fine Arts, 2010. Also see the more recent work of Adelina Modesti, such as her article "The Self-Fashioning of a Female 'Prince': The Cultural Matronage of Vittoria della Rovere," in *Representing Women's Authority in the Early Modern World: Struggles, Strategies, and Morality*, ed. Eavan O'Brien (Rome: Aracne, 2013), 253–98. Tarabotti dedicated her 1644 *Antisatira e antisatira* to the grand duchess and exchanged several letters with her; see Meredith Ray, "Letters and Lace: Arcangela Tarabotti and Convent Culture in Seicento Venice," in *Early Modern Women and Transnational Communities of Letters*, ed. Julie D. Campbell and Anne R. Larsen (Burlington, VT: Ashgate, 2009), 45–74. For Vittoria's relationship to Borghini, see Maria

was similarly a multi-generational affair, particularly with regard to one of the era's most revolutionary figures, Galileo Galilei (1564–1642). Three successive grand dukes lent their support to the astronomer, beginning with the first Ferdinando de' Medici and concluding with the astronomer's former pupil, Ferdinando II.[121] The apex of Margherita Costa's literary production coincided with Galileo's final years in Florence, a period that he spent under house arrest following his condemnation by the Inquisition. Copies of two of Costa's publications, *Li buffoni* and *Flora feconda*, have in fact survived in Galileo's library.[122] Evidence of Galileo's influence can also be found in Costa's work. A telescope, the kind of fine-tuned instrument used by Galileo to peer into the heliocentric heavens, is clearly discernable in the frontispiece for *Li buffoni*, which, like the frontispiece for Galileo's *Dialogue Concerning the Two Chief World Systems*, was produced by Stefano della Bella.[123] The artists, intellectuals, and performers associated with the Medici court during this period formed a small, closely-interrelated circle, placing an acquaintance between Costa and Galileo within the realm of possibility.

Though the overall number of dramatic performances sponsored by the Medici declined during this period, the princes nonetheless remained enthusiastic patrons of the theater. Ferdinando, Giovan Carlo, Mattias, and Leopoldo acted as impresarios, each negotiating with performers, academies, and foreign powers to bring all manner of spectacular entertainment to the grand duchy. As one critic has noted, during this period "harmony among the brothers became an extremely efficient instrument of the collective cultural policy that bestowed

---

Pia Paoli, "'Come se mi fosse sorella': Maria Selvaggia Borghini nella Repubblica delle lettere," in *Per lettera: La scrittura epistolare femminile, tra archivio e tipografia*, ed. Gabriella Zarri (Rome: Viella, 1999), 491–534.

121. The bibliography on Galileo and the Medici is too vast to cite here, but for a start see Mario Biagioli, *Galileo Courtier: The Practice of Science in the Culture of Absolutism* (Chicago: University of Chicago Press, 1993); J. L. Heilbron, *Galileo* (Oxford: Oxford University Press, 2010); and David Wootton, *Galileo: Watcher of the Skies* (New Haven: Yale University Press, 2010).

122. Margherita Costa's two publications are catalogued in Antonio Favaro, *La libreria di Galileo Galilei descritta ed illustrata* (Rome: Tipografia delle matematiche e fisiche, 1887), entries 394 and 438. Meredith Ray has recently written on Galileo's interest in female authors in her *Daughters of Alchemy: Women and Scientific Culture in Early Modern Italy* (Cambridge, MA: Harvard University Press, 2015) and *Margherita Sarrocchi's Letters to Galileo: Astronomy, Astrology, and Poetics in Seventeenth-Century Italy* (New York: Palgrave Macmillan, 2016.)

123. Galileo Galilei, *Dialogo sopra i due massimi sistemi del mondo, tolemaico e copernicano* (Florence: Gio. Batista Landini, 1632). Della Bella's etching represents Aristotle and Ptolemy engaged in a debate with Copernicus over heliocentrism. Della Bella also produced the frontispiece for the posthumous collection of Galileo's works, *Opere di Galileo Galilei*, 2 vols. (Bologna: per gli heredi del Dozza, 1656). For more on the subject, see Jaco Rutgers, "A Frontispiece for Galileo's *Opere*: Pietro Anichini and Stefano della Bella," *Print Quarterly* 29, no. 1 (2012): 3–12. The figure holding the telescope on the frontispiece of *Li buffoni* is likely Tordo, Ferdinando's lens maker (III.ii); for more on this figure, see below.

on Florence a mixed theatrical system... [incorporating] court theater, academic theater, and commercial theater."[124] In addition to sponsoring what we might call "official" theater for large-scale public celebrations and visiting heads of state, all three Medici princes were deeply engaged in music and drama. Leopoldo lent out his private apartments to at least two theatrical companies to use for rehearsals.[125] Mattias supported the famed castrato Atto Melani and his family.[126] Giovan Carlo enlisted the talents of the court architect Ferdinando Tacca to build Florence's first opera house, the Teatro della Pergola, also known as the Teatro degli Immobili. He also had a hand in creating the Teatro del Cocomero, which housed the Accademia degli Infocati and staged a repertoire of classical tragedies and comedic operas written in dialect.[127] Furthermore, the princes were known to have been caught up in the lives and intrigues of their protégés from time to time. Anna Francesca Costa, for example, bitterly complained to Giovan Carlo about Margherita, dragging the prince into a squabble between sisters over some missing items of clothing.[128] As their correspondence with each other and their clients reveal, the Medici brothers were intimately involved with nearly every aspect of theatrical production in Florence.

The brothers' shared love for the stage was no doubt instilled in them by their mother, Maria Maddalena. As children they were trained by court musicians and performed in plays for the archduchess. The Medici princesses benefited from an analogous exposure to theater in their cloister at La Crocetta. Maria Maddalena's youngest daughter, Anna de' Medici, and Vittoria della Rovere frequently attended court theatricals in and outside of the convent walls, and most likely studied music together under Francesca Caccini.[129] The court diarist Cesare Tinghi recorded their frequent visits to the court to enjoy some of the many ballets,

124. Mamone, "Most Serene Brothers-Princes-Impresarios," 4.1–2. Mamone retraces the correspondence exchanged between the brothers as they relate to theatrical patronage. Much of the same ground is also covered in her "Accademie e opera in musica nella vita di Giovan Carlo, Mattias e Leopoldo de' Medici, fratelli del Granduca Ferdinando," in *Lo stupor dell' invenzione: Firenze e la nascita dell'opera; Atti del Convegno Internazionale di Studi, Firenze, 5–6 ottobre 2000*, ed. Piero Gargiulo (Florence: Olschki, 2001), 119–38.

125. Acton, *The Last Medici*, 50.

126. Roger Freitas, *Portrait of a Castrato: Politics, Patronage, and Music in the Life of Atto Melani* (Cambridge, MA: Cambridge University Press, 2009).

127. Frank A. D'Accone, et al., "Florence," *Grove Music Online* (Oxford University Press); <http://www.oxfordmusiconline.com/subscriber/article/grove/music/09847> .

128. Megale, for example, analyzes the interrelationship between the Medici princes and Anna Francesca Costa. See "Il principe e la cantante," especially 212–13. Mamone dedicates some space to scandals involving the Medici and their performers in her article, "Most Serene Brothers-Princes-Impresarios."

129. Cusick, in *Francesca Caccini at the Medici Court*, 55, reveals the permeable nature of the La Crocetta's walls and the relative ease with which the Medici princesses were allowed to come and go in order to enjoy music, dancing, and theatrical performances.

jousts, *intermedi* (brief entertainments performed during intermissions), pastorals, comedies, and dramas that were being staged for the rest of the Medici youth. Also included within Tinghi's notes are accounts of Maria Maddalena inviting troupes of comic actors known as *zanni* to perform *commedie all'improvviso*, or what today is commonly referred to as the *commedia dell'arte*, for her children in the various great halls of Palazzo Pitti.[130] One entry from October 23, 1623, even tells of the staging of a *commedia ridicolosa*, or "ridiculous comedy":

> The Most Serene Archduchess, wanting to bring a little pleasure to His Most Serene Highness and to her other sons and daughters, had the *zanni* comics from the troupe of Fritellino and Flaminia come up to the hall where a backdrop has been set up in order to perform a *commedia ridicolosa*.[131] At 23 hours the aforementioned comedy began and within an hour it had ended, all much to the delight of their Most Serene Highnesses, who were hidden behind a screen in said hall.[132]

Respectably shielded behind a screen, the dowager and her children were free to privately enjoy the slapstick humor of the visiting *zanni*. It is easy to imagine the laughter of the young princes filling the halls of the Pitti, and why theater, including comedy, was in the Medici's blood.

Court pageantry under the *tutrici* was a decidedly more decorous affair. During their co-regency, Maria Maddalena and her mother-in-law used the visual and performing arts to publicly lend authority to their rule. They selected religious dramas featuring saints and biblical heroines, and staged their carefully orchestrated displays of feminine piety before visiting dignitaries.[133] They

130. Excerpts from Tinghi's *Diario di Corte* can be found in Angelo Solerti's *Musica, ballo e drammatica alla corte Medicea dal 1600 al 1637: Notizie tratte da un diario, con appendice di testi inediti e rari* (Florence: R. Bemporad e figlio, 1905).

131. Fritellino and Flaminia can most likely be identified as the famed actor and commentator Pier Maria Cecchini and his wife Orsola, who were known to have performed *La Pazzia di Flaminia* in Florence at this time. The Fritellino mask was associated with buffoon and carnival performances, and is featured in Jacques Callot's c. 1622 *Balli di Sfessania* etchings. See Ferdinando Taviani, "Cecchini, Pier Maria," in *DBI* 23 (1979): 274–80; <http://www.treccani.it/enciclopedia/pier-maria-cecchini_(Dizionario-Biografico)/>.

132. "[…] volendo la Ser.ma Arciducessa dare un poco di gusto a S.A.S et a' sig.ri fillioli et filliole fece venire e' comedianti di Zanni della compagnia di Fritellino et della Flaminia, su alla sala dove è ritto la prospettiva et fece recitare una commedia ridicolosa et alle 23 ore cominciò detta Comedia et a un'ora era fornita, con molto gusto di loro A. Ser.me, le quale erano incognite dreto a uno ingraticolato in detta sala." Tinghi, *Diario di Corte*, in Solerti, *Musica, ballo e drammatica*, 170.

133. Kelley Harness notes that between the years of 1621 and 1628, ten court spectacles featuring biblical heroines were staged at the Uffizi, Palazzo Pitti, and the Casino Mediceo, eight of which

also sponsored secular pieces with strong roles for women. Maria Maddalena in particular pushed for female themes and performers when designing her courtly divertissements. Most famously, when Prince Wladyslaw Sigismund of Poland visited Florence in 1625, the archduchess commissioned *La liberazione di Ruggiero dall'isola d'Alcina* from Francesca Caccini—an opera which boldly privileged the voice of the sorceress Alcina from Ariosto's *Orlando furioso* while still celebrating the martial prowess of the Medici princes.[134] With Ferdinando's ascent to the throne on July 14, 1628, however, the matriarchy officially came to an end, as did a preference for female-centered dramas. The return to patriarchy was honored, albeit indirectly, in the fall of that year in a grand opera organized for Margherita de' Medici's marriage to Odoardo Farnese. Staged in the Uffizi theater with sets by Alfonso Parigi, Marco da Gagliano's *La flora* was the centerpiece of the wedding festivities.[135] Maria Maddalena selected a libretto based on a tale from Ovid's *Fasti* (Book of Days) celebrating the union of the nymph Chloris to the god Zephyrus, and the consequent return of springtime fecundity to the Tuscan lands. The allegorical spectacle represented what some critics see as the symbolic transfer of power from female to male rule, and the reaffirmation of the continuity of the Medici patriline.[136] The event was also marked by a generic shift towards mythological themes and a pastoral mode which, Kelley Harness has argued, allegorically connected the theme of springtime renewal with the return of a male heir.[137] Accordingly, when Ferdinando's marriage to Vittoria was finally celebrated in July 1637, the couple was feted in the courtyard of Palazzo Pitti with *Le nozze degli dei* (The Wedding of the Gods)—a grandiose opera which culminated in the spectacular marriage of not one, but four pairs of Olympian deities.[138]

---

were performed for the benefit of high-ranking visiting dignitaries; see Harness, "*La Flora* and the End of Female Rule in Tuscany," *Journal of the American Musicological Society* 51, no. 3 (1998), esp. 445–49. However, Maria Galli Stampino cautions us against assuming that the regency court restricted its sponsorship to religious performances and promoted a "retrograde, stifling, and hyper-religious atmosphere." See Stampino, "A Regent and Her Court: Towards a Study of Maria Maddalena d'Austria's Patronage (Florence 1621–1628)," *Forum Italicum* 40, no. 1 (2006), 22. See also John Walter Hill, "Florence: Musical Spectacle and Drama, 1570–1650," in *The Early Baroque Era from the Late 16th Century to the 1660s*, ed. Curtis Price (Englewood Cliffs, NJ: Prentice Hall, 1994), 121–45.

134. See chapter 9, "*La liberazione di Ruggiero* amid the Politics of Regency," in Cusick, *Francesca Caccini at the Medici Court*, 191–212.

135. For more on the opera and the nuptial celebrations accompanying *La Flora*, see A. M. Nagler's *Theater Festivals of the Medici, 1539–1637* (New York: Da Capo Press, 1976), 139–61.

136. See Harness, "*La Flora*," esp. 451–53.

137. Harness, "*La Flora*," 458–60.

138. For more on *Le nozze* and Medici theatricals, see Nagler, *Theater Festivals of the Medici*, 162–74.

Large-scale operas and equestrian ballets were just one side of the spectrum of productions staged for the grand ducal family and their guests. Among the various dances, dramas, and tournaments organized for their amusement, spectacles involving dwarfs, hunchbacks, and other wondrous types of "human exotica" were also in high demand.[139] These natural "marvels" played an important role in the established culture of comic entertainment in early modern Europe, in and beyond the Medici court. Dwarf performers, in particular, were fashionable members of many a princely entourage and offered diversion and companionship to the lords to whom they were bound through ties of "abjection and affection."[140] As highly prized members of the courtly menagerie, they were rewarded for services that included all manner of grotesque entertainment. Commonly associated with mischief and merrymaking, they were frequently put on public display during feast days and carnival celebrations. Little people entertained crowds with elaborate jousts and races, and attempted to woo the ladies in the audience—all, supposedly, to comic effect.[141] There was also bloodsport. Dwarfs were known to wrestle and fight with knives at the feet of jeering courtiers and princes, stripped half-naked so that all could take in the spectacle of their astonishing bodies. The perceived absurdity of seeing their non-heroic forms engaged in chivalrous displays of skill and valor provoked contemptuous laughter from the crowds, yet granted them a livelihood as marginal performers. They were curiosities, monstrosities, deemed both repellent and attractive, and were often used to satirize the chivalric, the noble, and the beautiful at court.

The Medici's predilection for dwarf entertainment was documented by some of the leading artists of the day. The favorite dwarf of Grand Duke Cosimo I (1519–1574), Braccio di Bartolo, ironically known as *Il nano Morgante* after the eponymous giant of poet Luigi Pulci's epic, was immortalized in bronze, on canvas, and in several fountains across Florence.[142] Cosimo II was legendary for

139. See Pamela Allen Brown, "The Mirror and the Cage: Queens and Dwarfs at the Early Modern Court," in *Historical Affects and the Early Modern Theater*, eds. Ronda Arab, Michelle Dowd, and Adam Zucker (New York: Routledge, 2015), 137.

140. Brown, "The Mirror and the Cage," 137.

141. Sandra Cheng, "Parodies of Life: Baccio del Bianco's Comic Drawings of Dwarfs," in *Parody and Festivity in Early Modern Art*, ed. David R. Smith (Burlington, VT: Ashgate, 2012), 132.

142. Valerio Cioli's 1560 *Fontana del Bacchino*, or *Morgante*, features a nude, corpulent Braccio di Bartolo astride a turtle. Agnolo Bronzino's 1552 double portrait of *Il nano Morgante*, currently housed in the Uffizi, represents his nude subject before and after a bird hunt. Giambologna also cast a bronze of a nude *Morgante on a Dragon* for a small fountain above the Loggia dei Lanzi (1582, currently housed in the Bargello in Florence). For more on the subject, see Touba Ghadessi, "Lords and Monsters: Visible Emblems of Rule," *I Tatti Studies in the Italian Renaissance*, 16, no. 1/2 (Fall 2013): 491–523; and Robin O'Bryan, "Grotesque Bodies, Princely Delight: Dwarfs in Italian Renaissance Court Imagery," *Preternature: Critical and Historical Studies on the Preternatural* 1, no. 2 (2012): 252–88.

his love of dwarfs. During a long convalescence he is said to have locked himself away with only the company of his little people and buffoons, amusing himself by plying them with drink and watching them destroy his private chambers.[143] While in the service of the grand duke, Jacques Callot executed twenty-one engravings of dwarfs referred to as *Varie figure gobbi* (Various Hunchbacked Figures, c. 1621–1625). The series depicts a troupe of them singing, dancing, playing instruments, and making merry, some while wearing *commedia dell'arte* masks, and all displaying varying degrees of physical deformity (Figs. 4–6). Stefano della Bella followed suit in the early 1630s with four etchings of dwarfs engaged in parodic courtly displays for a festival book, as did other Florentine artists throughout the century.[144] Together, these prints provide visual testimony to the kind of dwarf spectacles that were *en vogue* when Margherita Costa arrived at the Medicean court, particularly during Carnival. But more to the point, these images of dueling, gallantly-attired dwarfs clearly anticipate the figures depicted in Della Bella's frontispiece for *Li buffoni* by just a handful of years. For as will be discussed in greater detail below, his etching (Fig. 7) deftly hones in on the comic incongruity between the diminutive stature of the players and the courtly roles they were assigned by Costa in her *commedia ridicolosa.*

Structure of The Buffoons

Costa sets her three-act comedy in the princely kingdom of Morocco. Despite this exotic locale, the reader-spectator glimpses nothing of the supposed African surroundings. The story largely centers on domestic disputes and court shenanigans, and the scenery to which it alludes is thus more familiar to a seventeenth-century Italian audience: a palace, its gardens, hunting grounds, and the windows of both a noblewoman and a prostitute. Reinforcing this proximity is Stefano della Bella's frontispiece illustrating a composite of the comedy's prologue and final scene (Fig. 7). Here the players dance and converse in a street whose surrounding buildings and far-off cypress trees are quintessentially Florentine.

Rather than offering a concrete geographic locus, the play's setting primarily allows Costa to map out the discord between warring spouses, Prince Meo and his bride, Princess Marmotta. Meo's realm in Morocco serves as a gendered foil for Marmotta's native kingdom, Fessa. The latter offers the reader-spectator a number of interpretations: Fessa refers to the historical realm and city of Fez,

143. Cheng, "Parodies of Life," 131.

144. For more on Callot's and Della Bella's etchings, and other comic drawings and dwarf parodies, see Françoise Viatte, "Allegorical and Burlesque Subjects by Stefano della Bella," *Master Drawings* 15, no. 4 (1977): 347–65 and 425–44, esp. 356–62; and the chapter "The Court and its Cruel Pleasures: 'Freaks' in Italy" in Barry Wind, *"A Foul and Pestilent Congregation": Images of "Freaks" in Baroque Art* (Burlington, VT: Ashgate, 1998), 19–48.

Figure 4. Jacques Callot, title page to *Varie figure gobbi.* c.1621/25.

Figure 5. Jacques Callot, dwarf playing the violin. From *Varie figure gobbi.* c.1621/25.

Figure 6. Jacques Callot, dwarf playing a wind instrument.
From *Varie figure gobbi*. c.1621/25.

while *fesseria* describes trifling nonsense and *fesso* or *fessa* indicates a fool.[145] As a word meaning "slit" or "crevice," however, it also alludes quite unmistakably to the female genitalia. While Fessa is a fertile land of sexual gratification in which women largely do as they please, Marmotta complains, in Morocco husbands shelve their wives and set aside their conjugal obligations for other pleasures. This incongruity between the dynastic couple's amorous proclivities constitutes the play's central plotline. Already exasperated by her husband's tavern escapades with the court dwarfs, hunchbacks, and buffoons, Marmotta reaches her breaking point when Meo pursues the unappealing prostitute Ancroia after having refused her own embrace. In her distress, Marmotta resolves to abandon her marriage vows and to return home to Fessa, where in the absence of any other successor she will ultimately rule. Husband and wife are reconciled only when it is discovered that Baldassarre, a Spanish buffoon and Ancroia's former lover, is Marmotta's long-lost brother and therefore the rightful heir to Fessa. Overjoyed at this revelation of an unexpected brother-in-law, Meo pledges to forego his previous diversions, to punish his court's most offending members, and to return to his wife and their conjugal bed.

145. Benedetto Croce questioned whether there might be a relationship between Costa's buffoonish *Fessa* and Jacques Callot's twenty-four drawings of *commedia dell'arte*-inspired figures, collectively titled *Balli di Sfessania*. See his remarks relayed in Luigi Rasi, *La caricatura e i comici italiani* (Florence: R. Bemporad e figlio, 1907), 33–34; and discussed in Strappini, *La tragedia del buffone*, 269n35.

Figure 7. Margherita Costa, *Li buffoni* (Florence, 1641).
Frontispiece by Stefano della Bella.

Costa likely adopted the Morocco-Fez pairing from the *commedia dell'arte*, already known to experiment with North African and Middle Eastern settings.[146] Most pertinently, Flaminio Scala's 1611 publication of *commedia* scenarios featured one tragedy, *La forsennata principessa* (The Mad Princess), about comparable sexual misalignments that is also set in Fessa.[147] In this case, the prince of Morocco throws over his beloved, the princess of Portugal (a figure perhaps played by Isabella Andreini), when he becomes enamored of the promiscuous princess of Fessa. While Costa's Marmotta remains love-starved until the comedy's final scene, in this scenario the prince of Morocco and the princess of Fessa consummate their lust. Left high and dry by her betrothed, the unfortunate princess of Portugal is driven to madness and suicide. In both works, however, a rightful spouse suffers her prince's dalliances with a woman of loose sexual morality. Several other similarities suggest that this, or a scenario like it, may have been Costa's source. In script and scenario alike, the princess of Fessa is (or is initially believed to be) the king's sole heir. And buffoonery plays a central role in each; while in Costa's comedy buffoons and other burlesque characters run amok until the prince finally reasserts his authority, Scala's tragedy instead ends with the buffoon Burattino and the citizenry assuming control over the kingdom after all the sovereigns either have been murdered or have taken their own lives. In both works, Fessa is a kingdom that risks being overrun by the absurd.

Although Costa dedicates the *Buffoni* plot *argomento* to the connubial narrative, her cast is populated by ridiculous characters. First among these is Tedeschino, who complicates the storyline through his antics and his ardor for the princess. Throughout the comedy, Tedeschino relentlessly pursues Marmotta. Plotting her revenge against her husband, Marmotta in turn tricks the buffoon into believing that she will finally succumb to his overtures and invites him to meet her in the palace disguised in women's attire. Supplying him with a set of Ancroia's clothes, she instead arranges for him to arrive at the spot where Meo has planned his sexual rendezvous with the prostitute. The resulting scene in which Tedeschino fights off Meo's libidinous advances incorporates stock elements of early modern comedy such as cross-dressing and same-sex erotic encounters. As Tedeschino's coverings come undone, however, so does Marmotta's plot. The buffoon suffers a thorough beating, and in the comedy's final scene he and Ancroia

146. For an overview, see Erith Jaffe-Berg, *Commedia dell'Arte and the Mediterranean: Charting Journeys and Mapping "Others"* (New York: Routledge, 2016).

147. Flaminio Scala, *Il teatro delle favole rappresentative,* ed. Ferruccio Marotti, 2 vols. (Milan: Il Polifilo, 1976), Giornata XLI. Also see the English translation with its additional commentary by Richard Andrews: *The Commedia dell'Arte of Flaminio Scala: A Translation and Analysis of Thirty Scenarios* (Lanham, MD: Scarecrow Press, 2008), here 264–73. On this point, also see Strappini, *La tragedia del buffone*, 269–71. Mediterranean settings such as Algiers and Alexandria also appear in Scala's scenarios *Isabella astrologa* (Isabella the Astrologer) and *La pazzia d'Isabella* (The Madness of Isabella).

both find themselves punitively locked in birdcages as Marmotta and Meo are reunited.

While Baldassarre (the missing brother) and Tedeschino are the two buffoons to whom the title explicitly alludes, in reality the comedy portrays a world populated entirely by bizarre and unconventional figures. In addition to a standard list of characters, Costa uses a letter to the reader to introduce her cast of misfits. Alongside Meo ("a born fool"), these range from the cook Grasso ("a fat, stupid person") to the bravo Scatapocchio ("a teeny-tiny little dwarf"). Accompanying these and other "freak[s] of nature" are a variety of linguistic outsiders. Joining Baldassare ("an Italianized Spaniard") is his servant Croatto (an "Italianized Turk") as well as the crazy valet Michelino and his servant Mantuano (both "Italianized German[s]"). While Baldassare speaks in a Spanish dotted with Italianisms, the others bring heavy accents and grammatical errors to their Italian. Costa winkingly excuses herself for the comedy's range of styles and languages, arguing that the representation of this outlandish band of courtiers necessitated such verbal play. The comedy reaches its peaks of slapstick ridiculousness in the final scenes of both Acts I and II when these same characters begin to brawl, resulting in a flurry of tongues and fists.

However absurd they may be, these characters do not represent figments of Costa's imagination but instead parody actual figures at the Medici court. Through substantial archival work, Teresa Megale has demonstrated that nearly all of the characters have historical counterparts who appear in the Medici financial registers.[148] For her parody of princedom, for example, Costa named her ruler Meo after a local Florentine madman supported by the grand duke. In fact, among Susterman's portraits immortalizing members of the Medici household, such as that of Ferdinando and Vittoria (Fig. 3), we find a painting of this "Meo Matto" (Mad Meo, Fig. 8). Although he faces the viewer in the bust-length, three-quarter view traditional to portraiture, the sitter's lack of conventional *dignitas* is communicated by his blotchy skin, hooded eyes, opened mouth, and suspended hands.[149] As the painting was likely executed sometime before 1640, its commission could have conceivably helped inspire Costa's *Buffoons*.

148. For the study of these registers from the Camera del Granduca, see Teresa Megale, "La commedia decifrata: Metamorfosi e rispecchiamenti in *Li buffoni* di Margherita Costa," *Il Castello di Elsinore* 2 (1988): 64–76. Unless otherwise noted, all of the character identifications that follow are made by Megale.

149. For the citation from the 1688 Palazzo Pitti inventories and a brief discussion of the painting, see Lisa Goldenberg Stoppato, *The Grand Duke's Portraitist: Cosimo III de' Medici and his "Chamber of Paintings" by Giusto Suttermans* (Livorno: Sillabe, 2006), 5; Anna Bisceglia, Matteo Ceriana, and Simona Mammana, eds., *Buffoni, villani e giocatori alla corte dei Medici* (Livorno: Sillabe, 2016), 78–79. The historical figure, "Meo Antonio di Domenico Matto," may also have been a buffoon; at the least, he was remunerated for performing buffoonish acts such as somersaults.

Figure 8. Justus Sustermans, *Portrait of a Buffoon (Meo Matto).* c.1640.

Servants in Ferdinando's employ also have clear comedic alter egos in the fictional Moroccan palace. A cook named Grasso worked in the kitchens of Meo and the Medici alike, for instance, while Michelino and Mantuano, here the prince's manservants, were members of Ferdinando's group of German mercenary bodyguards. The overlap between comedy and reality is especially apparent in those figures who historically were charged with providing revelry for the grand ducal family. Each of the comedy's four dwarfs are named after actual figures who were the objects of the kinds of crude and degrading courtly divertissements described above: Prince Meo's Captain of the Guard, Pedina (Pawn), and his Chief Huntsman, Gobbo (Hunchback), are modeled on the dwarfs responsible for the entertainment of Ferdinando and his guests, while Catorchia (here Ancroia's servant) and Scatapocchio (Catorchia's especially diminutive servant) similarly served the households of Giovan Carlo and Leopoldo de' Medici. The pimp Gobbo of the Violin shares the nickname of the famous hunched and musically-inclined buffoon Tommaso Trafedi, who was employed by Ferdinando's uncle Lorenzo.[150] The comedy's most extensive discussions about the nature of both buffoonery and courtliness are conducted by Prince Meo's Secretary of State and Advisor, Masino and Tordo, respectively. Like his fictional counterpart, Giovan Carlo's servant Masino suffered from a physical deformity, one that apparently made him a favorite participant in court games. One Ippolito, known as Tordo, worked at the Uffizi as Ferdinando's lens maker, providing the grand duke with new tools such as telescopes. Even he does not escape Costa's pen; his fictional equivalent admits to fraudulently passing off other men's goods as his own, while Masino professes a desire to use one of his telescopes as a chamber pot. Finally, the comedic rivalry between the play's two court buffoons, Baldassarre and Tedeschino, mirrors the relationship between the Spanish buffoon Don Baldassarre Biguria and Bernardino Ricci, the buffoon known as "il Tedeschino," both comic performers in the grand duke's employ.

The historical reality of "il Tedeschino" is especially important to the *Buffoni*. While the Prologue alludes in encomiastic terms to the Medici, the comedy is dedicated not to the grand duke or his brothers but to Ricci, one of the titular buffoons. Like Costa herself, Ricci (1588–1653) was a lifelong comedic performer with connections to the courts of Naples, Rome, Turin, and, above all, Florence, where he was first in the employ of Ferdinando and then Giovan Carlo.[151] Through the figure of Ricci/Tedeschino, Costa stages her world of buffoonery. On whom but he, she asks in the dedicatory letter, could she have based her comedy if she wished to "invent nonsense, represent hooey, and imitate poppycock"? While Costa's near contemporaries erroneously deduced that her dedication indicated a matrimonial bond between the singer and the actor, as noted above, she almost surely composed the comedy in response to a work of Ricci's own. Around the mid-1630s, Ricci published a dialogue entitled *Il Tedeschino, overo Difesa dell'Arte del Cavalier del Piacere* (Tedeschino, or A Defense of the Art of the Cavalier of Pleasure).[152] Incorporating his stage name and his self-stylized title of "cavalier"—

150. Though Megale was unable to find archival material on this character, the identification is made by Giuseppe Crimi, *Nanerie del Rinascimento: "La nanea" di Michelangelo Serafini e altri versi di corte e d'accademia* (Manziana [Rome]: Vecchiarelli, 2006), 310n. Crimi's suggestion is supported by the fact that the character is also repeatedly referred to in the text as Trafedi.

151. For Ricci's biography, see Megale's introduction to Bernardino Ricci, *Il Tedeschino, overo Difesa dell'Arte del Cavalier del Piacere* (Florence: Le Lettere, 1995), especially 61–63.

152. Berdardino Ricci's original *Il Tedeschino, overo Difesa dell'Arte del Cavalier del Piacere. Dialogo dal medesimo dedicato a tutti quelli principi, che si dilettano tenere buffoni appresso di loro* was printed in Venice by an unnamed publisher at an unspecified date. For a modern edition, and for notes on dating, see Ricci, *Il Tedeschino*, 8. For contemporary studies of buffoons and buffoonery, see Daniele Vianello, *L'arte del buffone: Maschere e spettacolo tra Italia e Baviera nel XVI secolo* (Rome: Bulzoni,

a parodied appellation common to buffoons—Ricci presents himself as both the subject of and an interlocutor in the discourse. Ostensibly written as a retort to critics of his profession, the dialogue sets out to establish the utility and, indeed, the necessity of buffoonery.[153]

Written with tongue-in-cheek sobriety, the dialogue showcases a Tedeschino who expounds upon the nature of the buffoon to his companion Pompeo. Through a series of clever citations of ancient and contemporary texts, from Plato to Castiglione, Tedeschino argues that buffoonery—which he defines as "the art of words and deeds fit to provoke laughter"—is comparable to art, music, and poetry in the delight it provokes in its audience.[154] Not only is buffoonery best identified as one of the liberal arts, he insists, but in fact the other arts (grammar, rhetoric, poetry) work in its service.[155] Similarly, it predates and transcends philosophy; those who call themselves philosophers criticize buffoonery out of a jealousy provoked by their inability to master the art.[156] If the buffoon has gained an unseemly reputation, it is because false practitioners—courtiers and other flatterers—have usurped and defamed his title.[157] The "good and true" buffoon practices a noble art by bringing laughter to his prince, who more than anyone else has need of mirth and happiness.[158] A Stefano della Bella portrait mirrors Ricci's parody of self-ennoblement (Fig. 9).[159] Presented to Vittoria della Rovere in 1637, the etching spoofs aristocratic equestrian portraiture by depicting Ricci mounted upon a steed and outfitted in a rich damask mantle and *galero* (a broad-brimmed hat often worn by clerics), the city of Florence clearly discernible in the background.[160] The caption below lauds "Bernardino Ricci, called Tedeschino, the most esteemed statesman of his day," an epithet that clinches the carnivalesque transformation of the entertainer into a ruler.

2005); Vianello, "Tra inferno e paradiso: Il 'limbo' dei buffoni," *Biblioteca teatrale* 49–51 (1999), 13–80; Piero Camporesi, *Rustici e buffoni: Cultura popolare e cultura d'élite fra Medioevo ed età moderna* (Turin: Einaudi, 1991); Robert Henke, *Performance and Literature in the Commedia dell'Arte* (Cambridge: Cambridge University Press, 2002), 50–68.

153. Ricci, *Il Tedeschino* (1995), 86.

154. Ricci, *Il Tedeschino* (1995), 85. Examining Tedeschino's faltering signature to his letters, and comparing those texts to the dialogue, Megale convincingly argues (at 9–12) that Ricci likely dictated the former and received assistance from someone more learned with the latter.

155. Ricci, *Il Tedeschino* (1995), 91.

156. Ricci, *Il Tedeschino* (1995), 80–83.

157. Ricci, *Il Tedeschino* (1995), 73, 77, 105.

158. Ricci, *Il Tedeschino* (1995), 77, 105.

159. On this portrait, see Massar, *Presenting Stefano della Bella*; and Anna Forlani Tempesti, *Mostra di incisioni di Stefano della Bella* (Florence: Olschki, 1973).

160. For a detailed analysis of the etching, see Ricci, *Il Tedeschino* (1995), 55–57.

Figure 9. Stefano della Bella, portrait of Bernardino Ricci, called "il Tedeschino." 1637.

Il Tedeschino was by no means the first publication associated with a professional buffoon; the famous Venetians Taiacalze and Zuan Polo were the subject (and in the case of Zuan Polo, the occasional author) of printed texts, while books of jokes and other "buffoonery" circulated throughout the sixteenth century under the names of famous performers like the medieval Gonnella.[161] The figure of

161. On the Venetian context, see Henke, *Performance and Literature*, 63–66. Publications of jokes and gags were available, such as the *Facecie del Gonnella* published by Giustiniano da Rubiera in 1506 and

the buffoon loomed even larger as the object of writing, however. He emerged as a figure of entertainment in accounts of civic life, such as the diaries of Marin Sanudo, and a figure of debate in analyses of courtly circles and comedic practices.[162] These discussions reveal concerns about the overlap between buffoons and courtiers (as both survived by pleasing the prince) and between buffoons and actors (as both were paid performers).

Tedeschino himself contests the equation of buffoons and courtiers, flipping the debate on its head by seeking to insulate the former from the ignominy of the latter. He makes less mention of debates on the nature of performance and actors, aside from his insistence that the buffoon is a private, not public, figure.[163] Yet with the rich world of diverse players that co-existed and often co-mingled in the same theatrical spaces, from mountebanks hawking medicines to the new Cinquecento divas, generic boundaries often blurred.[164] The medieval chronicler Filippo Villani offers an early example in his *De origine civitatis Florentie et de eiusdem famosis civibus* (The Origins of the City of Florence and Its Famous Citizens), including among his chapters on illustrious figures within the Florentine community a section "On Actors" that focuses primarily on buffoons like Gonnella.[165] With the emergence of professional acting troupes in the mid-sixteenth century, the suggestive similarities between the rowdy and clownish buffoon doing imitations, ad-libbing music, and executing acrobatic routines and the improvisational stage actor playing a part—especially a comic role—became uncomfortable. Actor-authors in this period took pains to distinguish their craft from what they disparaged as buffoon antics. In his treatise on *commedia dell'arte* dedicated to Ferdinando II, for example, Pier Maria Cecchini distinguishes between "serious" and "ridiculous" parts, such as the *innamorati* and the *zanni*, but stresses that the latter should be clever but never clownish.[166] Despite—or, better, because of—his own beginnings as a popular performer, Nicolò Barbieri bristled at the association of the two typologies of actor. "The comedian is different in each and every way from the buffoon, even when he represents one," he argued, because the ac-

---

reprinted throughout the century. For an example, see *Facezie, motti, buffonerie et burle del Piovano Arlotto, del Gonnella, et del Barlacchia* (Florence: Giunti, 1565).

162. See, for example, M. A. Katritzky, *The Art of Commedia: A Study in the Commedia dell'Arte 1560–1620, with Special Reference to the Visual Records* (Amsterdam: Rodopi, 2006), 35–37.

163. Ricci, *Il Tedeschino* (1995), 105.

164. On the diva's emergence in Italian theater, see especially Rosalind Kerr, *The Rise of the Diva on the Sixteenth-Century Commedia dell'Arte Stage* (Toronto: University of Toronto Press, 2015).

165. See the more modern edition: Filippo Villani, *Liber de civitatis florentiae famosis civibus*, ed. Gustavo Camillo Galletti (Florence: Mazzoni, 1847), 156–58.

166. The servant, for example, should be "astute and clever" and play his part spiritedly but "without buffoonery"; Pier Maria Cecchini, *Frutti delle moderne comedie, et avisi a chi le recita* (Padua: Guaresco Guareschi, 1628), 23.

tor temporarily plays the fool (or whatever persona he so wishes) through the sustained fiction that is theater, while the buffoon is always, and exclusively, just a buffoon.[167]

Not everyone found such distinctions convincing. In his criticism of the immoralities and excesses of contemporary theatrical practices, the Jesuit Giovanni Domenico Ottonelli directly challenged Barbieri: those actors who played—but were not themselves—buffoons were merely "ridiculous charlatans" who, like their clownish peers, engaged in a "diabolical" seduction of audiences.[168] Before him, Tommaso Garzoni deplored in *La piazza universale di tutte le professioni del mondo* (The Universal Piazza of All the Professions of the World) the tomfoolery and ribaldry he saw in public performances, though he exempted eminent and "proper" figures like Isabella Andreini from his condemnations. Not only had shenanigans and charlatanism taken over the piazzas, he added, but the buffoons' influence had so swelled that they filled the tables at court, leaving poets and orators exiled to the mess halls. "One can no longer find the lord without his buffoon," he lamented, "nor the buffoon without his lord."[169]

Costa responds to actors' endeavors to ennoble their art and critics' push to purify it by fashioning a stage populated not by the giants of professional troupes but instead almost exclusively by the *parti ridicole* (ridiculous characters), real buffoons and dwarfs. If Cecchini had imagined a comedy "without dishonest material, obscene words, and gross acts," Costa offers instead one composed entirely of those elements.[170] At the same time, however, she also mocks Ricci's postured self-aggrandizement by inventing a comical, carnivalesque world in which the Tedeschino character nevertheless cannot get ahead. Clearly working from Ricci's text—repeating, for example, the story of how he earned the stage name "il Tedeschino" ("the little German") as a child by popping out of a large pie while dressed in Teutonic grab—she transforms the character from an erudite exponent of the art of buffoonery to a bombastic and universally despised stooge.[171] Recalling the description of Tedeschino in the Della Bella portrait caption, her Tedeschino prides himself on being a politico, a statesman shrewd in the ways of rule and diplomacy. Not only is he unable to influence anyone at court, however, but he is punished for his airs. While the other buffoon Baldassarre (who,

167. Nicolò Barbieri, *La supplica, discorso famigliare a quelli che trattano de' comici*, ed. Ferdinando Taviani (Milan: Il Polifilo, 1971), 24–26.

168. Giovanni Domenico Ottonelli, *Della christiana moderatione del theatro* (Florence: Giovanni Antonio Bonardi, 1652), 452.

169. Tommaso Garzoni, *La piazza universale di tutte le professioni del mondo* (Venice: Giovanni Battista Somasco, 1585), 352.

170. Cecchini, *Frutti delle moderne comedie*, 13.

171. For a description of the pie scene, see Ricci, *Il Tedeschino* (1995), 74–75, and I.x.63–77 in *The Buffoons*.

as noted, represents Ricci's historical rival at the Medici court) is largely spared any clownish behavior beyond braggadocio and a brawl or two—being of noble blood within the fiction of the comedy—Tedeschino performs acrobatic stunts and dances against his will, improvises poetry and dons a dress, receives innumerable blows, and ends up encaged. He becomes, in short, a failed caricature of the persona Ricci had created with his own publication.

The Buffoons' *Place in Seventeenth-Century Comedic Traditions*

Students of Renaissance drama will no doubt recognize the strong generic resemblances between the *Buffoni* and the *commedia dell'arte*, or *all'improvviso*, which then dominated the popular stage. Costa's play is built around a number of modular scenes in which characters exchange quips and at times punches, much as they would in the performance-driven improvisational tradition.[172] Discrete comic routines, or *lazzi*, involving acrobatics and obscene gags abound, and it is not hard to imagine how the risqué slapstick of the *arte* stage might have inspired Costa's lewd references to chamber pots, enemas, and excrement.[173] At the same time, many of the theatergrams found in the *Buffoni* and *commedia dell'arte*—the cross-dressing paramour, the long-lost brother, the unhappily married wife, the controlled chaos leading up to a final recognition scene—all would be equally at home in *commedie erudite* (erudite comedies) of the humanists.[174] Writing for the courts or the academies, literati including the famed Ariosto and Machiavelli looked back to ancient drama for inspiration, particularly to the Roman comedies of Terence and Plautus. Erudite playwrights adopted ancient comedy's strict

172. A bibliography on the *commedia dell'arte* would be far too voluminous to attempt here. We instead direct the reader to Robert Henke's invaluable *Performance and Literature in the Commedia dell'Arte*, and particularly 216 for his notes on Costa's *Buffoni*. Other fundamental studies include Richard Andrews, *Scripts and Scenarios: The Performance of Comedy in Renaissance Italy* (Cambridge: Cambridge University Press, 1993); Ferdinando Taviani, *La commedia dell'arte e la società barocca*, 2 vols. (Rome: Bulzoni, 1969, 1991); and Roberto Tessari, *Commedia dell'arte: La maschera e l'ombra* (Milan: Mursia, 1981). Also useful are several of the essays included in Domenico Pietropaolo, ed., *The Science of Buffoonery: Theory and History of the Commedia dell'Arte* (Ottawa, Canada: Dovehouse, 1989). On the relationship between music and *commedia*, particularly in the case of women, see MacNeil, *Music and Women of the Commedia dell'Arte*; and Emily Wilbourne, *Seventeenth-Century Opera and the Sound of the Commedia dell'Arte* (Chicago: University of Chicago Press, 2016).

173. For more on *lazzi* in the *commedia dell'arte* tradition, see Mel Gordon, "Lazzi," in *The Routledge Companion to Commedia dell'Arte*, ed. Judith Chaffee and Oliver Crick (New York: Routledge, 2015), 167–76. Costa makes a "piss-pot" one of the sources of contention between warring spouses in Act I (I.i .80–81) and later makes scatological references to the telescope in Act III (III.ii.105–13).

174. The term "theatergram" is developed by Louise George Clubb in her *Italian Drama in Shakespeare's Time* (New Haven: Yale University Press, 1989). For more on these theatergrams in learned comedies, see Richard Andrews, "Erudite Comedy," in *A History of Italian Theatre*, ed. Joseph Farrell and Paolo Puppa (Cambridge: Cambridge University Press, 2006), 39–43.

five-act structure and maintained its unity of time and place; all dramatic action unfolded in a single exterior setting and was neatly resolved within the span of a day. Ghosts of ancient character types like the Plautine *miles gloriosus* (braggart soldier) and the crafty slave were transplanted into a "variegated Italian social landscape," making servants and Spanish braggarts recurring figures in humanists' works and later in the *commedia dell'arte*.[175] Furthermore, the protagonists of the erudite comedies were drawn from the professional classes, and set into motion in streets and piazzas that would have seemed familiar to contemporary audiences. One look at Stefano della Bella's frontispiece and its vaguely Florentine cityscape reminds us that the *Buffoni*, though ostensibly set in the distant kingdom of Morocco, is essentially an urban comedy, far removed from the arcadian landscapes of pastoral drama (Fig. 7). While elements from both the humanist and *arte* traditions echo throughout the *Buffoni*, Della Bella's etching as well as the play's title page clearly advertise its particular genre. Costa calls the *Buffoni* a *comedia ridicola*, that is, a *commedia ridicolosa*, and as such it straddles the line between improvised and erudite forms.[176]

The *commedia ridicolosa* then favored in Rome was a subgenre of *commedia dell'arte*.[177] Traditionally composed as light entertainment for carnival season, marriage celebrations, or festive get-togethers between friends, these three-act scripted comedies drew their humor from crass puns and bawdy gags. They were staged in the public piazzas, academies, and private salons of papal Rome, and before audiences of nearly every social extraction. It was a humble form of entertainment, broadly appealing and devoid of any lofty pretensions, and widely enjoyed by popes and peddlers alike.[178] *Ridicolose* playwrights drew their characters from a derivative repertoire of stock *arte* masks. There were a few new additions—a Frenchman and a female innocent, for example—but authors of these works were generally content to reshuffle their cast of *innamorati* and

175. As Donald Beecher and others note, it is hard to separate the distinct hallmarks of erudite comedy from other comic genres of the day since there is considerable overlap in their generic forms. See his "Introduction, From Italy to England: The Sources, Conventions and Influence of 'Erudite Comedy,'" in Beecher, ed., *Renaissance Comedy: The Italian Masters*. 2 vols. (Toronto: University of Toronto Press, 2008–2010), 2:4.

176. Both the frontispiece and title page of Massi and Landi's 1641 edition present the work as "Li buffoni | Comedia ridicola di Margherita Costa romana."

177. The fullest treatment of the genre can be found in Luciano Mariti's *Commedia ridicolosa: Comici di professione, dilettanti, editoria teatrale nel Seicento; Storia e testi* (Rome: Bulzoni, 1979). Other works on the *commedia ridicolosa* include Massimo Ciavolella's "Text as (Pre)text: Erudite Renaissance Comedy and the *Commedia Ridicolosa*: The Example of Gian Lorenzo Bernini's *L'impresario*," *Rivista di studi italiani* 10 (1992): 22–34; and Jackson Cope, "Bernini and Roman *Commedie Ridicolose*," *PMLA* 102, no. 2 (1987): 177–86.

178. Mariti, *Commedia ridicolosa*, cxx.

vecchi (old men) around within a limited range of tried-and-true scenarios.[179] While the *commedia ridicolosa* closely resembled the *commedia dell'arte* in plots, structure, and *dramatis personae*, its extreme plurilingualism set it apart from its sister genres. *Commedia dell'arte* masks came with their own distinct dialects, most notably the Bolognese Doctor, the Venetian Pantalone, the Neapolitan Pulcinella, the Bergamask *zanni*, and the Tuscan lovers. Foreign characters also donned linguistic "masks"—the Captain peppered his boasts with Spanish, while exotic slaves delivered their lines in broken Turkish.[180] But in the *commedia ridicolosa*, the multiplicity of languages competing for attention on the stage, or page, reached hyperbolic heights. Linguistic difference became exaggerated or garbled, resulting in a verbal cacophony ripe with opportunities for comic misunderstandings. One of the most prolific authors of *ridicolose* comedies, Virgilio Verucci, published one play featuring ten distinct languages and dialects.[181] True to form, much of the verbal play in the *Buffoni* comes from the macaronic hurly-burly produced by Costa's "crazy Italianized German," "Italianized Turk," and "Italianized Spaniard."

Authors of *commedie ridicolose* were often academics, painters, bureaucrats—learned yet amateur dramatists familiar with both the *commedia erudita* and the vivacious spectacle of the *commedia all'improvviso*.[182] They wrote their comedies on a lark, as a carnivalesque escape from the formal constraints of their professions, and claimed to throw them together in a matter of days. The Roman polymath Gian Lorenzo Bernini wrote and staged several of these ephemeral comedies. Though only one survives today, he is known to have created the sets, costumes, machines, music, and even to have performed in his own *ridicolose* from the comfort of his home.[183] Much like the dramatists behind the scripts, the actors cast in these short plays were also non-professionals. Writers enlisted their friends, colleagues, and clients to act in their comedies—amateurs who often lacked the improvisational techniques of the trained *arte* performer and relied on scripts for their dialogues and prompts. Engaged in only occasional, limited-run productions, the performers of *commedie ridicolose* took off their masks and went back to their day jobs after the final curtain fall.

179. Cope, "Bernini and Roman *Commedie Ridicolose*," 181.

180. For more on foreign characters and dialects in *arte* performance, see Henke, *Performance and Literature*, especially 58–60, 175; Erith Jaffe-Berg, *The Multilingual Art of Commedia dell'Arte* (Toronto: Legas, 2009); and Allardyce Nicoll, *The World of Harlequin: A Critical Study of the Commedia dell'Arte* (Cambridge: Cambridge University Press, 1963), 46.

181. Virgilio Verucci, *Li diversi linguaggi* (Venice: Spineda, 1627).

182. Mariti, *Commedia ridicolosa*, clxv.

183. Ciavolella, "Text as (Pre)text," 29–30.

Unlike most unscripted *commedia dell'arte* productions, scripted *commedie ridicolose* enjoyed a second life as literature for mass consumption.[184] They were printed and reprinted as cheap duodecimos in seventeenth-century Rome and its surrounding provinces, and sold next to almanacs and other leaflets on the city streets.[185] They were popular little books, within reach for most literate consumers, and as such became an attractive medium for another class of author: the professional actor. While dilettante playwrights penned these comedies as a diversion from their careers as doctors and lawyers, seasoned performers and *capocomici* (troupe leaders) also wrote *ridicolose* in order to reach a broader audience through print.[186] As discussed above, popular theater was often treated with scorn and distrust by moralizing ecclesiastics and classicizing academics, and print offered actors the opportunity to add a patina of respectability to their profession by melding it with "literary discourse."[187] Always at the ready with a toolbox full of narrative, verbatim, and thematic units which could be combined and recombined almost without limit for the stage, comic actors had an abundance of raw material to bring to print. They collected their scenarios and fixed their plays on the page, using them as platforms from which to publicize their achievements and arm their defenses against critics of their profession. The scripted *commedia ridicolosa* was thus the natural extension of commercial theater. It gave avid consumers the means to enjoy, and imitate, the improvisor's comedic repertoire while providing an additional source of income for its performers-turned-playwrights.

Though the *ridicolosa* genre was most closely associated with Rome, print culture made the plays accessible to readers far beyond the Roman capital.[188] Published *ridicolose* were used as scripts by largely amateur actors and staged in the academies and private salons of the nobler classes on festive occasions. In Florence, for example, *ridicolose* were organized in connection to the Medici court. Not officially patronized by the grand dukes for ceremonial affairs but nonetheless written for their approving eyes, such comedies were regularly performed by semi-professional troupes at the Pergola theater.[189] As noted above, at

184. Mariti, *Commedia ridicolosa*, xli. Cope explores the print and distribution of *ridicolose* comedies by smaller presses outside of Rome and Viterbo, along with their lower and middle-class target audiences, in "Bernini and Roman *Commedie Ridicolose*," 179–81.

185. Roughly a third of works published in Rome were dramatic works, nearly three-quarters of which were *commedie ridicolose*. Cope, "Bernini and Roman *Commedie Ridicolose*," 180.

186. Mariti, *Commedia ridicolosa*, cli. Henke studies publications by *commedia dell'arte* actors trying to rise above the stigma of their profession in his *Performance and Literature*, 175–216.

187. Henke, *Performance and Literature*, 4.

188. Cope notes in "Bernini and Roman *Commedie Ridicolose*," 180, that reprints of *commedie ridicolose* were distributed as far north as Bologna and Venice.

189. Mamone explores various manifestation of this semi-professional and unofficial theater, including the *ridicolose*, in early seventeenth-century Medicean Florence. See Sara Mamone, "Tra tela e

least one professional troupe crossed over the threshold into the Pitti palace to put on a command performance of a *commedia ridicolosa* for Maria Maddalena and her princely children. Staged in the private apartments of the Medici and their associates, and later in the commercial theaters they helped establish, the *commedia ridicolosa* entertained even the loftiest of spectators.

It is easy to see why a genre that originated in Rome and was popular with both spectators and readers might have appealed to Costa. She would have likely seen the *ridicolose* performed in the streets and salons of her native city during her youth. The *ridicolose*'s non-academic pretensions were also perfectly in keeping with Costa's predilection for popular themes. Though she published several elegiac and pastoral poems brimming with classical and Petrarchan allusions, Costa was just as quick to lampoon these very same conceits. Satirical poems from her *Lettere amorose*, *La chitarra*, and *Lo stipo* range from the risqué to the grotesque and show her willingness to associate herself with burlesque comedy in print. She was at times, though not always, an iconoclast, often extolling the mimetic virtues of her uncouth verse. The *ridicolosa* genre, unfettered by the constraints of Terentian and Plautine comedy, was thus a fitting vehicle for an ambitious author with a gift for naturalistic speech and bawdy humor.

While the *Buffoni* is closely aligned with the *ridicolosa* brand of comedy emblazoned on its title page, it does nonetheless differ from it in significant ways. Unlike the *commedie ridicolose* that were typically printed as inexpensive pocket editions and peddled to middle-class buyers, Costa's publishers appear to have made a considerable investment in her comedy.[190] *Li buffoni* was printed in quarto, not duodecimo format, as were all of her works with the exception of *Gl'amori della luna*. It was accompanied by a detailed frontispiece etched by Florence's leading printmaker, Stefano della Bella, and not with the modest woodcuts commonly associated with cheaper editions.[191] The play's dedication to the professional buffoon Bernardino Ricci was also a radical departure from the norm, while Costa's implicit Medicean audience further set her work apart from comedies designed primarily for popular consumption. No less noteworthy is her cast of characters. As discussed above, Costa populated her play with historical figures connected to the Medici court. Her distinctive cast of loons, buffoons, and dwarfs were marginal figures, actual performers and dependents of the princely family, and appear much as they would have in real life, albeit in comically distorted roles. Though Costa modeled some, like the braggart Baldassarre and the

---

scena: vita d'accademia e vita di corte nel primo Seicento fiorentino," *Biblioteca teatrale* 37–38 (1996): 213–28.

190. See Cope, "Bernini and Roman *Commedie Ridicolose*," 180, for more on the class of buyers in the market for *commedie ridicolose* in seventeenth-century Italy.

191. The famed author of *ridicolose* comedies, Giovanni Briccio (1579–1645), published his *La tartarea* with woodcuts of his own design; see Cope, "Bernini and Roman *Commedie Ridicolose*," 180.

go-between Filippetta, on stock *commedia* types, the *Buffoni*'s cast is said to have been represented *al naturale*, unmasked.[192]

While *Li buffoni*'s first publishers gave her text a material existence beyond what was customary for a *ridicolosa* comedy, Costa positioned her own work closer to the slapstick of the buffoons than to the classicizing dramas of the humanists. The tension between erudite and popular comedy is in fact dramatized in the play's Prologue and given human form in Stefano della Bella's frontispiece. Foregrounded house right on the stage in his etching, Buffoonery is represented as an attractive young woman with flowing hair who holds an instrument as she addresses the audience.[193] In contrast, placed to the left of the scene and partially cropped out of the picture, Ancient Comedy appears hunched over her cane with a pair of shears hanging from her waist. She is the precise visual equivalent of the severe, captious old hag that first commands the stage in Costa's Prologue, excoriating the audience with her razor-sharp words. She upbraids several classes of men, including the servile courtier, until she is finally interrupted by Buffoonery. The two personifications engage in a verbal sparring match, or *contrasto*, that pits the old against the young, the canonical against the irreverent.[194] Ancient Comedy calls Buffoonery "the laughingstock of the wise" and derides her opportunistic, lowbrow antics. Buffoonery in turn calls her a pedant, a hypocrite, an unwelcome outcast. Their agonistic exchange has no expository function, and we learn nothing about the characters or plot about to unfold. Costa instead uses the Prologue to deflect anticipated criticism of her work.[195] Acting as a mouthpiece for the playwright, Buffoonery staves off any prudish detractors by praising the laughter generated by her clownish farce. She makes no didactic claims for the piece and suggests no value other than delight and merriment. The public's taste for novel witticisms and buffoonery, she proclaims, has simply triumphed over Roman comedy. The play's receptive public, we then learn, includes none other than the grand duke. Both Buffoonery and Ancient Comedy celebrate the Medici as exalted heroes and

192. See note 4 of the translation. Claims at verisimilitude were also not uncommon in erudite comedies. For example, "real" characters from papal Rome are satirized in both Pietro Aretino's *La cortigiana* and Annibal Caro's *Gli straccioni*. On the verisimilar in Renaissance comedies in general, see Beecher, *Renaissance Comedy*, 1:18–19, and more specifically his introductions to these two works, at 1:101–10 and 1:207–15.

193. Teresa Megale advances the identification of these two figures as *Buffoneria* and *Commedia antica* in her notes on the frontispiece in "Sproporzioni: Il teatro dell'assurdo buffonesco all'ombra dei Medici," in Bisceglia et al., *Buffoni, villani e giocatori*, 71.

194. Eugenio Refini offers a chronological list of prologues to dramatic works featuring personifications spanning the Cinquecento and concluding with *Li buffoni*; Eugenio Refini, "Prologhi figurati: Appunti sull'uso della prosopopea nel prologo teatrale del Cinquecento," *Italianistica* 35, no. 3 (2006): 69n1.

195. For more on the defensive function of the prologue in Italian comedy, see Emilio Goggio, "The Prologue in the *Commedie Erudite* of the Sixteenth Century," *Italica* 18, no. 3 (1941): 124–32.

Augustan rulers, thus implicitly acknowledging the princes as the play's unofficial addressees. For this irregular brand of comedy, the customary Medicean encomia of Costa's other Florentine publications has been moved to the Prologue, making praise of the family part of the dramatic performance. In their place in the dedication stands Bernardino Ricci, a buffoon to whom Costa ironically entrusts her Buffoonery, and who boldly signals the play's unconventional and satirical nature.

Themes in The Buffoons

The Court

Central to the *Buffoni* is a discussion of courtly life. While Costa's other Florentine works typically lauded the Medici and participated in their message campaigns to greater and lesser degrees, her comedy offers a more bitingly satirical perspective.[196] In addition to caricaturing historical personages connected to the grand ducal family, the play pits the world of courtly divertissement against the obligations of governance. As the comedy's title would suggest, lowly pleasures nearly trump loftier duties. In the opening scene, Prince Meo abdicates his authoritative responsibilities to Princess Marmotta in order to dedicate himself entirely to his appetites: "It falls on you to keep an eye | on matters pertaining to the kingdom | and not to figure out if I'm on the hunt or want to love" (I.i.125–27). Marmotta does not console herself for her husband's negligence by embracing this opportunity to rule in his place but instead responds with incredulity ("Oh lord, it's up to me | to govern the state?" [I.i.128–29]) and begins contemplating a flight back to her native Fessa. Morocco is a principality left entirely unregulated as its two sovereigns abandon themselves to either delight or despondence.

Meo engages his governing corps—a ragtag group composed almost exclusively of comic dwarfs—in the pursuit of their shared pastimes of hunting, feasting, imbibing, reveling, and fornicating. These entertainments predictably lead to misunderstandings, brawls, and general mayhem. Meanwhile, Marmotta spends much of the play in tearful lament as she tries to upend Meo's debaucherous plans, but she also employs the buffoon Tedeschino to distract her through song, dance, and acrobatic routines. The rule of law returns to the court only when it is revealed that Baldassarre is Marmotta's brother and Meo's in-law. Reformed by this new male companionship, Meo reassumes his role as monarch by promoting Baldassarre from buffoon to ruler, pronouncing orders to his subjects, and planning for the well-being of his court and kingdom.

196. Debates on the nature of courtly life, including from a satirical perspective, were heated in the seventeenth century. For a survey and case study, see Paola Ugolini, "Paradoxical Virtues: Intellectuals Between the Court and the Academy in Agostino Mascardi's *Che la corte è vera scuola non solamente della prudenza ma delle virtù morali* (1624)," *The Italianist* 34, no. 1 (February, 2014): 54–72.

In addition to this royal couple disinterested in matters of state, the comedy takes satirical aim at the figure of the courtier. In the Prologue, Ancient Comedy decries the figures she spots around the new courtly theater: drunks, gamblers, pretty boys, misers, pilfering soldiers, and, finally, the courtiers. Impoverished and pathetically eager to live off the scarce attentions and scraps offered by his prince, the courtier is "like a snail | [who] wears his entire wardrobe on his back | … | [and] stows in his shell what's left of his wages" (lns. 46–51). Hardly a sympathetic figure, however, he is repeatedly associated with hypocrisy, freeloading, and backstabbing. When encountering the mad German valet Michelino, for example, the character Tordo proclaims, "He has no brains | and yet that too lends itself | to the style of the court, to the courtier | who's always arranging for his fellow | to be sent off to the bordello," that is, to hell (I.vii.63–67).

The only one of Morocco's courtly characters interested in the art and practice of governance is a buffoon, the asinine Tedeschino. More than an entertainer, Tedeschino fancies himself a political mind, an advisor to the prince. "I am a shrewd statesman," he professes to Marmotta, "and in the affairs of state | I know how to shuffle the deck as well as anyone" (II.iii.54–55), echoing Bernardino Ricci's comical epithet of *politico*. Tedeschino's companions mock such posturing. Marmotta categorically dismisses his ambitions ("If you want to be a statesman, | you fool, you don't know what you're saying. | And if you fancy yourself a great entertainer of guests, | you're an ass, since it's more likely | you'll drive them away" [I.xii.96–100]) and concludes that he is not fit to stay at court (lns. 133–34). Similarly, Tordo and Masino lambaste him as the "dimwit of diplomacy" (III.ii.24). Their animated inventory of Tedeschino's shortcomings develops into the play's most protracted discussion about the nature of courtiership. The only courtiers who get ahead in the palace, they agree, are the buffoons, who crack jokes, do imitations, play a little music, and, most importantly, serve as the prince's yes men. Debating which of the two would be better suited to replace Tedeschino at court, Tordo and Masino ultimately conclude that neither of them can hold their liquor nor unleash their tongue enough to be a proper courtier-buffoon.

In short, while Costa sets her fictionalized Tedeschino as the comedy's whipping boy in a way that undermines Ricci's treatise on the nobility of the buffoon, her other characters nonetheless maintain that the inner circles of a court are populated by clowns whose antics serve only to facilely entertain the prince. The comedy parodies the seventeenth-century Medici court, but it also participates in a tradition that, departing largely with Pietro Aretino's 1525 comedy *La cortigiana*, mocked the courtier himself.[197] Costa concretized longstanding

197. Pietro Aretino, *Cortigiana; Opera nova; Pronostico; Il testamento dell'elefante; Farza*, ed. Angelo Romano (Milan: BUR, 1989). In 1534, Aretino revised and republished this comedy about a Sienese bumpkin who tries to become a Roman courtier.

accusations that the courtier was a debased and ridiculous figure by transforming him into an actual buffoon.

Sexual Euphemisms

Costa's *Buffoni* is in many ways a sex comedy.[198] The play's plot revolves around Prince Meo's amorous pursuit of the prostitute Ancroia to the complete neglect of his wife. Sexual possession is the explicit goal and source of conflict between warring spouses, driving the comedy through a series of laughable escapades towards its predictably happy resolution. The very first act begins with the royal couple squabbling over Meo's refusal to satisfy Marmotta's wifely needs—needs which she makes clear are as much physical as they are political. Nearly all of the secondary characters are entangled in the pair's erotic misalliance: Tedeschino angles to possess Marmotta; Filippetta conspires to bring Ancroia and Meo together; Bertuccia urges Marmotta to find a lover, and so on. Explicitly sexual themes thus dominate Costa's conjugal farce and are expressed through a baroque array of ribald puns and metaphors drawn from the "material bodily lower stratum."[199] While many of the comedy's most ludic moments involve physical gags such as slapstick, dancing, and crossdressing, bawdy allusions to sex and scatology are what give the *Buffoni* its comedic bite.[200]

Of the many erotic themes contained within the *Buffoni*, the *banchetto* (banquet) motif is the most pronounced. It serves a crucial function within the play as the literal site for Meo and Ancroia's projected tryst as well as the primary metaphor for the sexual consummation of their affair. Historically, feast imagery was a staple of comic theater, as were the drunkards and the gluttons that dominated its carnivalesque scenes. The ever-hungry Harlequins and *zanni* of the stage

198. Though most commonly associated with popular cinema and seventeenth-century Restoration comedy, the term "sex comedy" can be used to describe all matter of farcical works, past and present, dealing with sexual themes and gender relations. For more on the subject, see Laura J. Rosenthal, "'All injury's forgot': Restoration Sex Comedy and National Amnesia," *Comparative Drama* 42, no. 1 (Spring, 2008): 7–28.

199. Mikhail Bakhtin, *Rabelais and His World*, trans. Hélène Iswolsky (Bloomington: Indiana University Press, 1984), 109.

200. Roger Thompson's study of seventeenth-century erotica offers useful distinctions between the lewd or obscene, and the ribald or bawdy. According to Thompson, the obscene is "intended to shock or disgust, or to render the subject of the writing shocking or disgusting. This seems to be the purpose in our period of the use of taboo words or casual descriptions of sexual perversions, and is often the companion of satire." The bawdy is instead "intended to provoke amusement about sex." Roger Thompson, *Unfit for Modest Ears: A Study of Pornographic, Obscene and Bawdy Works Written or Published in England in the Second Half of the Seventeenth Century* (London: Macmillan, 1979), ix–x. For a discussion on eroticism and obscenity in the *commedia dell'arte* and other forms of comedic theater and art, see Anna Sica, *Eros nell'arte: Lo spettacolo delle maschere* (Palermo: L'epos, 1999).

were familiar guests at the theatrical banquet table, keeping audiences in stitches by drinking, guzzling, belching, and engaging in similar expressions of crude humor. Table talk, or rather speaking and writing about feasting, often linked oral consumption to verbal production, resulting in the frequent analogy between "theatrical and gustatory taste" in Renaissance comedies.[201] Quite fittingly, the *Buffoni* is framed by a banquet metaphor that likens the comedy about to unfold to a festive meal fit for particular tastes. As Buffoonery informs her audience in the closing lines of the Prologue:

> Comedy is like a supper,
> and its stage resembles a large table
> where savory dishes
> are seasoned with nothing but mirth.
> May it thus be sprinkled only with playful banter
> so that its zesty wit and merry words
> may feed the soul and nourish the passions.
> Indeed, if the buffoon is the salt of the meal,
> without buffoonery the scene has no appeal. (Prologue, lns. 138–46)

The banquet is a metaphor for the play, and Costa promises to delight her reader's palate with a tasty mix of buffoonery and witticisms. It is an analogy that signals the comedy's festive atmosphere and provides the framework for the dizzying array of alimentary euphemisms that follows.

In carnivalesque literature, the trope of feasting collapses contiguous appetites and functions, making hunger and the consumption and expulsion of food thinly veiled metaphors for erotic desire and gratification. Accordingly, references to food, drink, urine, excrement, intercourse, and reproductive organs abound in the *Buffoni*, mixing the sexual and digestive in a grotesque confusion of bodily functions to humorous effect. In Act II, for example, plans for a feast in the garden serve as a pretext for a series of running jokes involving a variety of dishes. In Scene v, Gobbo informs the cook Grasso of Meo's desire to host a banquet for Ancroia—a feast that is doubly intended to be made for her and, with a wink, of her. Grasso is told to cook up the wagtail, owl, crow and cat—a curious assortment of animals no doubt chosen more for their function as sexual euphemisms

201. Chris Meads, "Narrative and Dramatic Sauces: Reflections upon Creativity, Cookery, and Culinary Metaphor in Some Early Seventeenth-Century Dramatic Prologues," in *Renaissance Food from Rabelais to Shakespeare: Culinary Readings and Culinary Histories*, ed. Joan Fitzpatrick (Burlington, VT: Ashgate, 2010), 146. For more on the metaphorical association between eating and speaking in ancient and Renaissance comedy, see Erith Jaffe-Berg, "Language, Food and the Hierarchy of Values in the *Commedia dell'Arte* Performance from the Renaissance to the Eighteenth Century," *European Studies Journal* 17–18 (2000–2001): 115–30.

than for their culinary appeal (II.v.10–14).[202] Gobbo then instructs Grasso to roast and cover the game in sauces that evoke epicurean fantasies of indulgence but also suggest sexual positions and fluids. The food metaphors reach a crescendo in the scenes that follow. Having just learned from Grasso about Meo and Ancroia's imminent *al fresco* rendezvous, Tedeschino longingly compares the object of his own desire, Marmotta, to a suggestive menu of poultry, wines, figs, and pastas smothered in cheese (II.vi.33–44). A love-starved Marmotta in turn denounces her philandering husband using a reiterative series of food-based *double entendres* (II.viii.46–69). Measuring Ancroia's feast against her own famine, her privation against the whore's physical abundance, Marmotta makes the erotic subtext of the banquet impossible to miss.

The cornucopia of meats, vegetables, and dairy products referenced within the play is more emblematic than edible. Instead of serving any of the succulent meats and fresh fish one might expect to find on a princely table, Grasso dishes up the grotesque quarry of cats and crows caught by Meo's inept hunting party.[203] These strange trophies are, at the very least, a send-up of the wild game that was traditionally associated with elite hunting and dining and, by extension, of Meo's capacities as a virile lover. Marmotta, in turn, expresses her sexual tastes through a series of metaphors drawn from the largely vegetarian fare consumed by the women of her native Fessa. In Act I, Scene viii, Marmotta fondly relates how Fessa's ladies eat their share of greens but much prefer a variety of unequivocally phallic root vegetables (lns. 261–66). Milk products are plentiful since the city's hardworking shepherdesses are practically swimming in dairy (lns. 268–72). Sexually suggestive herbs and cheeses have replaced Meo's cats and crows. While modern readers might fail to catch the obscene reference hidden within, say, an innocuous lettuce patch, contemporary readers were long familiar with the iconography of erotic produce. Bulbous gourds, sliced melons, juicy peaches, and overripe figs suggesting male and female genitalia hid in plain sight in works by some of the day's leading artists.[204] Pietro Aretino, who could make almost anything sound

202. Incidentally, cats were known to have been consumed in times of scarcity but were hardly considered appetizing fare. See Ken Albala's note on Giovanni Bertaldi's commentary on the 1618 *Regole della sanità* in *Eating Right in the Renaissance* (Berkeley: University of California Press, 2002), 265n75.

203. Ken Albala and Laura Giannetti both discuss the social significance of different types of food during the Renaissance and to some extent the Baroque, and note that despite the preference for meat-based dishes among the noble classes, fruits and vegetables played an increasingly important role in the diets of the Italian courts. See Albala, *The Banquet: Dining in the Great Courts of Late Renaissance Europe* (Urbana: University of Illinois Press, 2007), 73–89, and Giannetti, "Italian Renaissance Food-Fashioning, or The Triumph of Greens," *California Italian Studies* 1, no. 2 (2010): 3. Giannetti adds (8–9) that by the early seventeenth century, the eating of salads and raw vegetables had even become a sign of refinement and social prestige.

204. John Varriano discusses visual erotica by Caravaggio and Raphael in his brief survey, "Fruits and Vegetables as Sexual Metaphor in Late Renaissance Rome," *Gastronomica: The Journal of Food and*

dirty, used salads in his *Dialogues* as a sign for the female genitalia and a variety of sexual positions.[205] Members of literary academies such as the Vignaiuoli, or Vintners, penned farcical encomia to fruits and vegetables brimming with sexual innuendo.[206] Costa's erotic edibles were thus more the norm than the anomaly, and formed part of an established culture of verbal play involving food.

Marmotta's praise for her native kingdom also contains a number of *double entendres* involving fashion, commerce, agriculture, and architecture. Fessa is undoubtedly a gendered space—the name itself, we are reminded, is a vulgar euphemism for the pudendal cleft. It seems to have been designed with women's pleasure in mind: its streets are long, straight, and clean (lns. 144–45); its superb palaces stand erect (lns. 148–150); and its houses all have fountains where lovers can quench their desire (lns. 177–86). This sexualized architecture is matched by equally suggestive descriptions of the kingdom's gardens and fields. Fessa's lands are regularly hoed, its furrows are filled, and its hills are well tilled (lns. 218–225). Its fertile earth also yields fruit without the help of intermediaries, or "dung-brokers" (lns. 229–36). Fessa, as Marmotta drives home, is everything that Morocco is not (137).

Sexual themes in Meo's court are instead presented as comically anti-generative. The prince literally will not fulfill the conjugal obligations of his dynastic union, choosing instead to waste his energies on an aging prostitute. Interestingly, the fruitlessness of his attractions is framed using agricultural terms that ironically recall Marmotta's erotic utopia. In Act II, Tedeschino angles to gain Marmotta's confidence by warning her about Meo's plans to pluck Ancroia's "malformed and over-ripened fruit," "hoe" her "sodden fields," and "cultivate" her "sand" (II.viii.10–16). The lewd meaning is lost on no one, save Marmotta. Never one for brevity, Tedeschino piles on additional euphemisms: Meo wants to "water the soil" and "sow a variety of seeds" in Ancroia's dried-up lands, or rather, extinguish his burning desire for her in the garden (lns. 21–34). Marmotta, incredibly, still does not grasp his meaning. In a last-ditch effort, Tedeschino spits out a slew of crude puns that at long last deliver their intended message. These two complementary sets of agricultural metaphors, antithetical yet equally risqué, display Costa's creative mastery over ribald wordplay.

Birds also assume a conspicuous role in Costa's burlesque comedy. The menu for Ancroia's garden banquet features different types of fowl bearing phallic

---

Culture 5, no. 4 (2005): 8–14.

205. See Giannetti, "Italian Renaissance Food-Fashioning," 8–11.

206. Francesco Berni famously wrote in praise of peaches; Annibal Caro wrote on the subject of figs; and Francesco Maria Molza wrote in praise of both figs and salads, each referring to a variety of sexual objects and practices. For more on the subject see Giannetti, "Italian Renaissance Food-Fashioning," 9–10; and David O. Frantz, *Festum Voluptatis: A Study of Renaissance Erotica* (Columbus, OH: Ohio State University Press, 1989), 9–42.

connotations. But ornithological innuendos appear well beyond the context of the feast, serving as metaphors for both male and female genitalia throughout the comedy. They are products of a common erotic culture in which, as Guido Ruggiero observes, "virtually everyone, from the humblest peasant to the most refined humanist or patron of art knew, understood and could appreciate that a bird was not simply a bird."[207] On this point, Allen Grieco's study of Renaissance bird imagery is illuminating.[208] Avian innuendos are found in most European languages—even today, the anglophone 'cock' and the Italian *uccello* (bird) are commonly used as phallic euphemisms.[209] Such allusions were more prevalent, and varied, in the art, literature, and oral traditions of medieval and Renaissance Italy. In Costa's day, several species were associated with the male member, as evinced by the long list of sexually suggestive birds stirring within the pages of the *Buffoni*: the *civetta* (owlet), *colombo* (dove), *cornacchia* (crow), *cucù* (cuckoo), *fringuello* (finch, or chaffinch), *gufo* (long-eared owl), *merlotto* (blackbird), *ortolano* (ortolan bunting), *quaglia* (quail), *starna* (partridge) and *tordo* (song thrush).[210] The *civetta*, however, was doubly suggestive and could be used to allude to either the phallus or, as will be discussed at greater length below, to a flirtatious or promiscuous woman. At the same time, contemporary sources might refer to the female genitalia as nests, cotes, or bird cages.[211] For example, Ancroia ironically notes in the final scene of the play that she, who had once been the metaphorical "cage to so many birdies," will now be trapped within in an actual cage (III.ix.42–44). Compared to the large number of bird-themed phallus jokes scattered throughout the play, many of the verbal forms associated with the practice of hunting *with* birds are gendered female.

References to fowling run parallel to images of specific types of birds throughout the *Buffoni*. The rhetorical connection between hunting for game and the erotic chase is as much of a commonplace today as it was in seventeenth-century Florence. In fact, the *Buffoni* is filled with a number of provocative references to hounds, hunters, and weapons. Meo's first overtures towards Ancroia come in the form of an invitation to join him on a hunt, or *caccia*, a sport which immediately appeals to the well-practiced prostitute (I.iv.123–32), and can easily be understood as a not-so-thinly veiled sexual proposal. But Seicento authors could use a greater degree of specificity when describing the metaphorical pursuit of a desired prize.

207. Guido Ruggiero, "Introduction: Hunting for Birds in the Italian Renaissance," in *Erotic Cultures of Renaissance Italy*, ed. Sara F. Matthews-Grieco (Burlington, VT: Ashgate, 2010), 3.

208. Allen J. Grieco, "From Roosters to Cocks: Italian Renaissance Fowl and Sexuality," in *Erotic Cultures of Renaissance Italy*, 89–140.

209. Grieco, "From Roosters to Cocks," 89.

210. Grieco, "From Roosters to Cocks," in Appendix A on 126, provides a useful catalog of birds commonly used in fourteenth- to seventeenth-century Italian as euphemisms for the male genitalia.

211. Grieco, "From Roosters to Cocks," 94 and 108. Grieco notes that the use of *nido* and *gabbia* as vaginal euphemisms stretches back to Dante and Boccaccio.

The lexicon of bird hunting, or *uccellare*, was particularly suggestive.[212] Women on the metaphorical hunt were said to draw "birds" into their metaphorical "nets," to stuff them in their "cages," and to pluck their prey clean of their wealth.[213] The use of owlets as bait to attract other birds gave rise to the common association between *civette* and loose women, along with any number of variations on the theme to describe their womanly wiles.[214] Similarly, the practice of manipulating live, tethered decoys (*zimbelli*) to lure (*zimbellare*) other birds into an open net was also frequently sexualized.[215] Given the manifold erotic associations ascribed to bird hunting, and the sheer number of ornithological euphemisms already discussed above, it should then come as no surprise that sexual innuendos involving venery in *Buffoni* overwhelmingly point to the hunt with and for birds.

The cluster of burlesque quips delivered by Filippetta in Act I, Scene v, for example, is packed with euphemisms involving fowling. Having just orchestrated a meeting between Prince Meo and Ancroia, Filippetta listens in as the two exchange fulsome declarations of desire. Filippetta marvels at Ancroia's ability to trap Meo in her "net" with her beauty (lns. 44–45); at her skill at stringing him up like a bird; and at all those who, like Ancroia, know how to use their *zimbelli* to capture finches (*fringuelli*) (lns. 80–86). Filippetta then eggs the would-be lovers on—she spurs the prince by calling him to arms (lns. 108–110) and exhorts her mistress to strike before her quarry suspects a trap (lns. 111–16). At the scene's end, Ancroia handles her weapons of seduction masterfully and easily lands her prey. Later, a jilted Marmotta reveals that she had been eavesdropping on the exchange and recalls how Filippetta's frenzied efforts to lead Meo to Ancroia resembled those of a *civetta* hopping around to draw in the "birds" (I.viii.119–121). These consistently burlesque references to birds, food, and game, or, for that matter, ribald allusions to hats, baskets, and gardening tools would not have been lost on an original audience proficient in the doublespeak of carnivalesque theater.

Music and Dance

As might be expected, given both Costa's own background and the Medici's interests in performance, music and dance are key elements in *The Buffoons*.[216]

212. Grieco, "From Roosters to Cocks," 101.

213. Grieco, "From Roosters to Cocks," 104–5.

214. Grieco, "From Roosters to Cocks," 106, lists the following variants: *civettagine, civettamento, civettante, civettare, civetteggiare, civetterìa, civettesco, civettinare, civettino, civettòne, civettuola, civettuolménte*, and *civettuòlo*.

215. Grieco, "From Roosters to Cocks," 104–5.

216. To give but a few bibliographic examples covering an expanse of Medici rule, see Anthony M. Cummings, *The Politicized Muse: Music for Medici Festivals, 1512–1537* (Princeton, NJ: Princeton University Press, 1992); Cummings, *The Maecenas and the Madrigalist: Patrons, Patronage, and the*

Several characters break out in song throughout the comedy: Tedeschino sings when commanded to do so by Marmotta (II.iii.98–107); crazy Michelino belts out nonsensical tunes about hunting and food (I.vii.7–17; III.i.1–15); and Marmotta performs a more formal lamentation song at Bertuccia's urging (III.iv.16–60). Allusions to dance are frequent, with a preference for spirited and exotic choreographies such as the *moresca* and other high tempo steps such as the *saltarello*. In the Prologue, Ancient Comedy complains about the lure of dance and grumbles that the new theatrical culture is overrun with the *canario* and *spezzata*, popular stomp dances thought to have arrived from the Canary Islands by way of Spain (ln. 19). As noted, in the final scene of the comedy, Meo orders Tedeschino and the prostitute Ancroia placed into large cages and encourages his companions to dance a taunting *ciaccona*, or chaconne, around them. Performed to the music of guitars and castanets, this dance had Latin American and Spanish roots and, appropriately for Costa's context, was imaginatively associated with locales such as northern Africa.

Della Bella's frontispiece dramatizes this scene, showing four sprightly dancers kicking up their legs and, on the bottom right, Buffoonery, guitar in hand.[217] Costa appends the text of her *canzonetta* to the end of the publication, as well as two additional *canzonette* to be sung at the end of the first and second acts. Such *intermedi* were staples of early modern theater, providing entertainment through music, dance, and, in the case of comedies, buffoon performances between acts.[218] Each of these songs comments on the scene that would have preceded it: the first for Act I highlights the pains of unrequited love; images of beatings in the second correspond to the melee at the end of Act II in which the assorted male characters pummel each other; and for the Act III finale, the last *canzonetta* revels in the punishment of Tedeschino and Ancroia. The *intermedi* for comedies were often ephemeral parts of a performance and tended not be included in publications. Costa's decision to print the texts for hers, as well as a *canzonetta* for three voices to be sung before the Prologue, would have therefore been somewhat unusual

Origins of the Italian Madrigal (Philadelphia: American Philosophical Society, 2004); Nina Treadwell, *Music and Wonder at the Medici Court: The 1589 Interludes for* La Pellegrina (Bloomington: Indiana University Press, 2008); and Cusick, *Francesca Caccini at the Medici Court*.

217. The dancers in Della Bella's frontispiece bear a close resemblance to several of the figures in Jacques Callot's etching *La Ronde* (The circle dance) in his *Capricci* series. On this work, see *Le incisioni di Jacques Callot nelle collezioni italiane*, Exhibition Catalogue (Milan: Mazzotta, 1992), 153–64, cat. II.10.

218. On the inclusion of buffoons, see Henke, *Performance and Literature*, 51, 60–61. For official court functions such as weddings, these *intermedi* became increasingly extravagant parts of the production. See, for example, James M. Saslow, *The Medici Wedding of 1589: Florentine Festival as Theatrum Mundi* (New Haven: Yale University Press, 1996); and Treadwell, *Music and Wonder*.

for a comedy and underscores her investment in the performative nature of the work.[219]

Even music and dance cannot escape Costa's satirical pen, however. In Act II, Scene iii, Marmotta entreats Tedeschino to help distract her from her tribulations with some lighthearted entertainments. Despite his protests that he is a cavalier and not a clown, she wheedles him into dancing a *ciaccona*, strumming a guitar, performing acrobatics, and improvising a song. Heartened by these antics, she further provides him with a stick and commands him to ride it as if it were a dressage horse. In the lines that follow, Costa parodies the same kind of baroque equestrian ballet that she had explored in her *Festa reale per balletto a cavallo* manuscript of the previous year. Appearing first in France in 1581 and popular until the mid-eighteenth century, the equestrian ballet was especially dear to the Medici court, which staged performances on the occasion of grandiose festivities throughout the seventeenth century, including the wedding of Ferdinando II and Vittoria della Rovere.[220] Straddling his hobbyhorse, Tedeschino mimes the complex dressage movements known as airs above the ground to comic effect until his so-called steed sends him tumbling into the dirt. Through the buffoon Tedeschino, in other words, Costa pokes fun at the very courtly performative amusements that she elsewhere showcases and even lauds.[221] The result is a text that gives a broad sampling of the period's musical, dance, and theatrical offerings across high and low registers.

The Afterlife of Text and Author

Margherita Costa enjoyed warm praise from contemporaries for both her performances and her publications. The seventeenth-century Roman bibliographer Prospero Mandosio applauded her "rich and delightful talent" and catalogued

219. On the inclination not to publish *intermedi* texts, see Nino Pirrotta and Elena Povoledo, *Music and Theater from Poliziano to Monteverdi*, trans. Karen Eales (Cambridge: Cambridge University Press, 1982), 173.

220. For a general survey, see Helen Watanabe-O'Kelly, "The Equestrian Ballet in Seventeenth-Century Europe—Origin, Description, Development," *German Life and Letters* 36, no. 3 (1983): 198–212, as well as Kelley Harness, "Habsburgs, Heretics, and Horses: Equestrian Ballets and Other Staged Battles in Florence During the First Decade of the Thirty Years War," in *L'arme e gli amori: Ariosto, Tasso, and Guarini in Late Renaissance Florence: Acts of an International Conference, Florence, Villa I Tatti, June 27–29, 2001*, ed. Massimiliano Rossi and Fiorella Gioffredi Superbi, 2 vols. (Florence: Leo S. Olschki, 2004), 2:255–83. For the festival book printed for Ferdinando's and Vittoria's wedding, which includes a description of the equestrian ballet, see Ferdinando Bardi, *Descrizione delle feste fatte in Firenze per le reali nozze de' serenissimi sposi Ferdinando II, Gran Duca di Toscana, e Vittoria, Principessa d'Urbino* (Florence: Zanobi Pignoni, 1637).

221. On this scene and its relationship to both the genre and Costa's appeal to her patrons, see Goethals, "The Patronage Politics of Equestrian Ballet."

the numerous male intellectuals whose support she had won, both before and after her death. These included the noted Florentine court librarian Antonio Magliabechi, who wrote Mandosio a favorable assessment of the fame and honor Costa had enjoyed in his city.[222] A few decades later, the critic Giovanni Mario Crescimbeni described Costa in similarly glowing terms, deeming her "no less wise than learned" and touting the great admiration she earned "both in Italy and abroad."[223]

Despite these successes, Costa's literary and cultural activities have gone largely unknown and underappreciated until quite recently. Of all her published works, the *Buffoni* alone has enjoyed a full modern edition through its inclusion in Siro Ferrone's *Commedie dell'arte* anthology.[224] Costa has fared somewhat better in anthologies. Selections from her letters appeared in a *Scielta di lettere amorose* (Collection of Love Letters) published towards the end of her life, and more recently one features in an English translation of early modern Italian women's epistles.[225] Her lyric poetry has also graced several volumes assembled between the nineteenth and the twenty-first centuries. Curiously, these typically draw on a small set of verse from Costa's Florentine publications, a cluster that was partially canonized by the early eighteenth century following the selections made by Luisa Bergalli (herself a poet and a playwright) in her survey of women's writing.[226] In other words, anthologizers, particularly those of female authors, helped Costa maintain something of an enduring legacy but did so through a comparatively narrow subset of her admirably expansive and diverse oeuvre. More distinct were the choices in Jolanda de Blasi's early twentieth-century anthology, which notably

222. Prospero Mandosio, *Bibliotheca romana, seu Romanorum scriptorum centuriae.* 2 vols. (Rome: Ignati de Lazzaris, 1682–1692), 2:26–27.

223. Crescimbeni, *Comentari*, 2:323.

224. Margherita Costa, *Li buffoni*, in *Commedie dell'arte*, ed. Siro Ferrone. 2 vols. (Milan: Mursia, 1985- 1986), 2:234–359.

225. As noted above, this *Scielta di lettere amorose* was repeatedly republished throughout the century. For the modern example, see Lisa Kaborycha, ed. and trans., *A Corresponding Renaissance: Letters Written by Italian Women, 1375–1650* (Oxford: Oxford University Press, 2015), 179–82.

226. The most frequently anthologized poems are *La mia musa è svegliata e già ripiglia; O miei vaghi sorrisi, o dolci sguardi*; and *Lasciatemi morire*, all drawn from *La chitarra* (1–5, 449, 544–45). For the anthologies, see Luisa Bergalli, ed., *Componimenti poetici delle più illustri rimatrici d'ogni secolo* (Venice: Antonio Mora, 1726), 149–54; Antoine Ronna, ed., *Parnaso italiano: Poeti italiani contemporanei maggiori e minori*, 2 vols. (Paris: Baudry, 1843), 2:1025–27; Natalia Costa-Zalessow, ed., *Scrittrici italiane dal XIII al XX secolo: Testi e critica* (Ravenna: Longo, 1982), 146–52; Angelo Gianni, ed., *Anch'esse "quasi simili a Dio": Le donne nella storia della letteratura italiana, in gran parte ignote o misconosciute: Dalle origini alla fine dell'Ottocento* (Viareggio [Lucca]: M. Baroni, 1997), 89–90; and Giuliana Morandini, *Sospiri e palpiti: Scrittrici italiane del Seicento* (Genoa: Marietti, 2001), 114–24, 238. A pair of her poems appear most recently in a world poetry anthology aimed at a general audience: Elvira Marinelli, ed., *Poesia: Antologia illustrata* (Florence: Giunti, 2002), 266.

include an excerpt from the *Buffoni*'s Prologue.[227] Costa's terrain has been expanding as of late, however. For example, Natalia Costa-Zalessow and Joan E. Borrelli have recently published a volume of facing-page translations of select poems from across Costa's career, helping to make her works more accessible to Italian- and English-speaking audiences alike.[228]

A medley of factors has contributed to Costa's spotty presence on the pages of Italian literary history. First, even during her lifetime she seems to have been bedeviled by accusations over the authenticity of the texts published under her name. She countered such attacks in a poem from *La selva di Diana* addressed to "the person who says there are those who fear that the author does not write her own works." Just because the current era is plagued by others' ignorance and lethargy, she argues, does not mean her own devotion to Apollo should be thrown into doubt.[229] While later in the seventeenth century Magliabechi wrote with warm praise of Costa's talents, as noted above, his successor Antonfranceso Marmi claimed that in truth the famed bibliophile had doubted her authorship. Her poetic volumes were the work of her reported lover, Marmi alleged, a bandit known by the name Fra Paolo who worked as henchman to the Barberini and the Medici before being imprisoned in the Bargello of Florence.[230] More difficult to navigate than groundless rumors of this sort were the questions raised by Costa's first publication, the history of Ferdinando's travels to Germany. The volume stands out from the rest of her oeuvre, as it appears in print nearly a decade before her other Florentine compositions, and because of all her works it alone lacks poetic elements. Moreover, the history recounts a meeting between the grand duke and the emperor in 1627, presumably before Costa's arrival in Florence. Costa herself frames the text as a creative assemblage of notes entrusted to her by Ferdinando's secretary, Benedetto Guerrini, who accompanied him on the voyage—but she is quick to highlight her honor at being given the chance to undertake such a composition, hinting at an invitation of sorts.[231] Citing her introduction, Magliabechi later described Guerrini as having played a significant role in the history's composition, but a comparison of Guerrini's notes and the text of the history itself demonstrate that a process of reworking and revision has

227. Jolanda de Blasi, ed., *Antologia delle scrittrici italiane dalle origini al 1800* (Florence: Nemi, 1930), 334–41.

228. Costa, *Voice of a Virtuosa and Courtesan.*

229. "A persona che dice esservi chi teme che l'autora non operi da sé nelle sue compositioni." In Costa, *La selva di Diana*, 60.

230. BNCF, MS Magl. VIII 16, Antonfrancesco Marmi, *Miscellanea di diverse notizie letterarie e storiche*, fols. 51r–51v. While Costa's modern biographer Dante Bianchi, in "Una cortigiana rimatrice del Seicento," 29:2, has little positive to say about either the woman or her literary activity, he does note that this assertion that Fra Paolo authored Costa's works has no basis.

231. Costa, *Istoria del viaggio d'Alemagna del serenissimo Gran Duca*, 5.

been undertaken.[232] While ascertaining the authenticity of the *Istoria* as one of Costa's works falls beyond the scope of the present volume, it should be acknowledged that the attributional questions raised by this publication opened the door to accusations about the legitimacy of her literary activity. With the exception of the *Istoria*, however, the stylistic continuity of her works across time, genre, and geography make it highly unlikely that an unknown second party was publishing under Costa's name.

More problematic for Costa than this slight shadow cast upon her first entrée into the world of Florentine letters has been a moralizing response to her possible, perhaps even probable, activity as a courtesan. Several of her critics have been less concerned with the authenticity of her works than the virtuousness of her comportment. Accusations on this front emerged during her lifetime, most prominently in the satirist Erythraeus' work *Eudemia* (1645) in which an unsavory character is revealed to be the father of "the noted prostitute *Pleura*"—an appellation that puns on the Greek *pleura* and the Italian *costa*, both meaning "rib."[233] Some years later Magliabechi acknowledged that Costa had perhaps at one time plied the "art of the meretrix" (that is, prostitute), but concluded that such things had more to do with personal circumstance than literary merit and that the "many excellent and learned" men who supported her—including, he underscored, in print—would not have done so if she were not "adorned with virtues."[234] Her detractors proved less generous. One nineteenth-century commentator expressed indignation that his predecessors had taken Costa seriously at all, for "who could ever believe that the courtesan Margherita and the bandit Fra Paolo were two literati and should be the subject of bibliographic writing?" Presenting the various secondhand gossip associated with Costa as grounds to dismiss her out of hand, he concluded without irony that "in bibliographic works it seems to me that one needs conclusive facts and not pandering words."[235] In his study of Italian musicians in France from the same period, Agostino Ademollo scoffed at references to Costa's widowhood, contending that surely her erotic dalliances precluded her from ever having married or merited the ennobling title of "widow." His palpable disdain for Costa on the basis of her presumed lifestyle led him to decry her verse, describing her 1647 poems on the French music scene as "ugly" works that "without any merit of their own have the honor of being

232. BNCF, MS Magl. IX 14, Antonio Magliabechi, fol. 7r. Also see BNCF, MS Magl. VIII 15, Marmi, *Miscellanea di diverse notizie letterarie e storiche*, fol. 39r.

233. Erythraeus, *Eudemiae*, 86.

234. October 22, 1680 letter to P. d'Aprosio, transcribed in C. Arlia, "Un bandito e una cortigiana letterati," *Il bibliofilo*, nos. 8–9 (1881): 165.

235. Arlia, "Un bandito," 166. Arlia provocatively uses the word "lenocinio," which describes not only flattering language but also the crime of pimping.

remembered as historical documents."[236] Her most engaged biographer to date, Dante Bianchi, dedicated most of his one-hundred-page survey to combing through her publications for evidence of her sexual partners' historical identities, setting aside her volumes' actual contents and objectives as secondary.[237]

Like many of her contemporaries, Costa has also surely suffered from later readers' and critics' distaste for baroque writing. Importantly, however, the scorn shown to Costa specifically both underscores her prominence as a baroque figure and places her within a community of male peers. Francesco Saverio Quadrio, for example, reluctantly included seventeenth-century writers in his survey of poetic history, *Della storia e della ragione d'ogni poesia* (1739–1752). When introducing the notable practitioners of the baroque style—despite his aversion to them—he listed Costa alongside canonical male poets like Marino and disapprovingly conceded that, though he found little wisdom in her works, she nevertheless was "acclaimed by the literary men and princes of her day."[238] Two centuries later, however, Benedetto Croce—who famously disparaged the baroque aesthetic as an "artistic perversion"—stripped Costa of even such grudging accolades. Categorically criticizing Seicento women writers in comparison with their foremothers of the previous century, he accused Costa in particular of "scribbling" bad works of all sorts and insisted that she stood out primarily for her ignorance and lack of culture.[239] More recently, Costa's modern biographers Martino Capucci and Natalia Costa-Zalessow have suggested that she merits some consideration but in "sociological terms," with her works primarily "hold[ing] only historical value as a documentation of seventeenth-century taste and as a source of information about her contemporaries."[240]

236. Ademollo, *I primi fasti*, 37–38.

237. Bianchi, "Una cortigiana rimatrice del Seicento." In one of the few article-length studies dedicated to the comedy, Marcella Salvi similarly reads *Li buffoni* almost entirely in terms of prostitution, arguing that Ancroia—rather than Marmotta—is the work's female protagonist and associating the city of Fessa with the prostitute and not the princess. She concludes that Morocco represents a place of order in contrast with the disorder of Fessa, an inversion perhaps due to her unfamiliarity with Megale's work on the historical models for Costa's characters and thus the comedy's satirization of the Florentine court. Salvi, "'Il solito è sempre quello, l'insolito è più nuovo': *Li buffoni* e le prostitute di Margherita Costa fra tradizione e innovazione," *Forum italicum* 38, no. 2 (2004): 376–99. Also newly available is a coda in Alexandra Coller's *Women, Rhetoric, and Drama in Early Modern Italy* (New York: Routledge, 2017), 41–53.

238. Francesco Saverio Quadrio, *Ragione e storia d'ogni poesia* (Milan: Francesco Agnelli, 1739–1752), 2:310.

239. Benedetto Croce, *Storia della età barocca in Italia: Pensiero-poesia e letteratura vita morale* (Bari: Laterza, 1929), 33; and *Nuovi saggi sulla letteratura italiana del Seicento* (Bari: Laterza, 1931), 161.

240. Capucci, "Costa, Margherita"; Costa-Zalessow, "Margherita Costa," 118. In her later anthology of Costa's poetry, Costa-Zalessow subsequently did add that a smaller number of Costa's works "deserve to be studied for their Baroque peculiarities, originality, and humor" and walked back some of her earlier, primarily negative assessments, stating that Costa should be included in a survey of women's

The sidelining of Margherita Costa over concerns about her authenticity, her sexuality, and her baroqueness has begun to change course, however, and scholars are increasingly reassessing her role as a writer and a performer. Teresa Megale's aforementioned archival work on *Li buffoni* was an important early step in this direction, since she approaches Costa as a substantive figure within the Florentine court and the dramatic tradition. In her landmark survey of early modern Italian women writers, Virginia Cox insists upon Costa's singularity in terms of content, genre range, and position within the field of female authorship, and concludes that Costa's works are "deserving of a far closer critical scrutiny than they have hitherto received."[241] Recent work also has initiated the process of locating Costa within both the tradition of women's writing and the cultural milieu of late sixteenth- and early seventeenth-century Europe. Just as Cox detects an indebtedness to authoritative and innovative predecessors like Isabella Andreini in Costa's poetic endeavors, Meredith Ray highlights a similar continuity in the two women's unusually fluid appropriation of both male and female voices within their epistolary publications.[242] Similarly, the *Buffoni* appeared in a 2012 exhibit at the Folger Shakespeare Library entitled *Shakespeare's Sisters: Voices of English and European Women Writers, 1500–1700*, which placed Costa alongside approximately fifty early modern European peers such as Vittoria Colonna, Marguerite de Navarre, and Margaret Cavendish.[243] More recently, the comedy joined other seventeenth- and eighteenth-century burlesque works in the 2016 exhibit *Buffoni, villani e giocatori alla corte dei Medici* at Palazzo Pitti.[244] Given the expansiveness of Costa's literary and theatrical production, these represent but the first salvos in a much needed exploration of her biography, creative influences, and cultivated relationships to patrons and protectors. It is the editors' hope that the current volume will contribute to this ongoing process of reclaiming Margherita Costa from the shadows of neglect and prudish dismissal, helping to position her instead as a bold and inventive figure who moved deftly between registers and genres, and between the patrons and courts of seventeenth-century Europe.

Note on the Italian Text

While Amadore Massi and Lorenzo Landi published the Italian text of *Li buffoni* in 1641, there are in reality two editions whose identical cover pages bear

literature due to her relationship to theater, dance, and female-authored comedic writing; see her introduction to Costa, *Voice of a Virtuosa and Courtesan*, esp. 40.

241. Cox, *Women's Writing in Italy*, 204–27, citation on 213–14.

242. Ray, *Writing Gender in Women's Letter Collections*, 181–82.

243. February 3–May 20, 2012; see <http://folgerpedia.folger.edu/Shakespeare's_Sisters:_Voices_of_English_and_European_Women_Writers,_1500-1700#Shakespeare.27s_Sisters_exhibition_material>.

244. See the exhibition catalog Bisceglia et al., *Buffoni, villani e giocatori*, 69–71.

this date. We have consulted copies held at the Biblioteca Nazionale Centrale di Firenze, in the Fondo Palatino (12.5.3.14) and in the Fondo Magliabechiano (3.1.89), as well as additional copies held by the Biblioteca Nazionale Marciana and the Folger Shakespeare Library, and digitalized by the Beinecke Rare Book and Manuscript Library and the Bibliothèque Municipale de Lyon. A series of revisions distinguish the Magliabechiano volume from all other consulted copies of the comedy, indicating a subsequent moment of publication.[245] These alterations range from simple changes in punctuation and spelling, to rewording of expressions or verses, and even to the removal of full passages.

The most extensive—but by no means the only—revisions are found in the Act I, Scene viii dialogue between Marmotta and Bertuccia. In this scene, Bertuccia suggests that women have begun to enact revenge on their wayward husbands by engaging in extramarital dalliances of their own, and Marmotta launches into an extended series of *double entendres* regarding the nature of the city Fessa. Siro Ferrone has suggested that censorship was at play, by which "more or less openly obscene verses" were removed or replaced with "inoffensive ones."[246] This is evident, though it is important to not overstate the case. While the Magliabechiano edition somewhat tempers the vulgarity and the references to noblewomen's promiscuity in I.viii, both the scene and the comedy as a whole remain highly sexually suggestive. Moreover, all textual revisions save a few minor orthographic tweaks are confined to Act I, leaving the bawdiness of the other two acts untouched. In the absence of documentary evidence, we are left with several unanswered questions as to the source and motive of these revisions. Did a secondary party order the modifications, or did Costa herself opt to pursue them? Whether this is an instance of official decree or self-regulation, why were the changes made only after the comedy had seemingly been approved by the censors and was already published and circulating?

The material evidence suggests that while we may not be able to rely absolutely on the stated 1641 publication date of the Magliabechiano edition, it is likely that little time lapsed between the two printings. The publishers took evident care to keep reprinting costs low by minimizing disruptions to pagination. Even in the case of the more drastic changes made to Act I, Scene viii, Massi and Landi played with layouts and spacing in order to limit the disparity to fifteen pages and thereby to allow the two editions to realign fully from that point forward. Indeed, subsequent glaring errors in both page and scene numbering go uncorrected. The evidence therefore suggests that the publishers needed to remove and replace selected impacted sheets from Act I rather than generate an entirely fresh printing.

As did Ferrone in his 1985 edition of the comedy, we have opted to transcribe and translate the more widely available version. This is clearly the earlier

245. Ferrone, *Commedie dell'arte*, 1:64–65 for a similar conclusion.

246. Ferrone, *Commedie dell'arte*, 1:64.

of the two and, should the comedy have been staged (as Costa seems to suggest it was), it is the version with the greater likelihood of corresponding to the work as performed. With the goal of providing readers with as critical an edition as possible, however, we have also annotated and included all textual revisions from the later Magliabechiano edition as detailed below.

Note on the Transcription

We have sought to maintain the integrity of Costa's text by following the earlier edition as closely as possible while also including all subsequent published alterations. We have similarly attempted to keep the original layout in order to ensure a direct alignment between the Italian and the English translation, and to make the Italian text more accessible for the modern reader. The following changes have been made:

- Those passages that were altered or eliminated in the Magliabechiano edition have been set off with brackets, "[ ]", and put in italics. Notes on the Italian text explain the cuts and/or provide the textual revisions.
- The letters *u* and *v* have been distinguished.
- Abbreviations have been written out and punctuation has been modernized to reflect contemporary usage.
- The pseudo-etymological *h* has been removed and the resultant punctuation changes made as needed (e.g. *huomini* to *uomini*, *tal' hora* to *talora*), except in the case of Baldassarre's Spanish text.
- *J* in a final position has been changed to *i* (e.g. *sij* to *sii*).
- The use of accents, punctuation, and capitalization has been modernized. The capitalization of the word *Amore* has been maintained when it may refer to Cupid. The text uses a question mark to indicate both an interrogative and an exclamation. We have differentiated the two according to context. We have also added angled quotation marks indicating direct speech in order to facilitate readability.
- Latinate spellings have been modernized (e.g. *gratia* to *grazia*), except in the case of Baldassarre's Spanish text.
- Spelling inconsistencies within the text (e.g. the appearance of both *prencipe/principe*) have been corrected, typically in favor of the modern spelling, except in the case of macaronic speech. We have also adjusted small orthographic errors (e.g., *bellezza* for the erroneous *bellozza*).
- An error in the numbering of scenes in Act I (with "Scene Nine" mistakenly listed twice) has been corrected.

Note on the Translation

Any translation comes with unique challenges and negotiations, and Costa's *Buffoons* is certainly no exception. As translators, we were mindful from the outset that our edition would be the first to introduce anglophone readers to a comedy by a female dramatist without precedent among early modern Italian playwrights. Our translation therefore aims to render the quirks and conceits of her baroque Italian into an accessible yet appropriately colorful English. Costa reveled in mixing hackneyed Petrarchan affectations with crass puns, burlesque *double entendres*, and macaronic word play, and it is our hope that our translation conveys some of the flavor of her studied idiosyncrasies.

Our overriding priority has been to faithfully convey the content of Costa's play for modern readers. At times, however, we have moved away from the literal in favor of turns of phrase that (we hope) will make her text more accessible. We have also endeavored to preserve at least an echo of the rhythm and flow of Costa's original by translating *The Buffoons* in verse. Given Costa's unsystematic punctuation and often convoluted diction, we have taken a few liberties with her text where needed for the sake of readability. Lines and line breaks have also occasionally been shifted for syntactic clarity. Since Costa frequently uses rhyme to heighten comic and musical effect, whenever possible we have worked to mirror these elements with internal or concluding rhymes. With regard to meter, variations in verse length and rhyme scheme are the rule rather than the exception. While we have attempted to echo the sonorous quality of her verse through assonance and rhyme, Costa's meter has perforce been sacrificed in favor of intelligibility. However, in places where the meter is explicitly alluded to, such as in Act II, Scene iii, where Tedeschino announces that he will deliver his lines in tri-syllabic, or *sdrucciolo* verse, we have drawn attention to the metrical shift by highlighting the section in italics and concluding with rhyming couplets. Lines set to music, such as Marmotta's recitative verse in Act III, Scene v, are also set apart by italics.

The macaronic elements in Costa's *Buffoons* present a host of challenges for the translator. Many of the play's characters don "verbal masks"—character-specific linguistic tics marked by unique appropriations from other languages. Lines written for non-Italian characters are filled with distinctive verbal distortions, exaggerations, and confusions that are clearly manifest on the published page. In Act I, Scene xiii, for example, Tedeschino, Baldassarre, Michelino, and Mantuano verbally spar on the page using a cacophony of languages and accents that mirror the physical melee enacted on stage. Rather than flatten out their exchanges into a uniform English translation and suggest foreign pronunciations for the performance of each character, we have endeavored to mirror Costa's plurilingualism in our edition. Since English does not easily lend itself to the same kind of morphological twists possible in the Romance languages, we have created the following key for translating each one of these foreign inflections into English:

- Baldassarre—The buffoon-turned-brother speaks in a Spanish riddled with Italianisms. We have translated his lines in English and interspersed commonly understood Spanish cognates throughout (i.e. *medicina* for medicine).
- Michelino—This comically unintelligible character speaks with a thick German accent, which Costa communicates through botched verb, noun, and adjective endings (i.e. *siame* for *siamo*, *cavalle* for *cavalli*); mispronunciations (*pascie* for *pace*); and conjugation errors, particularly with imperatives (*fermare!* for *fermate!*). Michelino's often nonsensical utterances are also punctuated by song, including the refrain *tarantan tarantan ta ta*. In order to maintain something of the Germanized accent, we have replaced the letter *w* with the letter *v* (*v*retch for wretch), the English digraph *th* with the letter *z* (*z*roat for throat), the preposition *with* with *vis*, the conjunction *and* with *und*, and made every effort to capture the sing-song lunacy of his speech through rhyme. We have regularized his grammar for the sake of clarity.
- Mantuano—This German character maintains some of Michelino's verbal tics, albeit in a much reduced form. To offer readers a taste of his accent, we have replaced the conjunction *and* with *und* and added a suffix *-en* to verb forms (i.e. stopp*en* for stop).
- Croatto—This Turkish character's speech is distinguished by the substitution of the letter *p* with the letter *b* (i.e. *b*rince for *p*rince), spotty Italian grammar (such as speaking in unconjugated verbs), and gender inversions of nouns and adjectives. We have maintained his confusion of *p* and *b* but regularized his grammar for the sake of clarity.

All modified spellings and foreign words have been marked off in italics. Character names have been kept in Italian, except in the case of multi-part names (Gobbo del Violino) or where a translation is required within the context of the play (i.e. Act I, Scene viii, when Tedeschino explains how he earned the name "il Tedeschino," or "The Little German").

Note on the Stage Directions

Costa's stage directions for the *Buffoni* are sparse by modern standards, yet not atypical for her day. Explicit scene locations are limited to the opening reference to Morocco and later a window overlooking a street in an exchange between Ancroia and Filippetta (I.iii and iv), and Marmotta at her window (I.ii). The only note on costuming signals that Tedeschino is to appear dressed as Ancroia (II.xi and xii). There is no prop list. The few stage directions Costa does provide tellingly cue the characters to engage in physical or vocal performances. Marmotta sings (III.iv.15–60), Pedina sounds a horn (I.v.15), and Tedeschino sings, dances, and gallops on a wooden stick (II.iii). Michelino enters and exits with lines intended to be sung (II.vii.7–17 and III.i.1–5), and the whole play concludes with the performance of a *ciaccona* around the caged prisoners. The remaining stage directions must be inferred from the play's text. We have therefore reported Costa's original stage directions in the Italian transcription, but, following Ferrone's example, in our translation we have also added likely exits, asides, and actions within brackets to help orient the reader.

LI BUFFONI, COMEDIA RIDICOLA

THE BUFFOONS, A RIDICULOUS COMEDY

Li buffoni,
comedia ridicola
di
Margherita Costa
romana
a
Bernardino Ricci,
Cavaliero del piacere
detto il Tedeschino

Al Tedeschino Cavalier del piacere

Il solito è sempre quello, l'insolito è più nuovo; oltre che il far le cose a proposito vien da tutti lodato. Il dedicare questa mia Comedia de' Buffoni ad altri ch'al Tedeschino mi sarebbe posto a gran trascuragine, poiché se in essa non ebbi altra mira che d'inventar scioccherie, rappresentar balordagini ed imitar stoldidezze, a qual più di voi, vestito del mio pensiero, poss'io appoggiarla? Voi, schiuma de' buffoni, padre delle sciocche rie ed infine politico inventore d'ogni balordagine. Essendo dunque sicura che sotto l'ali d'un buffone vostro pari la mia buffoneria politicamente si manterrà viva, vengo sì a dedicarvi quella, come con novo assalto a ricomporre la vostra ira. Lo sdegnarsi a ragione è d'animo elevato, ma per l'opposito, quelli spiriti, che senza offesa per un mero capriccio o, per dir meglio, pazzia, tolgano ad altri quei termini di riverenza che anche fra nemici si devono, hanno più dello spiritato che dello spiritoso. Con tutto ciò, per farvi conoscere che altrettanta è la mia cortesia quanto la vostra sordidezza, senza riguardo del poco frutto ch'io cavai dalla ventaglia de' Buffoni a vostro onore data in luce, in questa mia burlesca composizione per scopo principale ho preso il vantar le vostre glorie, e postovi per uno de' principali soggetti di essa, mi sono dilatata in rappresentar vivamente le vostre virtù, in dinotar quegli onori che forsi in palese altrove ricevesti, e con viva copia dimostrare in voi que' talenti che in un cavalier del piacere della vostra tacca si richiedono. Gradite dunque il mio affetto, e se per la mia penna si esaltano i vostri meriti, confessandovi di quella obligato, datemi campo, che con essa possa perseverare a lodarvi, con che assicurandovi che la mia musa sempre via più m'infonderà materia, con che per le rime risponda alle vostre cortesie, vi augurio ogni staggione in Carnovale. Firenze, li 10 di gennaro 1641.

Margherita Costa

The Buffoons,
A Ridiculous Comedy
by
the Roman
Margherita Costa,
to
Bernardino Ricci,
The Cavalier of Pleasure,[1]
Known as Tedeschino[2]

Dedication

To Tedeschino, The Cavalier of Pleasure

The usual is always the same, but the unusual is far more novel. Not only is it opportune, it is praised by all. To dedicate this, my Comedy of Buffoons, to anyone other than Tedeschino would have been a grave oversight on my part. For if I had no other aim than to invent nonsense, represent hooey, and imitate poppycock, who else could I have based it on other than you, clothed in my very thoughts? You, scum of buffoons, father of absurdity, and cunning[3] inventor of all sorts of stupidity? Thus certain that under the wings of a buffoon of your stature my Buffoonery will shrewdly keep itself alive, I dedicate it to you and rekindle your anger with this fresh assault. Though righteous anger is the mark of a lofty mind, those souls who have not been insulted yet on a whim (or, rather, frenzy) deny others the respect shown even between enemies are more possessed than spirited. Keeping all of this in mind, in order to show you that I am as courteous as you are churlish, and with no regard for the paltry fruits I reaped from bringing a performance of the *Buffoons* to light in your honor, I have made praising your glories the main goal of this burlesque composition of mine. And having made you one of its principal characters, I have strained to vividly represent your virtues, to note those honors which you evidently received elsewhere, and with this animated likeness of you to display those gifts required of a cavalier of pleasure such as yourself. Therefore enjoy my affection, and if your merits are exalted by this pen to which you are indebted, give me some room so that with it I may continue to praise you. Having thus assured you that my Muse will infuse me with ever more material so that I may respond to your kindness with verse, I wish you a Carnival without end. Florence, January 10, 1641.

Margherita Costa

A' lettori

Lettore, se in questa mia Comedia de' Buffoni troverai con la varietà de' linguaggi l'inconformità dello stile, non me ne dare accusa, poiché solo il mio pensiero è stato d'imitare i personaggi che rappresenta, i quali per esser de' pazzi, buffoni, e nani, come qui sotto vedrai, non d'altro abito potevo vestirli, volendo rappresentarli del naturale. Il Cielo ti salvi.

Meo è nato scimonito.
Masino è un storto di tutta la vita e del viso.
Michelino è un pazzo tedesco italianato.
Mantuano tedesco italianato.
Baldassarre spagnuolo italianato.
Pedina è un nano.
Gobbo è un scherzo di natura, che al nano somiglia, ma gobbo.
Grasso cuoco è una persona grossa e sciocca.
Croatto turco italianato.
Catorchia nano.
Scatapocchio nanetto piccolissimo.
Gobbo del Violino è un gobbo.

To the Readers

Reader, do not blame me if in this, my Comedy of Buffoons, you find an array of styles together with its variety of languages. My sole intention has been to imitate the characters here represented, whom, being loons, buffoons, and dwarfs—as you can see below—I could not have dressed in any other garb since I wanted to capture them *au naturel.*[4] May Heaven help you.

Meo[5] is a born fool.
Masino[6] is crooked in both stature and in appearance.
Michelino[7] is a crazy Italianized German.
Mantuano[8] is an Italianized German.
Baldassarre[9] is an Italianized Spaniard.
Pedina[10] is a dwarf.
Gobbo[11] is a freak of nature who looks like a dwarf but is hunchbacked.
Grasso[12] the cook is a fat, stupid person.
Croatto[13] is an Italianized Turk.
Catorchia[14] is a dwarf.
Scatapocchio[15] is a teeny-tiny little dwarf.
Gobbo of the Violin[16] is a hunchback.

Personaggi che parlano

La Comedia Antica
Buffoneria
Meo, principe di Marocco, innamorato d'Ancroia meretrice
Marmotta, principessa di Fessa, moglie del principe Meo
Bertuccia, damigella di Marmotta principessa
Masino, segretario di stato del principe Meo
Tordo, consigliero di stato del principe Meo
Michelino, scalco del principe Meo
Mantuano, servidore di Michelino
Pedina, capitan della guardia del principe Meo
Gobbo, capocaccia del principe Meo
Ancroia, meretrice, dama di Baldassarre buffone
Filippetta, serva di Ancroia
Tedeschino, buffone innamorato della principessa Marmotta
Grasso, cuoco servidore del Tedeschino
Baldassarre, buffone amante d'Ancroia
Croatto, servidore di Baldassarre
Catorchia, innamorato di Filippetta serva d'Ancroia
Scatapocchio, bravo di Catorchia
Gobbo del violino
Coro di cacciatori

La scena si rappresenta in Marocco.

Cast of Characters

Ancient Comedy
Buffoonery
Meo, prince of Morocco, in love with the prostitute Ancroia
Marmotta,[17] princess of Fessa,[18] wife of Prince Meo
Bertuccia,[19] lady-in-waiting of Princess Marmotta
Masino, secretary of state of Prince Meo
Tordo,[20] state advisor of Prince Meo
Michelino, valet of Prince Meo
Mantuano, servant of Michelino
Pedina, captain of the guard of Prince Meo
Gobbo, chief huntsman of Prince Meo
Ancroia,[21] prostitute and mistress of the buffoon Baldassarre
Filippetta, servant of Ancroia
Tedeschino, buffoon in love with Princess Marmotta
Grasso, cook and servant of Tedeschino
Baldassarre, buffoon and lover of Ancroia
Croatto, servant of Baldassarre
Catorchia, lover of Filippetta, Ancroia's servant
Scatapocchio, *bravo* of Catorchia
Gobbo of the Violin
Chorus of Hunters

The play takes place in Morocco.

Argomento

Meo, principe di Marocco, tutto rivolto all'osterie, agli amori, ed alli buffoni, dà cagione a Marmotta principessa, sua moglie, di voler partirsi dal regno, ed andare a' suoi stati paterni di Fessa, e starvi col padre, che non avendo più successione di maschi, lei resta sua erede; e dopo varii avvenimenti che la disturbano e la trattengono, determina mandar Baldassare (tra buffoni assai virtuoso) al padre in Fessa, e nel dargli i contrasegni di sè, lo trova essere suo fratello, ed erede successore del principato di Fessa. Meo in tanta allegrezza del cognato principe si distoglie dall'osterie, lascia gli amori, punisce i buffoni, e torna in pace con la moglie.

Argument

Meo, the prince of Morocco, is so entirely consumed by taverns, lovers, and carousing with buffoons that he gives his wife, Princess Marmotta, good cause to leave his kingdom for her father's lands in Fessa, where, in the absence of any male successors, she is the heir. After various incidents trouble and detain her, she resolves to send Baldassarre (the most virtuous of the buffoons) ahead to her father in Fessa. While revealing her secret countersign to him, she discovers that he is her long-lost brother and the rightful successor to the principality of Fessa. Meo, elated to have a prince as a brother-in-law, gives up the taverns, abandons his lovers, punishes the buffoons, and returns to live in peace with his wife.

Canzonetta
da cantarsi a tre voci al principio della comedia inanzi il prologo

Che rumori,
Stridori!
Che fracassi, che grida
Andate facendo,
Ridendo!
Deh, non più tante strida!
Son tutte baiate,
Son tutte risate
A ufo signori,
Se prima di fuori
Ciascun non vedete.
Ah, ora, ora ridete,
Ah, ora, tutti ridete.

Canzonetta

for three voices to be sung at the beginning of the comedy before the prologue

What's all this noise,
this howling?
What's all this shouting,
this racket you're making
with your laughing?
Ah, enough with all the shrieking!
All these antics,
all these laughs
are gratuitous, gentlemen,
before you see anyone
come on stage.
Ah, now, now you laugh!
Ah, now, you all laugh!

Prologo [i]

La Comedia antica e la Buffoneria

[Comedia]
Oh, voi mi rimirate? Io son pur dessa.
Non m'ha l'antichità cangiato aspetto,
E meco c'è la rigidezza istessa.
Ciascuno se l'aspetti; mal v'accolse
Questo teatro. Al cinto mio sospesa,
Sol per farvi la barba a vostro costo,
Ho la cesoia ed il rasoio ho posto.
Dormir nel letto altrui con l'altrui donna?
Oh buono! E poi voler dare ad intendere
Ch'ei 'l fa per rispiarmare i suoi lenzoli.
Gnaffe! Egli vuole che col conio suo
Sol la moneta, ch'è d'altrui, si stampi,
E gode arare in licenzioso modo
Non già co' boi, ma con la fronte i campi.
Ed altri di bocali è sanguisuca,
Ed a cannella suona il suo stromento.
Vede i colori or verdi, or rossi, or gialli,
Ed instabil di testa, e mal in piedi,
Fa di canarii e di spezzate i balli.
E v'ha chi tutto dì sopra i buffetti
Altro non fa co' dadi, e con le carte,
Che «dico paro» e «tengo», e l'infelice
I bastoni talor prende per coppe.
Ma più da vero che per gioco al fine
Perde i danari, e si riduce in toppe.
V'è chi la gatta di Masino finge,
E scaltro ippocriton per umiltade
Tutto riconcentrato in sé si stringe;
Ha torto il collo, ed abbassato il ciglio,
Ma poi, per arrivare un pover omo
Di cervo ha 'l piede, ed ha d'arpia l'artiglio.
Ed altri fa il Narciso, e 'l Ganimede,
E mille volte il dì more, e rinasce;
Sempre il suo amore in dubbio stato inforsa;
Di sonno è carco, e di cervel leggero,
Ma più che di cervel, lieve è di borsa.

Prologue

Ancient Comedy and Buffoonery

[**Ancient Comedy** *addresses the audience*][22]
Oh, are you looking at me? I am indeed she.
Antiquity has not altered my appearance,
and I maintain my usual severity.
You all have it coming to you,
for you've been poorly received by this theater.
Upon my belt I've hung my shears and placed my razor,[23]
just to give you a good lather at your own expense.
This guy here sleeps in another's bed with another man's woman?
Oh that's nice! And then he wants to act as though
he does it to save his sheets?
Hooey! He wants to press
other men's coins with his own stamp,
and he loves to lewdly plow other men's fields,
not with oxen but with his head.
He leeches off other men's jugs,
and, taking a swig, he plays his instrument.
He sees colors—now green, now red, now yellow—
and with an addled head and two left feet
he dances the *canario* and the *spezzata*.[24]
And there's that guy who, hovering all day above the tables,
does nothing more with dice or cards
than say "I call" and "I fold,"
and the wretch at times even mistakes clubs for cups.
But in the end he loses his coins
more for real than for play and is reduced to tatters.
And then this guy pretends to turn a blind eye,[25]
and in a show of humility
the sly hypocrite curls his whole body up into itself.
He has a crooked neck and a lowered brow,
but when he sets his sights on some poor stiff
he has the hoof of a buck and the claw of a harpy.
Another guy plays the Narcissus or the Ganymede[26]
and a thousand times a day dies and is reborn,
his love always thrown in a state of doubt.
He is heavy with sleep and light in the brains,
but even more than in brains he is light in the purse.

L'avaro poi, perché rispiarmi forse
Il funerale suo, con smorto volto
Pone tutti i pensier dentro una cassa,
E con l'oro vi giace anch'ei sepolto.
Il soldato pe 'l gioco, che l'abbatte,
Pugna più che per l'arme del nemico;
Spresato s'attraversa per le strade,
A prede avvezzo va tra rischi a porse,
E più che le città, piglia le borse.
E 'l cortegian, ch'a guisa di lumaca
Tutta la guardarobba indosso porta,
Co' denti asciutti in camera se n' torna,
Né, per spender, avendo entro lo scrigno
L'avanzo del salario, o ver del suo,
Si pasce ch'il padron l'ha fatto un ghigno.

Buffoneria
Oh vecchia sgangherata, e fatta a volta,
E ben come sei giunta in queste parti,
E sì ben cinguettar libera agogni,
Usa a viver ne' secoli vetusti
Quando il mondo mangiava agli e scalogni?

Comedia
Oh vil Buffoneria, scherno de' saggi,
Che, per mangiare, eserciti la lingua,
E bugie vendi, per comprar vivande.

Buffoneria
Tanto il boccone mio val più del tuo,
Quanto, ch'è 'l mio di gemme, e 'l tuo di ghiande.

Comedia
Tu con tanti stromenti saltellando
D'alocchi e di civette sei zimbello.

Buffoneria
E tu d'Apollo sei ne la cucina
Col secco lauro un smunto fegatello.

And then the miser,
perhaps in order to scrimp on his own funeral,
with a wan face locks all his cares in a coffer,
and there too he lies, buried with his gold.
And the soldier fights more at cards, which trounce him,
than he does against his enemy's arms.
He walks the streets an object of scorn,
and, accustomed to plunder, goes in search of danger,
but more than cities, it's purses he seizes.
And the courtier, who like a snail,
wears his entire wardrobe on his back,
with a parched mouth withdraws into his chamber.
In order to skimp, he stows in his shell
what's left of his wages (or in truth of himself),
and lives off his master's sneers.

Buffoonery [*enters*]
Oh you unhinged old broad, humped as a barrel vault,
so used to life in the olden days
when the world ate naught but garlic and scallion,
just how did you get here,
and why do you love to prattle on?

Ancient Comedy
Oh vile Buffoonery, laughingstock of the wise,
you ply your tongue in order to eat,
and to buy your viands you peddle lies.

Buffoonery
A mouthful of mine is worth more than yours,
since mine is of precious stones, and yours of acorns.[27]

Ancient Comedy
And you are but bait for owls and owlets[28]
with so many instruments tumbling hither and thither.

Buffoonery
The closest you'll get to Apollo is his kitchen.
Next to the dried laurel[29] you're nothing but chopped liver.

Comedia
Oh quanto meglio fora che gli specchi
Che porti per altrui, per te portassi.

Buffoneria
Ed il bastone, onde la destra appoggi,
La schiena a suon di colpi a te drizzasse.

Comedia
Può la lattuca tua pascer un campo,
Ma d'asini che ragghino nel maggio.

Buffoneria
E, se non altro, il tuo rasoio almeno
Può farti donna segnalata al mondo.

Comedia
Oh come agevolmente pigli vento!

Buffoneria
E tu com'entri facilmente in barca!

Comedia
Credimi, a te la gioventù non giova.

Buffoneria
Sappi ch'a te più la vecchiezza noce.

Comedia
Tu come un animal vivi a giornate.

Buffoneria
E tu la notte, come i grandi, mangia,
Razza apunto di nottola, ch'avanzo
Sei di quei greci, e di quei tuoi romani,
Ch'a la tua mala lingua il bando diero.

Comedia
Sempre ha la veritade i suoi nemici.

Ancient Comedy
If only you'd look in the mirror
you hold up to others!

Buffoonery
And if only that cane where you rest your right hand
were to straighten your spine with a chorus of blows.

Ancient Comedy
Your lettuce patch could feed
an army of donkeys braying in May.

Buffoonery
And if nothing else, your razor can make you
a woman a cut above the rest.

Ancient Comedy
Oh how easily you go overboard!

Buffoonery
And how easily you're thrown off course!

Ancient Comedy
Believe me, your youth does you no favors.

Buffoonery
And you should know that old age is bad for your health.

Ancient Comedy
Like an animal you live day to day.

Buffoonery
And you feed at night, you predatory beast,
just like some kind of owl.[30]
You're but a remnant of the Greeks and those Romans of yours
who banished your wicked tongue.

Ancient Comedy
The truth shall always have its enemies.

Buffoneria
E l'insolenza il suo castigo aspetta.
Altro è l'officio tuo che di pedante,
Ch'è di natura sua bestia proterva,
E tutto il mal, ch'in altri biasmar suole,
Ei per fidecommisso in sé conserva.

Comedia
Il dir mal oggi è l'arte del buffone?

Buffoneria
Ti duole ch'io ti tolga la tua parte.
Almen facciamo a mezzo, e amica godi
Che sia mio l'esercizio, e tua sia l'arte.

Comedia
Tu forse scherzi perch'hai pieno il ventre.

Buffoneria
E tu fa' come la cicala suole,
Che pria che non si pasca ella non canta,
E poich'ella è pasciuta in su 'l meriggio
Sì talor canta che ci lascia il fiato.
Va', va' di qui lontana. A' nostri eroi
Ed a' figli de l'Arno, o stolta vecchia,
Nocer non può il livor de' detti tuoi.

Comedia
Già so che ti risenti, perché scorgi,
Che scacciarti di qui sola poss'io.

Buffoneria
Tu m'hai più cera col tuo brutto ceffo
Di scacciar cani che cacciar buffoni.
Nella felicità di questo regno
Maledicenza non ha loco alcuno.
Torna ne la tua Grecia, e non più meco
Vanta le tue bontà, qui non ad altro,
Ch'a bersi in su 'l mattino è buono il greco.

Buffoonery
And insolence awaits its due punishment.
You play no other part than that of a pedant,
who is by his very nature a scornful beast.
All of the evil that he reproaches in others
he keeps in trust for himself.

Ancient Comedy
Speaking ill, is this the buffoon's art nowadays?

Buffoonery
It pains you that I've taken away your part.
Let's at least split the difference, my friend, take heart,
let mine be the practice, and yours be the art.

Ancient Comedy
Perhaps you jest because your belly's full.

Buffoonery
And you behave much like the cicada
who unless she has eaten will not sing,
and once she has had her noontide feast
will at times sing until her voice gives out.
Go on, get away from here, foolish old woman.
Our heroes and the children of the Arno
cannot be harmed by the venom of your words.

Ancient Comedy
Already I see how resentful you are,
for you know that I alone can chase you away from here.

Buffoonery
You'd chase away more dogs than buffoons
with that ugly mug of yours.
In this happy kingdom backbiting has no place.
Go back to your Greece,
and no longer brag to me about your virtues.
Here the only Greek[31] that's any good
is the one that's drunk in the morning.

Comedia
Forza di vino rende il senso infermo.

Buffoneria
Chi de' principi Medici a la cura
Dal cielo è dato non ha parte inferma,
Onde tua lingua risanare il vaglia.
Taci, che quivi la Comedia antica
Non ha da farvi tacca o ripresaglia.

Comedia
A sì gran nome, e non a' detti tuoi,
Ceder m'è forza, ché la lingua mia
Punger può ma non nocere agli eroi.
Se i Medici ancor essi da la Grecia
Trasser l'antico sangue, eroi sì degni
Fia che co' greci miei prezzi ancor io.
Usa a' maligni cieli, or da l'aspetto
De le Medicee stelle altrove io parto.
E inchino lui, che da' miei greci sceso,
Degli italici regni è gloria altera,
Ed agli Augusti unito a l'Arno impera.

Buffoneria
Così vada chi sdegna i detti arguti
Di più faceti e più giocondi ingegni.
Non più di grave suon voci malgrate,
Se soglion nel terren ridere i fiori,
Qui la città di Flora ami risate,
Non più severi ed importuni detti;
Suoni il teatro buffoneschi amori,
S'oda comica scena ordir diletti.
Roma, ch'ebbe di senno i vanti primi,
Odiava i Gracchi, ed ascoltava i mimi.
Ad una cena è simil la comedia,
E sembra il palco suo tavola grande
Ove non altri alfin che l'allegria
Condisce saporose le vivande.
Solo dunque di ciancie aspersa sia,
Poich' i faceti sali, e i lieti detti
Ciban l'alme, e nodriscono gli affetti:

Ancient Comedy
The strength of the wine sickens your senses.

Buffoonery
Whomever the Heavens have entrusted
to the care of the Medici[32] princes never falls sick,
whereas your tongue could use some healing.
Silence, for here Ancient Comedy
need not reclaim or advertise her wares.

Ancient Comedy
To this great name, and not to your words,
I am forced to yield, since my tongue
may prick but not harm heroes.
If even the Medici, worthy heroes indeed,
drew their ancient blood from Greece,
then may I too be valued along with my Greeks.
Accustomed to malignant skies, now from the aspect
of the Medicean stars[33] I take my leave,
and bow before he who descended from my Greeks.[34]
He is the exalted glory of the Italian kingdoms
and, united to the Augustans, over the Arno he reigns.[35]

Buffoonery
Be on your way, you who disdain the witty words
of sharper, merrier intellects.
Let's have no more unwelcome, solemn voices,
when the flowers laugh throughout the land.
Here in the city of Flora[36] may laughter be loved,
let's have no more harsh and bitter words.
May the theater resound with buffoonish loves
and hear this comic scene devise delights.
Rome, who in truth had the first bragging rights,
despised the Gracchi[37] and obeyed the mimes.
Comedy is like a supper,
and its stage resembles a large table
where savory dishes
are seasoned with nothing but mirth.
May it thus be sprinkled only with playful banter
so that its zesty wit and merry words
may feed the soul and nourish the passions.

E se ’l buffone è ’l sale de la cena,
Senza buffonerie sciocca è la scena.

Indeed, if the buffoon is the salt of the meal,
without buffoonery the scene has no appeal.[38]

Atto primo

Scena prima

Meo principe di Marocco, Marmotta principessa sua moglie

Meo
Che canchero o diavolo sarà?
Tutto il giorno co' barbotti,
Ch'io non vada, ch'io non stia,
Ch'io non faccia, ch'io non dica;
(Quasi che mi scappò)
Che venir vi ti possa
Il male del rovello
O 'l bruscior de l'ortica.
Io l'intendo a mio modo,
Portar voglio i calzoni;
Né v'avete a impacciare,
Se mi piace la zuppa o li buffoni.

Marmotta
Ancora hai tanto ardir? Non so se sai
Ch'io son di Fessa erede, e che non venni
In Marocco per farti la fantesca?

Meo
O Fessa o Sfessa, io non so che ti vogli,
Ch'Ercole non son io
Che vanti qui per te portar la gonna.

Marmotta
Ancora questo, ancora?
Io dico che non voglio
Più durarla così! Voglio esser moglie.

Meo
Così non fussi tu; sia maledetto
Chi mi fece dir sì per una volta.

Marmotta
Oh testa di zuccaccia senza seme,
Cervellaccio di gatta, uomo da niente:

Act One

Scene One

Prince Meo of Morocco, his wife Princess Marmotta

Meo
Bloody hell, what the devil is it now?
All day long you've been grumbling:
that I shouldn't go, that I shouldn't stay,
that I shouldn't do this, that I shouldn't say that
(so much so that I almost lost it).
May you be struck mad
or get stung by nettles!
I plan on doing things my way,
I want to wear the pants 'round here.
You shouldn't meddle
if buffoons and sauces[39]
are what I hold dear.

Marmotta
You have some nerve! I don't think you understand
that I am the heir of Fessa, and that I didn't come
to Morocco just to be your maid!

Meo
Fessa, Shmessa, I don't know what you want.
I'm no Hercules
prancing about in a skirt for your pleasure.[40]

Marmotta
Again with this, again?
I tell you I can't go on like this!
I want to be a wife.

Meo
If only you weren't!
Cursed be whoever made me say "I do" once and for all.

Marmotta
Oh, you seedless squash-for-brains,
you lousy numskull, you worthless man.

Oh ve' s'io l'ho trovato il buon marito!
Tutto il giorno con gli osti a frugnolare
Qualche vil baronaccia, o fra guidoni
Fra mille scioccherie buffoneggiare.
Maladetto di te l'orbo cervello,
Maladetto l'umor, la frenesia,
Maladetto il tuo prence e principato
E di Marocco la geneologia.

Meo
Tu sola maladetta, e tutta Fessa.
Maladetta di te la troppa rabbia,
Maladetto chi fetti principessa,
[*E chi mi fece uccel de la tua gabbia.*[ii]]

Marmotta
Oh balordo cervel da far lunari.
A fé, a fé, ch'io ti vuò far vedere
Chi è Marmotta e chi sono i Fessanti.

Meo
E di grazia non fate.
Oh ve' chi vuol bravare in casa d'altri.
Orsù, volete voi farla finita?

Marmotta
Io mai non finirò finché non veda
Finito te reo prence e mal marito.

Meo
A fé, a fé, Marmotta,
Ch'io disciorrò li bracchi a tuo mal grado.

Marmotta
Oh pazzo, scimonito!
E quanto è che gli hai sciolti a tuo mal pro?
Fa' quello che ti pare,
Io voglio esser trattata da mia pari.
Vuò che mi sii marito
In altro che buon dì, m'intendi tu?

Just look at what a fine husband I've found!
Out the whole day with the innkeepers,
prowling for some cheap hussy,[41]
or stupidly clowning around with lowlifes.
Curse your blind mind,
curse your humors, your frenzies,
curse your prince and principality,
and Morocco's ancestry.

Meo
You alone are cursed, you and all of Fess.
Curse your excessive rage,
curse whoever made you princess
and me a birdie in your cage.

Marmotta
Oh, you harebrained lunatic.
I swear, I swear I'll show you
just who Marmotta is and who the Fessians are.

Meo
Do me a favor, don't bother.
Just look who wants to strut about other people's houses!
Come now, can't you just be done with it already?

Marmotta
I won't be done until I see you done in,
wicked prince and lousy husband.

Meo
I swear, Marmotta, I swear
I'm going to unleash the hounds, I'm warning you.

Marmotta
Oh, crazy fool!
And since when has setting them loose ever troubled you?
Do as you please,
I want to be treated as my station demands.
I want you to be my husband
for more than just a "Good day," get it?

Meo
Io non t'intendo, che malanno vuoi?

Marmotta
Voglio che come il dì son principessa,
Anch'io mi sia la notte. M'hai tu inteso?

Meo
E chi ti leva che la notte ancora
Non sii la principessa di Marocco?

Marmotta
Ah ah, o non intendi o tu fai 'l sordo.
Dico ch'io vuò la notte
Che Meo stia meco, e non vuò dormir sola!

Meo
Oh questo non può stare. Io tutta notte
Mi sogno stravaganze e fernesie[;][iii]
Se tu mi fossi a canto,
Forse potrei sognar che una bertuccia
Mi morsicasse il naso, e sbalordito
Darti un pugno sul viso a questa foggia.

Marmotta
Tira più là, bestiaccia! Eh ci vuol altro,
Io non son paurosa. Io vuò star teco.

Meo
Marmotta, a fé, che te ne pentireste;
Talor mi sogno di far al pallone,
Potrei darti nel ventre e disconciarti
L'original di qualche scimonito.

Marmotta
[*Ti volterò la schiena*[iv]], e se mi dai
Risponderotti con un creppapancia.

Meo
V'è peggio. Ora ch'è freddo, io piscio a letto
Ogni notte, Marmotta, non ti burlo.

Meo
I don't get you. What's this cursed desire of yours?

Marmotta
Just as I am a princess by day,
so too do I want to be one by night. Now do you get it?

Meo
And who says that at night
you aren't still the princess of Morocco?

Marmotta
Hah! Either you don't get it or you're playing dumb.
I'm saying that at night I want Meo to be with me,
and I don't want to sleep alone!

Meo
Oh, this can't be. All night long
I have wild, frenzied dreams.
If you were next to me,
I might dream that an ugly ape[42]
was biting my nose, and in a daze
punch you in the face like this. [*pretends to hit her*]

Marmotta
Get back, you brute! It'll take more than that.
I'm not daunted, I want to be with you.

Meo
Marmotta, I swear you'd regret it.
Sometimes I dream I'm throwing a ball,
I might whack you in the belly
and mangle some fool's misbegotten.

Marmotta
I'll turn my back on you, and if you get me,
in response I'll let one rip.

Meo
It gets even worse. Now that it's cold I piss in bed
every night, Marmotta, I'm not kidding.

Marmotta
So ben che non mi burli, che la sera
Prima ch'io venni me la caricasti.
A questo ci è rimedio, [*l'orinale*
Terrò sempre allestito per tal conto.[v]]

Meo
Pensa, [*se l'orinale*
Posso aspettare[vi]]; io dormo
Quando rovescio l'acqua ne' lenzoli.
Or finalmente solo
Io vuò dormir, che vuoi?
Vuò far quel che mi par, vuò quel che piace.

Marmotta
A fé, che non t'andrà sempre ben fatta.
Veramente l'è cosa
Da poterla soffrir (che sii appiccato),
Sentirsi tutto il giorno
Ch' un principe par tuo
Canta le mie bellezze a suon di corno.

Meo
Che corni o scorni? Oh tu l'intendi male!
Io non andai a moglie, ed a marito
Tu non venisti meco?
Oh guarda ritrovata!
Dunque s'a pranzo io vado,
Ho a domandar licenza
A la vostra eccellenza.

Marmotta
E pur lì: tu ben sai
Dove mi coce, ma tu fai lo sciocco
Principe di Marocco.
Io non presi marito
Per starmi con Bertuccia a sollazzare;
Lo presi, come fanno l'altre donne,
Per ritrovarlo pronto a' miei bisogni.
Tutto il dì tra gli amori e tra i buffoni,
E poi dir che portar tu vuoi i calzoni.

Marmotta
I know all too well that you're not kidding,
since the evening before I came you filled it up for me.
But for this I have a solution:
I'll always keep a piss-pot on hand.

Meo
You think I can wait
for a piss-pot? I stay asleep
even when I spill my waters in the sheets.
Now, once and for all,
I want to sleep alone. What's it to you?
I want to do as I please, I want what is pleasing.

Marmotta
I swear, things won't always go so well for you.
It really is too much
to have to endure—go hang yourself!—
hearing all day long
that a prince like you
sings my beauties to the sound of the horn.[43]

Meo
Oh horn, scorn, what are you talking about? You've got it all wrong!
I didn't go looking for a wife, and wasn't it you who came to me
looking for a husband?
Now listen here, you busybody!
If I'm going out to eat,
am I supposed to ask permission
from Your Excellency?

Marmotta
There you go: you know well enough
where it burns me,
and yet you play the moronic prince of Morocco.
I didn't take a husband
so I could amuse myself with Bertuccia.
I took one as do other women,
to find him ready to satisfy my needs.
You spend the whole day long with lovers and buffoons,
and then say that you want to wear the pants!

Meo
Facciamola finita:
Vuò stare in libertade,
Non ho bisogno di pedante attorno.
Oh ve' che bella tresca!
Io vuò darmi bel tempo, oh principessa,
Siamo in Marocco, e più non siamo in Fessa.

Marmotta
O in Fessa, o non in Fessa,
Io ho tolto marito per esser io la moglie,
E non perch'ad ogni ora
Vengan mille barone
A far la principessa.

Meo
Oh la puzza! Vuoi tu quietarti ancora?
Una donna tua pari
Non s'ha da dar pensiero
D'ogni cosa che sente,
A te tocca a badare
A le cose del regno
E non saper s'io caccio o voglio amare.

Marmotta
Signorsì, a me tocca
Di governar lo stato?
Oh d'Amor scimonito!
Oh sai come m'abbotta?
Oh padre, oh Fessa, oh povera Marmotta!

Meo
Andate, se volete;
Ho altro per il capo
Che le vostre parole!
Oh Meo, quanto gli è duro
Aver tai bestie intorno!
La donna? Oh ch'io m'affoghi
Se v'è 'l peggio animale.
Quand'ella viene in casa,
La par la buona cosa;

Meo
Let's cut to the chase:
I want to be free,
I don't need some know-it-all hanging around.
Oh what a fine mess!
I want to have a good time, oh Princess,
we're in Morocco and no longer in Fess.

Marmotta
Whether in Fessa or not in Fessa,
I took a husband in order to be the wife,
and not so that at every hour
a thousand tramps could could come around
to play the princess.

Meo
Oh this stinks! Will you quiet down already?
A woman of your station
shouldn't worry herself
about everything she hears.
It falls on you to keep an eye
on matters pertaining to the kingdom
and not to figure out if I'm on the hunt or want to love.

Marmotta
Oh lord, it's up to me
to govern the state?
Oh, man befuddled by Love!
Oh, isn't this rich?
Oh Father, oh Fessa, oh poor Marmotta!

Meo
Leave, if you want;
I have other things on my mind
besides your rants!
Oh Meo, how trying it is for him
to have such beasts about!
A woman? May I be struck down
if ever there be a worse animal.
When she first enters a home
she seems like a fine thing,

Ma quando ha fermo il piede,
È peggio d'un leone;
Quanto v'è, quanto trova,
Tutto mette in bisbiglio;
Né vi vogliono più nel vicinato
Che tre donne a compire un sol mercato,

Marmotta
A fé, a fé, che te ne pentirai,
Principe senza senno,
Cervel senza custode,
Pensier senza giudizio.
Oh guarda, ha tanto ardire
Di strapazzarmi ancora?
Tu me la pagherai.

Meo
Vattene in tua malora.

Marmotta
Io non mi vuò partire.
E che forse t'ho fatto
Qualche gran torto? Per rimproverarti
Ch'a un principe disdice
L'andar tutta la notte
Zimbellando civette?
Che gli è vergogna a darsi tanto in preda
Al vino a l'osterie,
E che ci vuol misura in ogni cosa?
Dunque, perch'io ti dico
Ch'attendi al tuo governo, e de lo stato
Sappi meglio gli affari,
Che non ti fidi tanto
Di questi masnadieri,
Mi devi discacciare?
Ah Prence, Prence, quanto un dì pentito
Ti troverai di non m'aver sentito!
Io parto, resta e godi, e tuo sia il danno:
Chi vuol la mala Pasqua, abbi il malanno.

but as soon as her foot comes to rest,
she's worse than a lion;
whatever there is, whatever she finds,
she sets everything abuzz;
and just three of them can make such a racket
that they sound like a busy market.

Marmotta
Oh I swear, I swear, you'll be sorry,
prince without wisdom,
brain without a keeper,
mind without judgment.
Look here, are you so brazen
as to mistreat me still?
You'll pay for this.

Meo
Go to hell!

Marmotta
I don't want to go anywhere.
Have I perhaps
done you some grave wrong by admonishing
that it's unbecoming for a prince
to spend the whole night long
ensnaring owlets?[44]
That it's a disgrace for him to abandon himself entirely
to wine at the taverns?
And that one needs moderation in all things?
So because I tell you
to attend to your government,
to better know the affairs of state,
and not to place such trust
in these ruffians,
you have to chase me away?
Ah, Prince, Prince, your regret will be great indeed
because my words you did not heed!
I'm off, stay and enjoy yourself, it's your loss.
The harm you wish will come back to bite you tenfold. [*exits*]

Meo
Oh la se n'è pur ita.
Oh ve', pazzo cervello!
Io ho tanto di capo.
Ahimè, che mai si quieta:
Poss'io morir se più la miro mai.
Moglie? Moglie, e to' guai!
Oh felice quel core
Che fuor di quel legame
In dolce libertà scherzo è d'Amore.
S'io dormo, la mi desta;
S'io mangio, la m'inquieta;
S'io vado, la mi stoglie;
S'io parlo, m'interrompe;
In fin la vita mia non ha mai posa.
La vorrebbe che sempre
Le stessi sopra i scherzi,
Ch'io fossi un covadonne, un animale,
E da mattina a sera
Io [*le pestassi*[vii]] l'acqua nel mortale.

Scena seconda

Filippetta, Meo

Filippetta
Oh ben trovata la Vostra Eccellenza!
A che contanta furia?
Con chi l'avete voi con tanto sdegno?
V'è forse macchinato
Qualcosa contra il regno?

Meo
Oh Filippetta, a punto
Tu giungi a tempo per spassarmi un poco.
Che si fa? Come va? In che la passi?
Com'hai de le facende?
Quant'è che da l'Ancroia
Non hai condotto qualche passarotto?

Meo

Ah, she's finally gone.
She's as mad as a hatter!
I have so much on my mind.
Woe is me, she never quiets down.
I would die a happy man if I never set eyes on her again.
A wife? He who takes a wife takes on trouble!
Oh, happy is the heart
that is unfettered by that yoke
and in sweet liberty is Love's plaything.
If I sleep, she rouses me;
if I eat, she bothers me,
if I go, she blocks me,
if I speak, she interrupts me.
My life has not a moment's rest.
She'd like me to always be
on top of her desires,
like some sort of lady-hatcher, an animal,
and from dawn to dusk
to grind water in her mortar.[45]

Scene Two

Filippetta, Meo

Filippetta

Oh, greetings, Your Excellency!
Where are you off to in such a rage?
Who do you have it in for with all this anger?
Has some plot been hatched
against our kingdom?

Meo

Ah, Filippetta, you're here just in time
to perk me up a bit.
What's happening? How's it going?
What have you been up to? How's business?
How long has it been since you've led some little sparrow
back to Ancroia's roost?

Filippetta
A punto or ora ve n'infilzai uno.
Ancroia è bella donna,
Graziosa, pulita e ha il più bel viso
Ch'abbiasi degli amanti
Il riposto comune.
Ha un occhio, com'un porco, disdruscito!
Una bocca longaccia e rilevata,
Un nasino ch'ancor non par finito,
La carne lustra come invitriata,
Infine gli è un boccon proprio da prence.
Se voi una sol volta
La vedeste vicino,
Direste ch'io ho studiato il Calepino.

Meo
Fammela un pò vedere, e se mi piace
Ti vuò dar non so che, ch'io non la trovo.

Filippetta
E che, per vita vostra?

Meo
Una cosa che gusta.

Filippetta
Eh volete la burla.
A la padrona si dan queste cose.

Meo
Io la vuò dare a te.

Filippetta
E se son Filippetta,
Non son come credete;
Ancroia è bella è vero,
Ma io non sono ancora
A fatto tra le brutte;
E se non ho bel viso,
Son però graziosa,
Polita, e più di lei,
Ne le cose d'amor sperimentata.

Filippetta
I strung one of them up there just this very moment.
Ancroia is a beautiful woman,
charming, unmarred,
and of all the lovers at the warehouse
her face is the loveliest.
She has eyes that are red like a pig's,
a long and prominent mouth,
a nose that goes on forever,
skin that glows like it's been glazed.
In short, she's a tasty morsel
fit for a prince.
If you were to see her up close even once,
you'd say that I studied my Calepino[46] well.

Meo
Let me get a peek at her, and if I like what I see
I'll give you a little something, since I can't seem to find her.

Filippetta
And what's that, pray tell?

Meo
Something you'll like.

Filippetta
Ah, you're teasing me.
These sorts of things are given to my mistress.

Meo
I want to give it to you.

Filippetta
Even if I am Filippetta,
I'm not what you think.
Ancroia is beautiful, it's true,
but by no means should I
yet be counted among the hags.
Even if I don't have a beautiful face,
I'm still charming, unmarred,
and more experienced than she
in the stuff of love.

Se le gote ho cadute,
Non son cadenti in tutto;
Quando va e quando vien è buono il frutto.

Meo
Orsù, siamo d'accordo.
Io voglio dare a te quel che t'ho detto.

Filippetta
E che m'avete detto?
Che cosa è quel che me volete dare?

Meo
Dirolti, e l'indovina.
Una cosa [*sì lunga,*
E grossa e dura, e sta cotanto tesa
Che pare uno spagnol quand'è in postura;
Si piglia con le mano, e vi si mette.[viii]]

[***Filippetta***
E che?

Meo
Quel che dentro vi va.[ix]]

Filippetta
Oh l'è la sporta. Io non la voglio, fiò.
Vi mancano le sporte in casa nostra?

Meo
La sporta? Non è sporta, né cistello.
Oh sciocca, l'è un cappello.

Filippetta
Un cappello, sì, sì:
Or che l'inverno piove, io son contenta.
Adesso adesso ve la meno qui.

Meo
Ed io intanto me n' vo verso la regia;
Fra poco spazio qui ci trovaremo.

Even if my cheeks do sag,[47]
they haven't gone entirely bad:
Whether it's coming or going, the fruit is still good.

Meo
Come now, we're in agreement.
I want to give you that thing I told you about.

Filippetta
And what did you tell me?
What is it that you want to give me?

Meo
I'll tell you, but first you have to guess.
It's something about yea long,
and thick and hard, and it's so taut
that it looks like a Spaniard when he's en garde.
You grab it with one hand and fill 'er up.

Filippetta
What?

Meo
Whatever fits in there.

Filippetta
Oh, it's a basket.[48] No way, I don't want it.
Do we really lack for baskets at our house?

Meo
A basket? It's neither a basket nor a box.
Oh silly woman, it's a bonnet.

Filippetta
A bonnet, oh yes, yes!
Now what with the winter rain, I'm pleased.
I'll lead her here right away!

Meo
In the meantime I am heading towards the palace.
We'll meet back here before long. [*exits*]

Filippetta
Oh l'è 'l dolce boccone
Per la mia padroncina.
Adesso adesso è 'l tempo
Ch'io seco mi guadagni una gonnella.
Gnaffe! Meo per amante?
E chi gli potrà piu toccar il naso?
Esser dama d'un prence di Marocco?
Ne caverà de' soldi,
Che per quanto s'intende,
Egli suol gettar via quel ch'altri spende.
Vuò picchiar l'uscio. Olà.
Che son tutti a dormire?
Ella ha ragione, chi la notte veglia
Convien che dorma il giorno per campare.
Tic, toc, tic, toc.

Scena terza

Ancroia alla finestra, Filippetta in strada

Ancroia
Chi bussa in su quest'ora?

Filippetta
Son io, son io, padrona,
Venite a basso che v'ho da parlare.

Ancroia
Oh ve', che bel partito!
Non ho altro che fare?

Filippetta
Oh se sapesse quel che v'ho da dire,
Voi non stareste tanto.
Oh via venite aprire,
È qual anguilla che tra diti sfugge,
L'occasion che viene, e non si piglia.

Filippetta
Oh, he is quite a sweet morsel
for my young mistress.
Now is the hour
for me to earn my skirt with her.
Yes indeed! Meo as her lover?
Now who will be able to ruffle her feathers?
Be the lady of a prince of Morocco?
She'll dig a bunch of money out him,
since from what I understand,
he usually throws away more than others have in hand.
I'm going to pound on the door. Hey there!
What, is everyone asleep?
She's right, though. Whoever stays watch all night
had better sleep all day to get by.
Knock, knock.

Scene Three

Ancroia ***at the window,*** **Filippetta** ***on the street***

Ancroia
Who's down there knocking at this hour?

Filippetta
It's me, Mistress, it's me.
Come down, I have something to tell you.

Ancroia
Oh look, what a lovely invitation!
What, I have nothing better to do?

Filippetta
Oh, if you only knew what I have to tell you,
you wouldn't take so long.
Oh, come on, open up.
This is your chance, but just like an eel
it will slip through your fingers if you don't grab it.

Ancroia
Eccomi qui, che vuoi?

Filippetta
Sentite. Meo, Meo.

Ancroia
Oh tu forse sei cotta.
Chi Meo dici? Chi Mea? Forse m'uccelli?

Filippetta
Meo il principe nostro,
Il vostro padronaggio,
Il principe di gnocco.

Ancroia
Di Marocco, in malora!
E ben, che cosa vuole?

Filippetta
Vi vuol fornir la casa
Di panni di cucina,
Ed addobbar la stalla
D'un porco grosso e due porchetti grassi.

Ancroia
Il malan che ti pigli: oh ve' regali?
Orsù vuoi altro, o tu sei pazza o cotta.

Filippetta
Son un campan da botta,
Io vi dico così, ch'adesso adesso
Verrà qui per vedervi,
E se gli piace il vostro bel modello,
M'ha promesso un cappello.

Ancroia
Un cancher che ti mangi.

Filippetta
Un cappello da vero.

Ancroia [*at the door*]
Here I am, now what do you want?

Filippetta
Listen. Meo! Meo!

Ancroia
What are you, sauced?
What Meo are you talking about? Mea who? Are you trying to screw me?

Filippetta
Meo, our prince,
your master,
the prince of Moronico.

Ancroia
Of Morocco, dammit!
Alright, what does he want?

Filippetta
He wants to dress up your house
with fine duds and tasty meats,
and fill up your stall
with a big hog and two fat piglets.

Ancroia
Damn you. What, gifts?
Come on, is that all you've got? You're either nuts or sauced.

Filippetta
Hell's bells I am![49]
I'm telling you, right this moment
he's coming here to see you,
and if he likes what he sees,
he's promised me a new bonnet.

Ancroia
Go to hell!

Filippetta
A real bonnet!

Son tanto fuor di me da l'allegrezza
Che non so dir parola.
Oh via, m'avete inteso?
Il signor di Marocco
Vi vuol per sua signora di piacere,
Ne sete voi contenta?
Sorella questo è 'l modo
Di procacciarsi il pane.
Un prence più in un'ora
Vi può dar ch'un privato in mille lustri.
E poi gli è liberale,
Non tien conto di nulla
E getta via ciò che li dà in le mani.

Ancroia
Filippetta mi burli o fai da vero?

Filippetta
Non vi burlo, a la fé: poco può stare
A mostrarne gli effetti, e lo vedrete.

Ancroia
Orsù, mi vuò lisciare,
Vuò rilustrarmi un poco,
Vuò farmi i ricciolini
E tutta linda comparirle avanti.

Filippetta
Avertite, padrona,
A non portar collaro,
Ch'egli v'ha simpatia molto diversa.

Ancroia
E perché? Non li piacciono i collari?
E che parrei senza collare al collo?

Filippetta
Ei non le vuo' veder, gli piace ignudo
Veder il collo de la cosa amata;
Venite scollacciata, e sia che vuole.

I'm so beside myself with joy
that I can hardly say a word.
Oh, come on, do you understand what I'm saying?
The Lord of Morocco
wants you for his Lady of Pleasure.
Aren't you happy?
Sister, this is the way
to win one's bread.
A prince can give you more in one hour
than a commoner could in a thousand decades.
And, oh, he's lavish,
he doesn't keep track of anything
and tosses away whatever comes into his hands.

Ancroia
Filippetta, are you mocking me or is this for real?

Filippetta
I'm not mocking you, I swear! He can hardly wait
to show you the effects, and then you'll see.

Ancroia
Alright then, I want to put my face on
I want to brighten myself up a bit,
I want to give myself some pretty little curls
and appear before him all spruced up.

Filippetta
Take heed, my lady,
not to wear a collar,
since he has very different tastes.

Ancroia
And why not? He doesn't like collars?
What would I look like without a collar around my neck?

Filippetta
He can't stand them. He likes to see
the bare neck of the object of his affection.
Come wearing something plunging low, and be what he desires.

Ancroia
Adesso adesso, me ne torno a basso.

Filippetta
In fin noi altre donne,
Come non siam lisciate
Né la gota s'inostra,
De la nostra beltà non facciam mostra;
Anzi in noi senza l'arte
La beltà non ha parte.
E bene, se la donna
Ha sempre finte l'opre,
Solo a sé co' difetti
Il sembiante ricopre;
E tra l'acque e tra l'ostro,
Di natura è prodigio, e d'arte è mostro.
Ed io se fosse amante
Vorrei tutte vederle la mattina,
Quando ancor con le mani
Non s'abbino lisciato il lor sembiante,
Per veder chi è Ciprigna e chi è Gabrina.
E la bellezza lor forza di braccia
E sette volte il dì mutan la faccia.
Padrona, oh via, non più, voi sete bella.
A che tanto fregare,
Che forse vi volete scorticare?

Ancroia
Eccomi! Che ti pare?
Son io quella di prima?
Guarda come campeggia
Sul bianco il purpurino!
Guardami un po' le labra!
Ti paion di rubino?

Filippetta
Sì, ma rubin che cade;
Se vi vien da sputare
Come farete voi?

Ancroia
Alright, alright, I'll be right back down. [*exits*]

Filippetta
In the end,
if we're not painted up
or have rouged cheeks,
we women don't make a great show of our beauty.
Or rather, in us without art
beauty has no part.
Well, even if a woman
always uses deceptive means,
she conceals the defects
of her appearance only from herself.
Between the perfumed waters and the crimson cosmetics,
she is a prodigy of nature and a monstrosity of art.
If I were a lover,
I'd want to see them all in the morning
when with their hands
they haven't yet painted their faces,
to see who's a Ciprigna and who's a Gabrina.[50]
Their beauty is their brawn,
and seven times a day they'll change their charms.
Oh, Mistress, c'mon, no more, you're beautiful.
Why all the scrubbing,
are you trying to rub your skin off?

Ancroia [*returning*]
Here I am! What do you think?
Notice anything different?
Look how the rouge is encamped
on a field of white!
Take a look at these lips!
Do they not look like rubies?

Filippetta
Yes, but rubies that droop.
If you get the urge to spit,
what will you do?

Ancroia
Perché? S'ad ogni sputo
Il cinabro cadesse (oh tu sei sciocca).
Oggi non s'usa altro che bocche tinte.
Egli è ben fatto, si posson chiamare
Trappole degli amanti,
Poiché in vece del labro
Se gli porge il cinabro.

Filippetta
Padrona, ecco qui il prence!
Fategli un bell'inchino a la spagnola.
Sogghignate un po' po' con l'occhio dritto.
Bisogna usar de l'arte in questo mondo.

Scena quarta

Meo, Ancroia, Filippetta

Meo
Signora Ancroia, molto ben trovata.
Certo ch'avea ragione
Filippetta a lodarvi.
Voi sete una bellezza,
Da ver, che mi piacete;
Ed io vi piaccio a voi?

Ancroia
Un prence sempre piace,
E per brutto che sia,
Pare bello ad ognuno.

Meo
Dunque io son brutto? Orsù, pur ch'io vi piaccia,
La sia come vi pare e la volete.

Ancroia
Non dico questo, dico che nel prence
Non si scorge bruttezza,
Ma fra cotanti lussi
Ogni cosa è bellezza.

Ancroia
Why? As if the cinnabar[51] would dribble down
with every drop of spittle! Oh, you're such a simpleton!
Nowadays everyone is staining their mouths.
It's quite becoming.
They're even called lovers' traps
since in place of lips
they offer up only some cinnabar.

Filippetta
Mistress, here comes the prince!
Give him a nice Spanish curtsy,
laugh just a touch with your eyes forward.
One needs to use a bit of art in this world.

Scene Four

Meo, Ancroia, Filippetta

Meo
Lady Ancroia, you are a most welcome sight.
Filippetta certainly was right
to praise you.
You are a real beauty:
in truth, I find you quite pleasing.
So … do I please you?

Ancroia
A prince is always pleasing,
and however ugly he may be,
he seems handsome to everyone.

Meo
So I'm ugly? Come now, as long as I please you
things can be however you believe or want them to be.

Ancroia
That's not what I'm saying, I'm saying that in a prince
one doesn't notice ugliness.
Rather, amid such luxuries
everything is beauteous.

Filippetta
Oh via, sete d'accordo; o brutto o bello,
Beltade e legiadria
Non si portano in capo per pennacchio.

Meo
Accostatevi un poco, o bella Ancroia.

Filippetta
Se si sta sì discosto,
Farem poco pan unto e meno arrosto.

Ancroia
Scusatemi signor vosignoria,
Ch'io non ho avuto mai
Principi in casa mia.

Meo
Ahi lasso, già mi pare
Di sentir dentro il seno
Tra 'l fegato e 'l polmone una gran scossa.
Già, già sento nel core
Suscitarsi le fiamme, e nel mio petto
Scolpita è Ancroia per le man d'Amore.
Oh come dentro il foco
Mi raffreddan le vene!
Come gli incendi tuoi, messer Cupido,
Senza soffietto accender sai ne l'alme.
Ancroia, Ancroia mia,
Tenebre de' miei lumi,
Raggio de la mia notte,
Noia de le mie gioie,
Affanno del mio seno,
Disturbo del mio core,
Anima de' miei mali,
Gelo de l'ardor mio,
Esca sempre insonne al mio desio.

Filippetta
È colto ne la rete.
Quanto puote un bel volto!

Filippetta
Oh, c'mon, you both agree: ugly or handsome,
beauty and grace
aren't worn like a plume on one's head.

Meo
Come a little closer, oh fair Ancroia.

Filippetta
If you don't get closer,
we'll make little larded bread and even less roast.

Ancroia
Forgive me, Your Lordship Sir,
I've never had
a prince in my home before.

Meo
Alas, already I seem to feel
a great tremor within my breast
somewhere between the liver and the lungs.
Indeed, I feel in my heart
the flames being fanned, and within my chest
Ancroia has been carved by the hands of Love.[52]
Oh, how within the blaze
my veins go cold!
Sir Cupid, without any bellows you know how to ignite
your fires in a man's soul.
Ancroia, my Ancroia,
darkness of my lights,[53]
sunbeam of my night,
tribulation of my delight,
sorrow of my breast,
disturbance of my heart,
soul of my misfortunes,
frost of my ardor,
never slackened lure of my desire.

Filippetta [*aside*]
He's caught in her net.
Oh, what a beautiful face can accomplish!

Oh quanto, oh quanto vale
Quel cattivel d'Amor ne l'alme amanti!

Meo
Ancroia, o bella mia,
Mio sol di mezzanotte,
Mia luna in quintadecima,
Mie stelle sempre infeste,
Soave acquaio de le mie minestre.
E qual per te prov'io
Pagliaio acceso dentro il freddo petto?
Qual nova brama (ahi lasso),
Mi rende sazio de' tuoi vaghi lumi?
Soccorrimi, ch'io moro;
E se troppo prolunghi a darmi aita
Mi vedrai nel dolor tornare in vita.

Filippetta
Come si raccomanda! Oh quanto può
Il figlio di Ciprigna!
Quanto puon far duo lumi!
Per quante vie la vigna altrui si zappa!

Ancroia
Prence, s'il volto mio
A te reca tormento,
Odio chi mi fe' bella.
Maledette bellezze,
Grazie mal dispensate,
Se voi sete cagione
Di far altri prigione.
Dunque di gioie in vece
Da me, mio bel difforme,
Ti si reca tormento?
Dunque quando gioire
Credea fra le tue braccia,
Dovrò nel mio dolore
Bestemmiar Meo e maledire Amore?
Ah! se tai danni io fo,
Ti lascio e me ne vo.

Oh, how great is Love's sway
over lovers' souls!

Meo
Ancroia, oh my beautiful one,
my midnight sun,
my mid-month's moon,
my ever inauspicious stars,
my sweet honeypot.
What do I now feel for you,
smoldering haystack[54] within a gelid breast?
What is this new desire, oh alas,
that leaves me satisfied by your fair lights?
Give me succor, I am dying,
and if you tarry too long to bring relief,
you'll see me in anguish revived.

Filippetta [*aside*]
How he begs!
Oh, what the son of Ciprigna can do!
What two lights can do!
Many are the ways to plow another's vineyard!

Ancroia
My Prince, if my countenance
brings you torment
I hate him who made me beautiful.
Damn you, my beauty,
my ill-dispensed charms,
if you are the cause
of another's imprisonment,
and so instead of delight,
my twisted beauty,
you bring only torment?
And so while I believed
I would find delight within your arms,
am I, in my anguish, instead to
curse Meo and blaspheme Love?
Ah, if these are the wrongs I sow,
I leave you now and off I go.

Filippetta
Oh la bella moresca, oh la sa fare!
Guarda come gli sa ben dar la corda!
Cappi. Vacci di sotto.
Infatti queste donne di bel tempo
Non si lascian scappare
De la ragna i fringuelli.
Non son da parolai i lor zimbelli.

Meo
Ah cruda non partire!
Mi son care le gioie,
Abborisco le pene,
E più per te desio provar contento,
Che per altra beltà pena e tormento.

Ancroia
Oh vita mia dolcissima,
Mio vago volto amabile,
Mio sole splendidissimo,
Mio foco e refrigerio
Per te, per te, mio core,
A poco a poco il seno
Si fa schiuma d'ardore.
Io ardo e più non posso
Stare a roder quest'osso.

Filippetta
Orsù, prence, e che nova? A che si bada?
Non è tempo di ciance, andianne un poco.
La stoppa a canto al foco
O bisogna abbruciarla o di là torla.
Questo è un parlare al sole,
Un liquefarsi al vento,
Un incordarsi senza aver la fune.
A le prese, a le prese, a l'arme, a l'arme.
Già del par son le voglie,
A che si tarda il desiato colpo?
Padrona, e che facciamo?
Che ti sei smenticata
Di su la pania frognolar gli augelli?

Filippetta [*aside*]
Oh, what a fine *moresca*![55] Oh, she sure knows how to do it!
Look how well she knows how to string him up!
What a knot![56] Get 'em from below.
To be sure, these good-time girls
don't let the finches
escape from their webs.
Their lures are not the stuff of empty boasts.

Meo
Ah, cruel one, don't go!
So dear to me are the delights,
so abhorrent the pains,
and more from you I yearn to feel content
than from another's beauty, pain and torment.

Ancroia
Oh my sweet, sweet life,
my lovely lovable countenance,
my super splendiferous sun,
my fire and relief,
for you, my heart, for you
little by little my innermost parts
get into a lather with ardor.
I burn, and I am unable to go on
gnawing away at this bone.

Filippetta
[*aside to Meo*] (Come now, Prince, what do you say? What are you waiting for?
Now's not the time for chitchat, give it a little try.
The kindling is next to the fire,
you need to either burn it or brush it away.
This here's like talking to the sun,
melting in the wind,
getting all tied up without any rope.
Attack, attack, to arms, to arms!
Your desires are already equaled,
why delay the longed-for blow?)
[*aside to Ancroia*] (Mistress, what are we doing here?
Have you forgotten
how to lure birds into your trap?

Scarica la balestra, egli è già tuo!
Che se s'avvede de la rete tesa
Non mai più per mia fé farai tal presa!

Ancroia
Prencipe, che più brami?
Ove vuoi ch'io t'aspetti?
Qual deve a' nostri amori
Esser la stanza de' piacer bramati?

Filippetta
Oh così! Conclusione:
Chi lascia correr tempo non fa preda.

Meo
Fammi un piacere, Ancroia,
Andianne a caccia insieme
Ed ivi a suon di corno
Diamo la notte a sì felice giorno.

Ancroia
Andianne dove vuoi:
Son pronta ad ubidirti, e de la caccia
Mi piacciono i piaceri;
Anch'io, anch'io talvolta
Mi diletto cacciare,
E so le reti e i bracchi maneggiare.

Filippetta
A la caccia, a la caccia! Oh la mi va:
Quel cominciar cacciando
Ne le cose d'amore
L'ho per buona derata tutto l'anno.

Meo
Andianne, ch'a Pedina
Capitan de la guardia
Ho commesso il partire
E 'l Gobbo capocaccia
Ne condurrà co' cani
Ogni ordigno che s'usa per la caccia.

Unload the crossbow, this one's already yours!
For if he suspects that the net has been cast
I swear to you that this catch will be your last.)

Ancroia
Prince, what more do you desire?
Where do you want me to wait for you?
Which chamber shall we use
for our love's desired pleasures?

Filippetta [*aside*]
Oh, that's it! What's the lesson here?
If you let time fly away, chances are you'll lose your prey.

Meo
Do me this pleasure, Ancroia,
let's go on a hunt together
and there, by the sound of the horn
we'll put the joyous day to bed.

Ancroia
Let's go where you wish,
for I'm ready to obey you.
I take pleasure in the pleasures of the hunt.
I, too, from time to time
enjoy the hunt
and know how to handle the traps and the hounds.

Filippetta
To the hunt, to the hunt! Oh, this I like:
starting off by hunting around
in matters of love
is good for business all year round.

Meo
Let's go, I've charged Pedina,
Captain of the Guard,
with arranging for our departure,
and along with the dogs
Chief Huntsman Gobbo will bring
all manner of guns for the hunt. [*they exit*]

Scena quinta

Pedina, Gobbo

Pedina
Oh ve' che fantasia d'andar a caccia!
E dice bene il vero,
Ch'in questo si conosce
Il servo dal padrone.
L'un al comando, e l'altro a l'obedire.
L'è una giornata da cacciar civette.
Oh che pochi pensieri!
Gobbo, che piglieremo?

Gobbo
De le ranocchie al certo.
Che ci vuoi far fratello?
E per acqua e per neve
Dee camminar chi deve.

Pedina
Orsù, noi che dobbiamo,
Andianne a cacciar botte.
Da' una sonata al corno. [*qui suona il corno*]
Gobbo, credimi certo
Che più d'ogni altro tono
Mi piace questo suono.

Gobbo
Hai tu moglie, Pedina?

Pedina
E perché me 'l domandi?

Gobbo
Te lo dirò dopoi.

Pedina
Io non ho moglie, né già mai pensiero
Mi verrà di pigliarla.

Scene Five

Pedina, Gobbo

Pedina
Oh, what a lark to go hunting!
Truth be told,
this is what separates
the servant from the master—
one in command and the other taking orders.
What a day to hunt owlets!
Oh how carefree!
Gobbo, what shall we catch?

Gobbo
Some frogs for sure.[57]
What can you do, brother?
Come rain or come snow,
he who must, a-walking he must go.

Pedina
C'mon, we who must,
let's go hunt some toads.
Give a blow on the horn. [*here the horn plays*]
Gobbo, believe you me
more than any other tune around,
I love this sound.

Gobbo
Do you have a wife, Pedina?

Pedina
Why do you ask?

Gobbo
I'll tell you in a moment.

Pedina
I don't have a wife,
and I never plan on taking one.

Gobbo
Tu fai bene a la fé, poiché quel gusto
Di quel suono di corno
Ti potrebbe riuscire
Invece di sentir, di farlo udire.

Pedina
Vuoi ch'io ti dica? L'è una certa usanza,
Ch'io non mi vanterei di non sonare.
Ma dimmi, Gobbo, sai tu chi son quelli
Ch'a la caccia se n' vengono col prence?

[Gobbo][x]
Io non lo so, e quando lo sapessi,
Io non te lo direi:
I fatti de' padroni
Non si van recitando per le piazze.
Attendiamo a servire,
Non tutti quei che fan, vuon lasciar dire.

Pedina
Ritocca un poco il corno. Eccoli a punto:
Oh l'è Ancroia a la fé.
Oh che le venga il morbo!
E chi diavol mai
Gliel'ha posta dinanzi?
Poveri prenci! Infatti
È questo mondo una gabbia de matti.

Gobbo
Badiamo a' fatti nostri, e non ci rompa
I casi altrui il sedere.
Siam qui per ubidire,
E non per ravvisor degli altrui botte.
Chi l'altrui fatti cerca,
Procura il sol di notte.

Gobbo
That's good, by God, especially since
that taste for the sound of the horn
may very well see you transform
from one who listens to one who must perform.

Pedina
What can I say? It's such a common practice
that I wouldn't brag too much about not playing.
But tell me, Gobbo, do you know who's coming
along with the prince on the hunt?

Gobbo
I don't know, and even if I knew,
I wouldn't tell you:
a master's goings-on
shouldn't be recited out in public.
Let's tend to the attending;
not everyone wants to air their dirty laundry.

Pedina
Play that horn a little more. Here they are!
Oh, upon my word, it's Ancroia.
Oh, may she be struck with the plague!
Who the hell dangled her before him?
Poor princes!
I'll say it again,
this world is a cage for the insane.[58]

Gobbo
Let's mind our own business
and not let other people's affairs bite us in the behind.
We're here to obey
and not to clean up someone else's mess.
He who pokes his nose in what others have done
ends up with nothing but the midnight sun.

Scena sesta

Meo, Ancroia, Filippetta, Gobbo, Pedina, Cacciatori

Cacciatori
A la caccia, a la caccia:
Chi la scioglie non l'allaccia.
Suoni il corno
Tutto il giorno,
Errin lepri,
Corran cani,
Cerchin bracchi,
Fuggan volpi,
Né c'ingombri orror di polve;
Chi la sa, non la risolve.

Meo
S'incammini la turba in ordinanza;
Oggi cervi e cinghiali
Da la mia voce forte
Avranno e vita e morte.
Voi tutti ad uno ad uno
Seguitatemi in schiera,
E voi, mia speme spenta,
A me sempre vicina,
Mirate in dolce guisa
Qual il mio piede gli spontoni avventa!

Cacciatori
E noi siamo cacciatori,
Buoni bracchi e curridori,
Tutti in fila
Ne la fila
Infilziamo,
E cacciamo.
Ognun fa quel che può più.
Turutu, turutu, tu, tu, tu, tu, tu.

Scene Six

Meo, Ancroia, Filippetta, Gobbo, Pedina, Hunters

Hunters
To the hunt, to the hunt!
He who unleashes it does not rein it in.
Sound the horn
from dusk till morn,
let the hares roam,
the dogs run,
the hounds track,
the foxes flee,
fear not a bit of grit;
He who knows it can never quit.

Meo
Let our throng set out in formation;
today deer and wild boar
will receive life and death
from my powerful voice.
All of you follow me
one by one in a row.
And you, my quenched hope,
always near to me,
look on in gentle fashion
at how I hurl pikes with my foot![59]

Hunters
And we are hunters,
good with hounds and swift-horses,
all in a row,
all in one row,
we file in
and we hunt,
everyone doing the best they can do.
Tu-ru-tu, tu-ru-tu, tu-tu-tu-tu-tu. [*they exit*]

Scena settima

Tordo, Michelino

Tordo
Oh l'è pur l'esser prence il bel mistiere,
Comandar, dominare,
E non sentir se piove o vuol fioccare.
Oh ve' tempo di caccia!
Giunon versa dal cielo gli urinali
E Meo principe nostro è gito a caccia.

Michelino [*cantando*]
E se voi vi dilettasse
Venir con esso noie …

Tordo
Oh ecco quel pazzon di Michelino.

Michelino [*cantando*]
… voi avreste mille spasse
A cacciar ancor voie.

Tordo
Oh felice pazzia!
Solo ne' pazzi è sempre l'allegria.

Michelino
E de le lepre e golpe poi
Gran quantità pigliame.
Piascevole noi siame.
Trandirà, trandira, tra.

Tordo
Oh bene, oh bene, che si fa Michelino?
Oh buono cacciatore
Di roba cucinata, e di buon vino,
Che fai de l'archibuso?
Oh ve' quant'arme porti! Hai le pistole?

Scene Seven

Tordo, Michelino

Tordo
Oh, being the prince sure is a nice job—
to dominate, to reign,
and to not care if it rains or pours.
Some time for a hunt!
Juno is dumping piss-pots down from the sky,
and our prince Meo has gone off to hunt.

Michelino [*singing*]
Und *if you should desire*
to bring your cares vis *you …*

Tordo
Oh, here comes that big loon Michelino.

Michelino [*singing*]
… amusements in zee *thousands*
vould be yours to pursue.

Tordo
Oh, what a joy to be mad!
Only lunatics are always glad.

Michelino [*singing*]
Und *of* zee *fox* und zee *hare*
great numbers vee *shall ensnare,*
pleasurable are vee,
tra-la-la, tra-la-lee.

Tordo
Well, well, what do we have here, Michelino?
Oh good hunter
of cooked fare and good wine,
what are you doing with that harquebus?
Oh, look how well armed you are! Do you have your pistols?

Michelino
Suscellenze principe di Marocche,
Ch'il ciel salve e mantenghe,
Ha ordinate un bellissime caccie.
E vuole ch'ie vade in Fesse
A casciar di notte columbascie
Servatiche e domestiche piscione,
E fare buon tempone.
Trandirà, trandira, tra.

Tordo
Ma come v'anderai? Forse per acqua?

Michelino
A cavalle con mie pistole a cante,
Con mie archibuse lunghe,
E con mie palloline,
Come pepe per far taffite tiffe.
E con mie palle grosse,
Per far boffiti toffi,
Con mie carniere e con un bel pan pianche.

Tordo
Infatti è l'esser pazzo,
Un piacer, un sollazzo.
Il mal non si conosce, il ben diletta,
E si gioca con tutti a la civetta.
Sta', vuò porlo in valice.
Michelino vien qua.
[*Dimmi il vero. Tu vai a cacciar gatte?*[xi]]

Michelino
Sì, tu mangi le gatte,
Scelerate, barone.
Va', va' sotto l'officie
A comperar gli occhiali
E poi vendele ad altre, e di' che fatte
L'hai con le tue manascie.
Che ti venghe le rabie, baronascie!

Michelino
His Highness prince of Morocco,
may *zee* Heavens save *und* keep him,
has ordered a *v*onderful hunt
*und v*ants me to go to Fessy,
to go hunting *v*hen night has come
*v*ild doves *und* domestic pigeons,
und be *zee* life of *zee* party.
Tra-la-la-la, tra-la-la-lee.

Tordo
But how will you get there? By water perhaps?

Michelino
By horse *vis* my pistols by my side,
vis my harquebus so long and *v*ide,
und vis my balls so itty-bitty
like pepper to go rat-tat-tat
und vis my balls so big *und* fat
to go boom, bam, smack,
vis a nice *v*hite bread *und* my own meat sack.

Tordo
[*aside*] (Truly, being insane
is a pleasure, a game.
One knows no evil, delights in the good,
and will play hide-and-go-seek with anyone.[60]
Watch, I want to make him blow his stack.)
Michelino, come here.
Tell me the truth. Are you going to hunt cats?

Michelino
Sure, you go eat *zee* cats,
you villain, you idiot!
Go on, go to *zee* Uffizi[61]
to buy *zee* glasses
und sell *z*em to others,
*und z*en say you made 'em *vis* your big ol' mitts.
I hope you catch rabies, you big hypocrite!

Tordo
Oh via, su Michelino, io ho burlato.
Facciam pace, vien qua, dammi la mano.

Michelino
Giove in ciel di Venere,
Marte e Saturne casciateme in terre.
Tu cascime tu nasascie di detre,
Su vie spesseme il cape,
Spiascie, sciocatore.
Prencipe di Marocche.
Ti vuò fare impiccar per un ginocchie.

Tordo
Fino ne' pazzi ha la superbia il loco:
Costui non ha cervello
E pur s'adatta anch'esso
A lo stil de la corte, al cortegiano,
Ch'è di procurar sempre, ch'il compagno
Sia mandato in bordello.
Michelino, non più, ti sono amico.

Michelino
Son contente, sempre buon compagne
Di Torde; un buon fiasche di perdee
Voglie, che biveme a l'osterie

Tordo
Costor son giti a caccia,
E tu non sei più a tempo di cacciare.

Michelino
Torde andiame a cacciare al grecaiole
Nelle studione buone fecatelle;
E 'l principe Marocche suscellenze
Vade con le sue [*drude*[xii]] nel pordelle.
Trandirà, trandira, tra.

Tordo
Andiam dove voi tu
Ch'io non ne posso più.

Tordo
Oh, come now, Michelino, it was a joke.
Let's make peace, come here, give me your hand.

Michelino
Jupiter in *zee* sky of Venus,
Mars *und* Saturn push me down to *zee* earth.
You're crushing me, you nosy meddler,
Shoo, away, you're on my last nerve,
you sneak, you trickster.
Prince of Morocco!
I *v*ant to have you strung up by *zee* knees.

Tordo
[*aside*] (Even in madmen pride has its place.
He has no brains
and yet that too lends itself
to the style of the court, to the courtier
who's always arranging for his fellow
to be sent off to the bordello.[62])
Michelino, enough, I'm your friend.

Michelino
I'm glad, a good mate I shall always be to Tordo.
I *v*ant a good flask of Verdea *v*ine[63]
*zat vee v*ill drink together at *zee* tavern.

Tordo
They've already gone off to the hunt,
and you're no longer in time to go hunting.

Michelino
Tordo, let's go hunting at *zee* tavern
for fine kabobs of *fegatello,*[64]
und may *zee* prince His Royal Highness
go *vis* his hussy to *zee* bordello.
Tra-la-la-la-la, tra-la-la-la.

Tordo
Let's go wherever you prefer,
since I can't take this any longer. [*they exit*]

Scena ottava

Marmotta, Bertuccia

Marmotta
Bertuccia, io più non posso
Soffrir le stravaganze del mio Meo.
Sventurata Marmotta, e che son io?
Forse un'orsa nel bosco,
Che cotanto mi fugge e mi disprezza?
Ah miseria dovuta
A donna spenserata!
Quanto meglio foria ch'ad ogni figlia
In vece di marito il padre desse
Un bichier di veleno,
Over tra tante doglie
Lecito fosse di pigliarne un altro.

Bertuccia
Oh quante non contente
Sarebbone le moglie,
[*E di nov'esca ciberian le voglie.*
Se ben son di parere
Ch'anco senza licenza
Si faccia a' tempi d'oggi tal mistiere.[xiii]]

Marmotta
Ah Meo, Meo, più crudo
D'una serpe d'inverno; e che t'ho fatto,
Che cotanto mi [*fuggi*[xiv]] e mi disami?
Che mi giova, infelice,
L'esser di te consorte,
S'io sempre da te lunge
Traggo vita felice?
Che mi val ne la regia
Fausta porre il mio piede,
S'infausto è 'l mio desio
E sempre senza te godo, Meo mio?
Ahi lassa, il duol m'uccide, e fra le pene
Sento d'insania invigorir le vene.

Scene Eight

Marmotta, Bertuccia

Marmotta
Bertuccia, no longer can I
take the eccentricities of my Meo.
Hapless Marmotta, and what am I?
Am I perhaps a she-bear in the forest,
that he flees and scorns me so?
Oh, the misery that awaits
a carefree young woman!
How much better would it be
if to each daughter a father were to give,
not a husband, but a glass of poison,
or if amid so many pains,
it were permissible to take another.

Bertuccia
Oh, there would be so many unhappy wives
who with new bait
would feed their drives.
In truth it seems to me
that even though it's not permitted,
nowadays such trades are practiced.

Marmotta
Oh, Meo, Meo, crueler than a winter snake.
What have I done to you,
that you flee and withdraw your love from me so?
What good is it for me, unhappy woman,
to be your consort
if I can only ever lead a happy life
far away from you?
What use is it for me
to step foot in a fortunate kingdom,
if my desire is unfortunate,
and if I am forever to take pleasure without you, my Meo?
Alas, the pain is killing me, and through the pangs
I feel madness quicken in my veins.

Bertuccia
Principessa, che fate? Eh state su!
Che tanto stralunar[?][xv] Che tanto affanno?
S'egli non sta con voi,
Voi non state con lui, e sia del pari,
E che v'importa al fine?
Dove non batte il sol, non mancan brine.
Lasciatelo sfogar, faccia che vuole!
Benché dilate errante
Ne l'occidente alfin ritorna il sole.

Marmotta
Eh Bertuccia, egli è vero.
Ma quello aver mai sempre
A calcetrar lenzola,
Quello abbracciar guanciali,
Adesso siam d'inverno,
È male di dormir co' capezzali.
Dunque sempre debb'io
Dibatter forsennata
Queste misere membra su le piume?
Non so come ch'il capo
Infranta non mi sono in ogni lato.

Bertuccia
Eh se voi nol battete
In altra pietra, che sui matarazzi,
Poco mal vi farete.

Marmotta
Eh Bertuccia, tu stai pur su le burle.
Non bastava a la sorte
D'avermi tolto (ahi lassa)
Il mio caro fratello, ch'i corsali
Su le rive di Fessa mi rapirno,
Ch'ancora del consorte
Volse farmi infelice.

Bertuccia
Che vi fu forse tolto da' corsali
Un fratello, signora?

Bertuccia
Princess, what are you doing? Hey, cheer up!
Why such hysterics? Why such sorrow?
If he's not with you,
you're not with him, and then you're even.
Besides, what does it matter in the end?
A rolling stone grows no moss.
Let him let loose, let him do what he likes best!
Though the sun may wander off course,
in the end it always sets in the west.

Marmotta
Oh Bertuccia, it's true.
But this always having
to kick the sheets?
This hugging the pillows?
Now that we're in winter,
it's wrong to have to sleep with long bolsters.[65]
Must I therefore always
frantically thrash
these miserable limbs against the down?
I don't know how I have survived
and not crushed my head on every side.

Bertuccia
Well, if you don't go beat it
against some other stone, instead of on your mattress,
you're not hurting anyone.

Marmotta
Oh, sure, Bertuccia, go ahead and joke.
It wasn't enough for Fate
to have taken—alas!—
my dear brother, whom the corsairs[66]
on the shores of Fessa carried away from me,
but once more it chose to increase my sorrow,
this time through my consort.

Bertuccia
What's this? The corsairs took
a brother from you, Mistress?

Marmotta
Ah così l'avess'io, che forse Meo
Pensarebbe a straziarmi?

Bertuccia
E dove? E quando? E come?

Marmotta
L'istoria è troppo lunga; basta solo
Che da' corsali in mare,
Mentre egli era bambino, in su la riva
Di Fessa ne fu tolto. Ahi duro fato.

Bertuccia
Oh gran caso! Né mai
Nova di lui sapeste?
Chi sa che nel paese de le scimie
Il povero bambin non erri ancora?
Soglion questi corsali
Talvolta ivi lasciarli, acciò ch'esperti
Diventin più degli altri in ogni cosa.

Marmotta
Io non lo so, so ben che più nol vidi,
E 'l mio povero padre,
Per levarsi di lui la rimembranza,
Mi diede (oh pensier sciocco)
Per vettovaglia al prence di Marocco.

Bertuccia
Non fu mai trista cena
Quella ch'in apparenza
Sa con il magro ancor mostrar la grascia.
Egli, se non con voi
Compie il gioir notturno,
Il giorno vuol che siate
Di Marocco signora e principessa.
Vi fa vestir di seta, e a la cintura
Il cingolo vi dà, qual soglion dare
De la villa i più grandi a le lor donne.

Marmotta
Ah, if he were still with me,
would Meo dare to mistreat me so?

Bertuccia
But when? But where? But how?

Marmotta
The story is too long.
I'll just say that when he was a boy,
on the banks of Fessa
he was taken by the sea-faring corsairs. Oh, cruel destiny!

Bertuccia
Oh, what an ordeal!
You never received any more news of him?
Who knows if in the land of monkeys
the poor child does not wander still?
These corsairs sometimes tend
to leave them there so that they'll become
more experienced than others in all respects.

Marmotta
I do not know, I know only that I never saw him again,
and my poor father,
to rid himself of any memory of him,
gave me—oh foolish thought!—
as victuals to the prince of Morocco.

Bertuccia
A supper is never sad
when one knows how
to pass off the lean for the fat.
Even if he doesn't satisfy
his nocturnal delights with you,
come daybreak he wants you to be
the lady and princess of Morocco.
He has you clothed in silk,
and for your waist he gives you a girdle,[67]
which the greatest lords customarily give their women.

Marmotta
Sì, ma non sai, Bertuccia, quel ch'inteso
Ho con le proprie orecchie a la finestra.

Bertuccia
E che sentiste voi?

Marmotta
Quel ch'intesi? Il buon prence
Ancroia, quella già di Baldassarre,
Per man di Filippetta ora ha per druda.

Bertuccia
Che ne sapete voi? Oh questa è brutta!
Ancroia, quella sozza, ben lisciata,
[*Quel naso di braccaccio a la francese,*
Che si tien Baldassarre a le sue spese.[xvi]]
Oh veder lo vorrei,
E poi lo crederei!

Marmotta
Non cercar altro, gli è quel che ti dico.

[***Bertuccia***
Ma come ciò v'è noto? Dite un poco!

Marmotta
Già che lo vuoi saper, stammi a udire.
Mi stavo poco dianzi a la finestra
Sopra pensiero, e mi tornava in mente
Ad uno ad uno i torti del mio Meo,
Quando sento di sotto bisbigliare.
Miro e mi tiro dentro, e vedo, e sento
Ch'è Meo con Ancroia, e Filippetta
Stringe d'amore il parentado indegno.
Sento ch'egli le dice
Che la vuol per signora, e ch'a la caccia
Vuol ch'ella vada seco a sollazzare.
E sai, quella monnaccia
Di quella Filippetta
L'andava tanto in sugo, e saltellava,

Marmotta
Yes, Bertuccia, but you don't know
what I heard with my own ears at the window.

Bertuccia
And what did you hear?

Marmotta
What did I hear? Thanks to Filippetta's doing,
the good prince has now taken as his lover
Ancroia, the one that used to be with Baldassarre.

Bertuccia
Are you sure? Oh, this stinks!
Ancroia, that greased-up alley cat
with a nose like a mangy French hound?[68]
The one Baldassarre keeps well fed?
Oh, if only I could see it,
then I would believe it!

Marmotta
Look no further. It is just as I'm telling you.

Bertuccia
But how did you find out? Tell me everything.

Marmotta
If you really want to know, listen to me.
A short time ago I was at the window,
lost in thought and remembering one by one
all of my Meo's faults.
Suddenly I hear whispering below.
I look out and I pull back in, and I see and I hear
Meo with Ancroia,
and Filippetta binding the disgraceful couple together in love.
I hear him tell her
that he desires her as his lady
and wants her to come frolic with him on the hunt.
And you know,
that floozy Filippetta,
was jumping all around, and getting all wet,

Che parea tra gli augelli una civetta.
Infine intesi e vidi, e vidi e intesi
Ch' [xvii]] egli Ancroia si gode a buona cera,
Ed io col flusso in man perdo primiera.

Bertuccia
Vi compatisco assai, ma che volete?
Bisogna aver pazienza, anco de l'altre
Qual voi sono infelici,
E forse ancor più belle, e più vezzose.

Marmotta
Pazienza? A fé ch'assai
Ho sopportato di costui gl'inganni.
Vuò tornarmene in Fessa,
Ed ivi in casa mia
Trarmi vita [*più lieta*[xviii]] e più noiosa.

Bertuccia
Signora, è bella Fessa?
Come vi sono di bei guardadonne?

Marmotta
Se Fessa è bella? Oh che tu non lo sai?
Ah, ch'altro è Fessa che non è Marocco.
Vi son donne bizzarre ed hanno tutte
Un modo di trattar [*ch'al forastiero*
Mostran di cortesia le voglie aperte,
Lo ricevono in casa volentieri
E di quanto ne puon gli fanno parte.[xix]]

Bertuccia
Come son belle strade, e bei palazzi?

Marmotta
Le vie son quasi tutte a una misura,
Son dritte, polite, e senza mota,
E non, come che qua, si porta rischio
[*Di dar ne la pozzangola a lo scuro.*[xx]]
Son superbi i palazzi, [*e perch'il luogo*
Ha de l'umido alquanto, han gran puntelli.

so that among the birds she seemed an owlet.
And so I heard and I saw, I saw and I heard
that while he blithely enjoys Ancroia,
I'm holding a flush but still lose the pot.[69]

Bertuccia
I really feel for you, but what do you expect?
You need to be patient.
There are others who are as unhappy as you,
and perhaps more beautiful and more fetching.

Marmotta
Patient? I swear, I've put up with
enough of that man's tricks.
I want to go back to Fessa,
and there in my own house
lead a more humdrum and happier[70] life.

Bertuccia
My lady, is Fessa beautiful?[71]
Are there fine men-in-waiting[72] there?

Marmotta
Is Fessa beautiful? Do you not know?
Oh! Fessa is everything that Morocco is not.
There are bizarre women,[73]
and they all have courteous ways
of showing a stranger their explicit desires.
They gladly receive him in their house
and do what they can to make him feel at home.

Bertuccia
What of the fine streets and beautiful palaces?

Marmotta
The roads are almost all of one length,
they are straight, clear, and free from mire,
and, unlike here, one doesn't run the risk
of stumbling into some puddle in the dark.
The palaces are superb,
and since it's a rather humid spot,

Questo lo fan perché s'attengan sodi.
E chi teme ch'il suo voglia cadere
S'approveccia del muro del compagno.[xxi]]

Bertuccia
Oh ve' cosa garbata! La mi piace.
Le donne son [*d'assai? Son casareccie?*[xxii]]

Marmotta
Come se son d'assai o casareccie?

Bertuccia
Voglio dir, se si sanno
Rimescolar per casa ne' lor fatti?

Marmotta
Oh quel che tu domandi!
Le donne fessatine
Son per le case lor sempre un mercato.
[*Son approveccie, e tengon tanto stretto*
Che se lor dà ne l'unghie un capitale,
Mio danno se gli scappa.[xxiii]]
Se 'l marito di loro in capo a l'anno
Tirasse ben il conto, ei trovarebbe
Che più una donna ha lor portato in casa
Che mille mercatanti al lor [*paese.*[xxiv]]
[*Gli uomini se ne stanno, e lascian fare,*
Se la donna rinova un bel vestito,
Una bella collana, un bello anello,
Non ha da darne conto al suo marito.[xxv]]

Bertuccia
Vi s'usa il far l'amore, come qua?

Marmotta
Tutto il mondo è paese;
È ben vero ch'in Fessa
S'usa di far l'amore a la francese.

Bertuccia
E come a la francese? È foggia nova?

they have great big buttresses so they stay erect.
And whoever fears that his own is going to fall
takes advantage of his fellow's wall.

Bertuccia
Oh my, could it be more delightful? I like it there.
Are the women haughty? Are they homey?

Marmotta
What do you mean, are they haughty or homey?

Bertuccia
I mean to ask if they know how
to get down to business 'bout the house.

Marmotta
Oh, the things you ask!
Fessatine women
are always setting up shop in their houses.
They are profit-minded, and they clamp down so tightly
that if they get a bit of capital in their clutches
let lightning strike me down if it gets away from them.
If the husbands were to keep good count
from the start of the year, they'd find
that one woman brought in more to her home
than a thousand merchants to their country.
The men stay put and let them do as they wish.
If a woman dons a beautiful dress,
a beautiful necklace, a beautiful ring,
she need not account to her mate for a thing.

Bertuccia
Are they in the habit of lovemaking, like here?

Marmotta
It's the same the world over.
Yet it is true that in Fessa,
they are in the habit of making love *à la française*.

Bertuccia
What do you mean *à la française*? Is this some new style?

Marmotta
Si fa l'amor con tutti a la scoperta.
Ma sai: modestamente.
Chiede l'amante core
A la sua dea [*che gli apra*
De' pensieri d'amor lo scattolino,
Che le mostri il zucchetto de' desiri,
E che lasci il suo foco
Smorzar ne la di lei cortese fonte.
E ciò perché ne le lor case han tutte
Una fontana[xxvi]: intendimi Bertuccia.

Bertuccia
Voi non parlate a' sordi. E come s'usa
Di regalare in Fessa le lor dame?

Marmotta
[*In Fessa il regalare è moto propio.*[xxvii]]
E qual città tu trovi
Che de la nostra sia più regalata?
[*È città ricca, e poi*
Ognun vi fa l'offerta del suo avere.[xxviii]]
Ma sai qual è quel don ch'è più prezzato?

Bertuccia
E che? L'argento e l'oro?

Marmotta
Ohibò, non no! Le femmine di Fessa
Di ciò non son bramose.
Che credi, ch'a le donne
Piaccia l'argento e l'oro? Tu t'inganni.

Bertuccia
Intesi sempre dir che de le donne
Quest'è la calamita che fa presa.

Marmotta
Questo succede in quelle
Che di pane e di vino
Han scarso il magazino.

Marmotta
They make love with everyone openly.
But, you know, modestly.
The loving heart
asks his goddess to open her little box
of amorous thoughts to him,
so that he can show her his *zucchetto*[74] of desire,
and to let him extinguish his fire
in her generous spring
since each has a fountain in her own home.
Do you get my drift, Bertuccia?

Bertuccia
This isn't falling on deaf ears.
And how do they usually bestow gifts on their ladies in Fessa?

Marmotta
In Fessa gift giving is *moto propro.*[75]
For where can you find
a city better endowed than ours?
It's a rich city, and, besides,
everyone offers what he has.
But do you know what gift is the most prized?

Bertuccia
What is it? Silver and gold?

Marmotta
Tsk, tsk! No, no! The women of Fessa
don't covet such things.
What do you think, that women like silver and gold?
You're fooling yourself.

Bertuccia
What I meant to say was that
this is the curse that takes hold of women.

Marmotta
This happens to those
whose larders
are low on bread and wine.

[*Ma s'avvien che ricchezza*
Possieda amante core,
Per altro che pecunia arde d'amore.[xxix]]
Non dassi a prezzo d'oro
Beltade ch'in amor prova martoro.

Bertuccia
Che si regala dunque? In che si dà?

Marmotta
Quando vuole un amante
Gustare la sua diva
Gli manda un ortolano con la [*piva.*[xxx]]

Bertuccia
Son grassi come i nostri, gli ortolani?

Marmotta
Eh tu sei pazza o fingi.
Non dico un ortolano da mangiare.

Bertuccia
E che ortolani dunque, e per che fare?

Marmotta
Perché talor zappando
La tratenga sonando.
[*Non sai che la mia patria è tutta ortaglia,*
Né a cosa più s'attende
Ch'ad empir fossi e coltivar terreni.
Insomma del mio regno
Son coltivate meglio le pianure
Che di questi paesi le colline.[xxxi]]

[***Bertuccia***
Puol esser circa a l'acque e l'ortolani,
Ma non alla pastura del terreno.

Marmotta
Che pastura di' tu? Cosa cingotti?

But if it happens that the loving heart
already possesses wealth,
it burns with love for something other than money.
No amount of gold can buy
the beauty for which love does cry.

Bertuccia
Then what do they gift? How is it delivered?

Marmotta
When a lover wishes
to enjoy his goddess, he sends her
a gardener with a pipe.[76]

Bertuccia
Are they fat like ours, their garden warblers?[77]

Marmotta
Oh, you're nuts, or pretend to be.
I'm not talking about the kind you eat.

Bertuccia
Well, which gardeners then, and to do what?

Marmotta
So that while he's hoeing
he can entertain her by playing.
What you don't know is that my country is one big garden,
and that no one enjoys anything more
than filling furrows and tilling the land.
In short, in my kingdom
the fertile plains are better tilled
than these countries' hills.

Bertuccia
It may be near water and gardeners,
but not by any grazing lands.

Marmotta
What grazing land? What are you jabbering about?

Bertuccia

In Marocco vi son gran cercastabbio,
E però i suoi terreni
Ingrassati gli stimo più degli altri.

Marmotta

Fiò, fiò, noi non usiamo
Simil coltivatura,
Poiché il nostro terreno
Non ha, come ch'il vostro, dell'asciutto,
E senza stabbi ne produce il frutto.[xxxii]]

Bertuccia

Come s'usa il vestire?
Che ne' nostri paesi
Ormai non so qual sia la vera usanza.

Marmotta

Di questo son cagione i genovesi
Che sempre trovan qualche stravaganza.
Hai visto come dietro la zimarra
Hanno ridotta stretta queste donne?
La par la coda del mio somarello.
E quel basto da mulo
Ch'elle portano in cinto,
Sotto le falde per mostrar ne' fianchi
Un seder rilevato da fachino.
Ed io aspetto ch'un giorno
Si vestan d'Arlecchino.

Bertuccia

Ancora non m'avete
Detto di lor l'usanza del vestire.

Marmotta

Si porta falda tesa, giobone lungo,
Veste sfibiata, e 'nvece [*de la coda,*[xxxiii]]
Che dietro già s'usava quattro braccia,
[*La portano*[xxxiv]] dinanzi quattro dita;
Questo serve per punta del giubbone.

Bertuccia
In Morocco there are great dung-brokers,[78]
and that's why I prize
their fattened fields above all others.

Marmotta
No, no, we don't use
the same kind of farming
since, unlike yours,
our terrain is without dry root,
and without manure it bears fruit.

Bertuccia
And how do they dress?
I can no longer even tell
what the true custom is in our own country.

Marmotta
The Genovese are to blame for this
since they always come up with some newfangled fad.[79]
Have you seen how these women
have tightly cinched back the *zimarra*?[80]
It looks like the tail of my donkey.
Or that mule's bundle
that they carry strapped
at the hip under their skirts
to show off a protruding bottom like a porter's?[81]
I expect that one day
they'll even dress up like Harlequin.[82]

Bertuccia
You still haven't told me
how they dress.

Marmotta
They wear a taut coat skirt, a long doublet,
an unbelted dress, and instead of the usual train
worn four arms length down the back,
they wear one four fingers long up in front.
This serves as the tip of the doublet.

Bertuccia
A fé, non mi dispiace.
Ella è più propria ed è di minor briga.
Come v'è de l'erbagio e lattecini?

Marmotta
De l'erbagio ve n'usa, ma non molto,
[*E tra l'altre del cavolo le donne*
Non ne voglion sentir né men parlare.[xxxv]]
S'usa mangiar di molta mescolanza,
De le radiche d'erba d'ogni sorte;
Del resto vuon del buono a crepapancia.

Bertuccia
E de' casci e ricotte come fanno?

Marmotta
Che mi domandi tu? [*S'usa altro in Fessa*
Che mugner capre e liquefar butiri.[xxxvi]]
Le fan tanto formaggio le pastore,
Che per le case loro
Si potrebbe notar ne' [*latticini.*[xxxvii]]
Ecco Masino, taci.

Scena nona

Masino, Tordo e li medesimi

Marmotta
Masino, che si fa? Dove n'andate?

Masino
Da vostra signoria eccellentissima.

Marmotta
Da la mia miseria miserissima.

Masino
E perché ciò signora?

Bertuccia
My word, that doesn't sound bad at all!
It's more suitable and less of a hassle.
How are they set for vegetables and dairy?[83]

Marmotta
There are some who eat their veggies, but not a whole lot.
And there are other women
who don't want to hear, much less speak, about cabbage.
They typically feast on a great mix
of tubers of every type.
After all, they want the good stuff till their tummies burst.

Bertuccia
And how do they make their hard and their soft cheeses?

Marmotta
What are you asking me?
All they do in Fessa is milk goats and melt butter.
The shepherdesses make so much cheese
that in their homes,
one could swim through all that dairy.
Here's Masino. Hush.

Scene Nine

Masino, Tordo, and the same

Marmotta
Masino, what are you up to? Where are you two going?

Masino
To see your most excellent ladyship.

Marmotta
To see my most miserable misery.

Masino
And why's that, Madam?

Marmotta
Perché? Tordo vien qua, statemi a udire.

Tordo
Eccomi eccellentissima Marmotta.

Marmotta
E pur lì con i titoli. Io vi dico
Ch'infelice è il mio nome, ed io son quella
Degna sol di miseria e non di gradi.

Tordo
E che sarà signora? E perché questo?

Marmotta
Dunque voi non sapete
Le mie sventure ancora?

Masino
Non, principessa, al certo, e che sarà?

Marmotta
Principessa di pianti e di sospiri.
Ancroia è in loco mio la principessa.
Ed io sono Marmotta,
Mal nata erede del Regno di Fessa.
E non v'è noto ancora
Ch'il prencipe a mio scorno
Dopo cotanti affanni
È d'Ancroia seguace?
Non sapete che Meo,
Non sazio de' miei mali,
Fatto è d'Ancroia amante?
Non sapete che l'empio,
Non affatto contento
D'avermi mille volte
E per il vino e pei buffon sprezzato,
D'Ancroia è innamorato?
Non v'è noto ch'il cane,
Vago di nuova sposa,
Vedovo ha fatto il suo ghiacciato letto?

Marmotta
Why? Tordo, come here, listen to me.

Tordo
Here I am, Most Excellent Marmotta.

Marmotta
Still with the titles! I'm telling you
that wretched is my name, and I am she
worthy only of misery and not of rank.

Tordo
But why? What's the matter, Mistress?

Marmotta
So you do not yet know
about my misfortunes?

Masino
No, Princess, certainly not. What might they be?

Marmotta
Princess of sobs and sighs.
Ancroia in my stead plays the princess,
and I am Marmotta,
the ill-born heiress of the Kingdom of Fess.
Are you not yet aware
that the prince, to my shame
and after so many tribulations,
is Ancroia's disciple?
Do you not know that Meo,
still not sated by my misfortunes,
has become Ancroia's lover?
Do you not know that the pitiless man,
not at all content
to have scorned me a thousand times
for buffoons and wine,
is Ancroia's inamorato?
Are you not aware that the dog,
desirous of a new bride,
has widowed his icy bed?

Non vi è fatto palese
Ch'egli, tra veltri, e fere, e reti, e cani,
Oggi con la sua Ancroia
Appaga i sensi insani?
Ah non più fia di Fessa il regio sangue
Così da Meo schernito!
Ritornerò al mio regno,
Andronne a la mia sede
Ed in Fessa io mi sia,
Io principessa de la patria mia.

Masino
Deh per Dio raffrenate
Così aspro martoro.
Chi sa, potreste ancora
Ingannarvi, signora?

Marmotta
Ingannarmi? Ingannarmi? Ah, ch'io fui quella
Ch'intesi e vidi (ahi lassa)
Le mie sventure e l'ignoranze altrui!
Io, io, Masino, intesi
Di caccia il suon de' corni,
Io fui presente a li miei propri scorni.

Tordo
Principessa, non più, quietate il duolo.
Non si pensi al partire.
Straportano talor gli sdegni e l'ire.
Non dee lasciarsi un regno
Per un freddo pensier di gelosia.
Troppo, troppo a gran prezzo
La libertà da voi si venderebbe.
Voi sete di Marocco
Principessa e signora,
Sete di Meo consorte,
Né puote Ancroia torvi il vostro grado.
È Meo troppo gran prence,
Non dovete sprezzare
Sì degna compagnia per vile sdegno.
Il ritornare in Fessa io non lo lodo.

Has it not been made plain to you
that he, amid greyhounds and beasts and nets and dogs,
today with his Ancroia
shall satisfy his mad passions?
Oh, let the royal blood of Fessa
be no longer mocked by Meo thus!
I shall return to my kingdom,
I shall go to my court,
and in Fessa I shall stand,
I, the princess of my land.

Masino
Ah, by God, refrain
from such harsh torment.
Who knows, could you be
deceiving yourself, Mistress?

Marmotta
Deceiving myself? Deceiving myself?
Oh, but I was she who heard and saw, alas,
my own misfortune and the ignorance of others.
Masino, I myself heard
the hunt commence to the sound of the horn,
and I bore witness to how I was scorned.

Tordo
Princess, enough, quiet your sorrow,
think not of leaving.
Ire and contempt can at times be misleading.
You should not abandon a kingdom
for the chilling misgivings of jealousy.
You would sell off your freedom
at far, far too great a price.
You are Morocco's
lady and princess,
you are Meo's consort,
and Ancroia cannot rob you of your station.
Meo is too great a prince,
you should not scorn
so worthy a companion out of unworthy disdain.
I do not advise you return to Fessa.

Che di voi si direbbe?
State, state in Marocco, oh Principessa,
Che qui godrete Meo, Marocco, e Fessa.

Marmotta
Sia che sia, vuò partire.
È meglio esser signora d'una villa
Che d'una gran città vana sibilla.

Masino
Deh pensatela bene.
Marocco è un bel paese,
Il prence di Marocco è un gran signore.
Ha di gran grossi aver, voi lo sapete.
Credete a me, ch'in Fessa senza Meo
Parreste esser a punto
Scopa senza bastone,
Fortezza senza botta di cannone.

Bertuccia
Oh che ti venga il morbo! Oh guarda gente
Da consigliar gli stati!
Ogni cosa al rovescio egli ha proferto.

Marmotta
Andar me n' voglio, se ben mi credesse
D'esser, lunge da Meo,
Pollo senza governo
Estate senza inverno.

Tordo
Ed io vi dico che se vi partite
Sarete (il dice Tordo)
Piede senza pianella,
Zoppo senza stampella.

Bertuccia
E capo senza cervella!
Oh che voi sete pure
Duo consiglier di stato di gran conto!
Oh ve' se voi gli date i buon ricordi!

What would be said about you?
Stay, stay in Morocco, Princess,
for here you will please Meo, Morocco, and Fess.

Marmotta
Be that as it may, I want to leave.
Better to be the mistress of some country estate
than the idle sibyl of a city, however great.

Masino
Ah, think it over.
Morocco is a beautiful country,
the prince of Morocco is a great lord:
he must have great *grossi*,[84] as you well know.
Believe you me, in Fessa without Meo
you'd seem like
a broom without its shaft,
a fortress without the cannon's blast.

Bertuccia
Oh, a pox upon you!
Oh look, isn't this a fine person to give advice of state?
Everything he's uttered is backwards!

Marmotta
I want to leave, even if he thinks
that far from Meo I would be
a hen where no one rules the roost,
a summer without winter's frost.

Tordo
And I say to you that if you go
you will be (so says Tordo)
a foot without its slipper,
a gimp without his crutch.

Bertuccia
And a head without a brain!
Oh, aren't you a fine pair
of state advisors?
Well aren't you doling out some good counsel?

Ed io vi dico che la mia padrona
Sarà, lunge da Meo,
Gonna d'ogni frittella
E d'ogni piè pianella.
E s'in Marocco stenta,
In Fessa al fin sarà poco contenta.

Tordo
E tutti dissero: oh bene, oh bene, oh bene.
Orsù, quieta Marmotta, io l'ho trovata.
Io vi prometto insieme con Masino
Di trovar Baldassarre e far ch'ei meni
Ancroia e Filippetta in altra parte.

Masino
È vero a fé, la ci riesce giusta.

Marmotta
Guardate quel che dite, non burlate!

Tordo
Non burliamo, a la fé. Volete voi?

Marmotta
Come s'io voglio? Se tal cosa fate
Io vi prometto, a fé da principessa,
Farvi venir dui barettin da Fessa.

Masino
Vi ringraziamo, senza nulla è fatto.

Marmotta
In Baldassarre pongo ogni mia fede.

Tordo
Andianne, e state pur di buona voglia,
Che per le nostre man risanarete
La non sentita, inaspettata doglia.

Marmotta
Per vita vostra fate ch'io ne senta

I tell you that once my mistress
is far from Meo, she will be
the smock for every greasy spatter,
and for every foot the slipper;
and if in Morocco she is miserably spent,
in Fessa she'll end up even less content.

Tordo
Everyone together: oh sure, sure, sure.
Come now, calm yourself, Marmotta.
I've got it!
I promise that Masino and I will find Baldassarre
and have him lead Ancroia and Filippetta somewhere else.

Masino
I swear it's true, we can manage it without a hitch.

Marmotta
Mind what you say, don't joke around.

Tordo
We're not joking around, I swear. Is this what you want?

Marmotta
What do you mean, is this what I want?
If you pull this off, I promise, upon my word as a princess,
that you'll get two little caps from Fess.

Masino
With our thanks, consider it done.

Marmotta
In Baldassarre I place all my faith.

Tordo
Off we go, but be of good cheer,
since by our hands you'll soon find relief
from this unexpected, unheard-of grief.

Marmotta
Upon your lives, make sure to bring me

Qualche novella in breve a modo mio.
Bertuccia, oh quanto il duolo
Per costor m'è scemato.
Chi sa? Forse ch'amore
Per tal via mi vorrà render men lieta.

Bertuccia
Signora, abbiate speme,
Che suol talor Cupido
Fabbricar con gli affanni in noi le pene.

Marmotta
Spero, credo, e desio,
E già parmi vedere
Ancroia in Fessa, ed in Marocco Meo.

Bertuccia
Si suol dire, anzi è certo,
Che moglie disperata,
Quanto meno lo crede,
È dal marito amata.
È Meo di buona pasta,
Potrebbe ritornarli il sentimento,
E questi suoi diletti
Dare a le forche per tratenimento.

Marmotta
Oh ecco quella bestia
del Tedeschin, Bertuccia.

Scena decima[xxxviii]

Tedeschino e le medesime

Tedeschino
E qual Saturno a me prepara gioie?
Ecco la principessa.
In su la vita, o Tedeschino, in tono.
Il figlio de la moglie di Vulcano,
Il Dio senz'occhi e con la schiena alata,

some good news without delay. [*Tordo and Masino exit*]
Oh, Bertuccia, how they have lessened my grief.
But who knows?
Maybe Love will still find a way
to make me unhappy.

Bertuccia
My lady, have hope.
Sometimes Cupid fashions
sorrows out of our worries.

Marmotta
I hope, believe, and long,
and already I seem to see
Ancroia in Fessa, and in Morocco Meo.

Bertuccia
It's often said, rather it's a fact,
that a desperate wife,
though little she may believe it,
is the love of her husband's life.
Meo is made of good stuff,
he could return your sentiment
and give these trifles of his
the heave-ho just for merriment.

Marmotta
Oh, here comes that brute
Tedeschino, Bertuccia.

Scene Ten

Tedeschino and the same

Tedeschino
What Saturn[85] prepares such delights for me?
Here is the princess.
Straighten up, oh Tedeschino, buck up.
Let the son of the wife of Vulcan,[86]
the sightless god with the winged back,

L'inventor de le gioie,
Il nume de' piaceri,
Lo scherno de' desiri,
Infine il fabro de la carne umana,
A voi, bella Marmotta,
Percota nel bel seno,
Qual a me diè, la botta.

Bertuccia
Oh, oh, ecco il pavone senza coda.

Marmotta
Che si fa Tedeschino? Che ci è di novo?

Tedeschino
Fo sempre senza fare, e sempre vecchia
È la nova: ch'io amo, e sono amante.

Marmotta
Il Tedeschino amante? Oh l'è dovizia.
E chi è la dama di cotanta sorte?

Tedeschino
La dama? Oh terra, oh stelle, Amore, aiuto.
Voi ben la conoscete, e sempre seco
Dimorate, signora, ch'ardirei
Quasi di dir, che voi fossivo quella.
Ah Marmotta, Marmotta, ahimè pietà.
Voi sete, quella, voi,
Ch'il fraschettin d'Amore
M'ha qual canna nel pozzo
Posto traverso il petto.
Voi sete sì, voi sete
Quella per cui Cupido,
Non con dardo, quadrella, arco o spontone,
M'ha sbusciato il polmone;
Ma del vostro uscio ha preso
Il più grosso stangone,
E con ambe le mani
Tra capo e collo (ahi lasso)
M'ha fatto altro ch'inceso.

the inventor of delights,
the numen of pleasures,
the derision of desires,
in short, the craftsman of human flesh,
who shot me through,
strike you, lovely Marmotta.
in your breast so fair.

Bertuccia
Oh, oh, here's a peacock without its tail.

Marmotta
What are you doing, Tedeschino? What's new?

Tedeschino
I do without doing, and the news is always old:
that I love, and that I am a lover.

Marmotta
Tedeschino a lover? Oh, that's rich.
And just who is the lucky lady?

Tedeschino
The lady? Oh earth, oh stars, Love, help!
You know her well,
and with her you always dwell,
so much so that I'd almost say that you were she.
Oh Marmotta, Marmotta, woe is me, have mercy.
You are she, you,
whom that little devil Love
set within my breast
like a flume in the well.
You are, yes, you are she
with whom Cupid,
not with a dart, arrowhead, bow, or javelin,
pierced my lung.
He grabbed the thickest rod
that barred your door,
and with both hands
along my head and neck, alas,
he left me all aflame.

Per voi, per vostri lumi,
Ch'a me le stelle son di mezzanotte,
Provo interrotte notte,
E son questi occhi miei
Duo disseccati fiumi.
Per voi l'anima mia
Sempre dormendo sogna;
La mente fa lunari,
Il pensier nulla pensa,
Il desir nulla brama.
Son stanche le voglie,
E sempre in ozio provo
Per tua beltà non conosciute doglie.
Per le tue labra, in cui
Havvi Amor sparso a gara
De le viole mammole il candore,
Sono quasi ne la bara.
Per quei d'ebano fino
Denti, che di mia morte
Portan pietosi il bruno,
Tra le piume disteso
Non dormo notte l'ore,
E son fatto per te mumia d'amore.

Marmotta
Orsù, non ti turbar, ch'ancor potresti
In amor non languire.
Ma dimmi qual tu sei e qual vivesti?

Tedeschino
Io mentre ero piccino,
Vestito da tedesco,
Fui messo entro un pasticcio;
Ma poi che col coltello
Fu quella pasta aperta,
Con improviso scherzo
Feci fuor capolino.
Tutte a l'apparir mio
Risero le brigate
Ed acclamaro: «Viva il Tedeschino».
Ond'ho poi sempre usato,

For you, for your lights,
which to me are like the midnight stars,
I suffer interrupted nights,
and these eyes of mine
are two parched rivers.
As I slumber, my soul
always dreams of you;
my mind builds castles in the air,
my thoughts think of nothing else,
my desire hungers for nothing more.
Weary are my yearnings,
and when I am at rest I suffer
for your beauty pains unknown.
For your lips,
which love has sprinkled lily white
to rival shrinking violets,
I am nearly in the grave.
For those teeth of fine ebony,
pitifully dressed in mourning for my death,
I do not sleep a wink all night long,
and so stretched out beneath my sheets,
I have become
your mummy of love.

Marmotta
Come on, don't get riled up.
You might still avoid languishing in love.
But tell me what you are and how you've lived.

Tedeschino
When I was a wee tike,
I was dressed up like a German
and placed in a savory pie;[87]
and when they cut the crust
open with a knife,
as a prank
suddenly out I peeked.
As I popped into sight,
the whole party laughed and cheered,
"Long live Tedeschino, the little German!"
Since then I always come running

Ove si faccion pasti,
Correr, qual bracco, al fiuto,
Scroccare a la gagliarda
Ed appoggiar per tutto l'alabarda.
Ne la corte di Roma,
Sempre per util mio,
Ho cangiato mantello,
E rinegando l'esser italiano,
Or spagnolo, or francese,
Secondo che venivano i dobloni
O pur vestiti vecchi,
Mutato ho setta e variato arnese.
E per vivere ho fatto
A suono di fischiate
Lo scopacorte e 'l frustacavalcate.

Marmotta
Ma vorrei pur sapere
Qual potevan cavar gusto coloro
Di vederti scherzare e far l'astuto?
Vien qui, facciamo un poco a dir il vero.
Che cosa è quella che si faccia in corte,
Che tu bene lo facci, e come va?
Se tu vuoi far de lo statista, sciocco,
Tu non sai che ti dici; e sei una bestia
Se ti picchi di bel trattenitore:
Certo de' forastieri in vece sua
Sarai discacciatore.
Se vuoi far il buffon, non lo sai fare!
A tal sorte di gente
Convien saper cantare,
Sonare, motteggiare,
Aver frasi galante,
Botte ridicolose,
Bei motti all'improvviso,
Saper tacere a tempo,
Non parlar fuor di tempo.
Infin vuole il buffone
Aver materia, scherzo, e discrezione.
Tu di ciò non sai nulla. In che si deve
Servir un prence de la tua persona?

to wherever meals are made
like a hound on the scent,
scrounging around *à la gagliarda*[88]
and cadging wherever I lay my halberd.[89]
At the court in Rome,
I always switched out my livery
to suit my needs,
and denying I was Italian,
I changed my sect and varied my attire,
now Spanish, now French,
according to the source of the doubloons[90]
or even old clothes.
And in order to get by,
I've played screw-the-court and flog-your-ride[91]
to the sound of their jeers.

Marmotta
What I'd like to know
is how they could find pleasure
in seeing you joke around like some wiseguy!
Come here, let's have a bit of straight talk.
What is it that one does at court,
which you do oh-so-well, and how does it work?
If you want to be a statesman,
you fool, you don't know what you're saying.
And if you fancy yourself a great entertainer of guests,
you're an ass, since it's more likely
you'll drive them away.
If you want to be a buffoon, you don't have a clue.
For that class of people
it's best to know how to sing,
to play music, to banter,
to have smooth sayings,
ridiculous retorts,
smart offhand quips,
to know when to keep silent,
to not speak out of turn.
In short, the buffoon needs to have
substance, whimsy, and discernment.
Of this you know nothing.
What use can a prince have for someone like you?

Se tu parli,
Straparli!
Se tu ridi,
Disfidi!
Se tu scherzi,
Disprezzi!
Se motteggi,
Guerreggi!
In fin tu non sai formar parola
Che non chiami il «ti menti per la gola»!
Il buffone non vuole esser mordace,
Vuol saper tra lo scherzo
Frappor qualche bottetta,
Ch'a tempo ella sia detta,
Che lecchi ma non morda,
Che punga e non offenda,
Che tocchi e non ferisca.
Ma tu sei come il gatto, o graffi o mordi,
E non sai far né dire,
Se non dir sempre mal di qualcheduno.
In somma tu non sei morto né vivo,
Il caso per la corte.
E se non hai altra virtù che questa
Vatti a far appiccar, razza di bestia.

Bertuccia
Turù tu tu tu.
Da tal paese non ne venga più.

Scena undecima

Tedeschino *solo*

Tedeschino
Ah cruda più d'un serpe,
Fera più d'un leone,
Mordace più d'un cane,
Ria più d'una pantera,
Più rozza d'una porca,
Maligna più d'un bue,

If you speak,
you misspeak.
If you laugh,
you sneer.
If you jest,
you scoff.
If you tease,
you wage war.
All in all, you can't utter a single word
that isn't called "lying through your teeth."
The buffoon shouldn't be mordant,
he should know to insert
a quip or two amid his jokes
so that he can be said to
lick but not bite,
sting but not offend,
strike but not wound.
But you're like a cat, you either scratch or bite,
and you don't know how to act or to speak,
unless it's to badmouth someone.
In short, dead or alive,
you're not fit to be at court.
And if you have no other virtue than this,
go to hell, you beast.

Bertuccia
Tu-ru-tu, tu-tu-tu.
Let's have no more of you! [*they depart*]

Scene Eleven

Tedeschino, ***alone***

Tedeschino
Oh, more cruel than a snake,
more fierce than a lion,
more biting than a dog,
more vicious than a panther,
more coarse than a swine,
more nasty than an ox,

Rabiata più d'un'orsa,
Perfida più di tigre,
E rigida più d'orca,
Di scorpione, di drago e di chelidro.
Così, così mi scherni?
Così, così te n' vai?
Così, così il Tedeschin s'offende?
Oh donna, avaro mostro,
Mostro d'ogni malizia,
Malizia d'ogni inganno,
Inganno d'ogni petto,
Petto nido di strage,
Strage d'ogni ruina,
Ruina d'ogni casa,
Casa de l'altrui pena,
Pena d'ogni alma amante,
Amante di rapina,
Rapina d'ogni bene,
Bene del re de l'ombre,
Ombra di ria bellezza,
Pianto, scherno, furor, rabia e tristezza.
E chi di me potrà farti maggiore?
Chi dar più ti potrà del Tedeschino?
Chi fia Marmotta ingrata,
Che sotto aurati auspici,
Possa senza rapina
De la vena de l'or farti regina?
Io, io sol era quello
Ch'a suono di martello
Potea con verghe d'oro
Far Bertuccia d'argento e te far d'oro!
Sì, sì, io col soffiare
Ti potevo indorare,
E far potea per sempre
Nume spennato di dorate tempre.
Che forse qual io sono
Troverai vago amante?
Forse qual me vedrai
Altri senza artificio aver vaghezza?
Nel mio corpo risplende
Lindo il piè, vago il lume, e snello il seno.

more enraged than a she-bear,
more treacherous than a tiger,
more savage than an ogre,
than a scorpion, than a dragon, than a viper.
Like this, you mock me like this?
Like this, you leave like this?
Like this, Tedeschino is insulted like this?
Oh woman, greedy monster,
monster of every malice,
malice of every deception,
deception of every breast,
breast a den of carnage,
carnage of every downfall,
downfall of every house,
house of another's pain,
pain of every loving soul,
lover of plunder,
plunder of every good,
good of the king of shadows,
shadow of vicious beauty,
tears, mockery, fury, rage, and sadness.
And who can do more for you than I?
Who can give more to you than Tedeschino?
Who will it be, ungrateful Marmotta,
that under golden auspices
and without plundering your goldmine
can make you a queen?[92]
With the pounding of my hammer
and with my golden rod,
I alone could forge
Bertuccia out of silver and you from gold!
Yes, yes, I could have gilded you
with just a blow of my breath[93]
and made you forever more
a plucked numen of quenched gold.[94]
Do you think you will find
as desirous a lover as I?
Do you think in another you will see
unaffected desire such as mine?
My body stands out
for its fine foot,[95] its desiring eyes, its lithe chest.

I principi con meco
Se la beccano male,
Ch'io certe regoluzze
Ho del governo, che non hanno eguale.
Quando aver negli stati
La pace non potiam, s'abbia la guerra.
E se v'è carestia,
Comprar cara la roba;
Lasciar passar le furie, quando vengono;
Per non sentir gridar, dar poca udienza.
Perch'altri non ti chieda delle grazie
Spesso mancar con tutti di parola.
Con chi tu non la puoi
A suo modo accordarsi e non al tuo.
Per aver men fastidii
Il non tenere mai conto di nulla.
E perch'altri non faccia
Più mai ne' regni tui,
Non tosar no, ma scorticare altrui.
E per far buontempone,
I regni dissipare e le corone.
Sol co' consigli miei
Far grandi in questo stato
La principessa e 'l principe saprei,
Ch'al par del mio sapere ogni altro è sciocco.
Né titolo potrei
Aver per me più degno
Ch'esser governatore di Marocco.
E pur con queste regole
Di gran politicone,
In Napoli mi fero
Scrivano di galea
Con una penna di cinquanta palmi.
E con un grave cambio,
Ch'a tutti mal riesce,
Mentre il fiero agozino
Me bastonava, io bastonavo il pesce.
Ed anco i merti miei
Ha conosciuto Roma,
Se ben s'è contentata,
(Per pietà forse del mio basso stato)

With me by their side
princes have it tough,
since I have certain little rules
of governance that are without rival.
When there cannot be peace between states,
let there be war;
and if there is famine,
buy goods at a high price;
when furies come, let them have a free pass;
in order to not hear shouting, do not lend an ear.
So that others do not ask for favors,
break your word often;
with those you cannot,
agree to do things their way and not yours.
To have fewer troubles,
never keep track of anything.
And so that others no longer harm your kingdom,
shear not, no, but rather fleece theirs.
And to really be the life of the party,
squander kingdoms and crowns.
I know how by my counsel alone
the prince and princess
could be made great in this state,
since compared to my knowledge
everything else is foolish.
I could have no other title
more worthy of me
than governor of Morocco.
And even with these rules
of a great, grand statesman,
in Naples they made me
a galley scribe,
with a fifty-palm long quill.[96]
And in a dreadful exchange
that went badly for all,
while the fierce galley-captain beat me
I beat the fish.[97]
And Rome too came to know my merits,
although perhaps out of pity
for my low station,
she was satisfied

Sol da le mura sue darmi l'esiglio.
Che la pentola ancor, mentre alza il bollo,
Ancor ella costuma
Fuori de l'orlo suo mandar la schiuma.
Oh ecco Baldassarre, il cicalone.

Scena duodecima

Baldassarre, Tedeschino

Baldassarre
Don Baldassarre, bravura del mundo!
Mi qualitad primiera es espagnolo.
Puor todas las provincias conossido,
Cavaglier del piaser,
Escamberada des prences,
Amigho y conseghiero de lo reis,
Entartenimiento de su gustos,
Utilitades d'eglios,
Para su recreacion,
Y passatiempo de mi persona,
Y cosa nechegharia puor la Cuerte.
Medigho, astrologho, herbolario,
Especial, compodista, negromantico,
Cherusigho valiente y madematigho,
Philosopho, teologho, buffone,
Ombre de reis des converciaciones,
Y todas qualitades de las sciencias,
Mapamundo real todas dottrinas,
Poeda, musigho y emprovisador
Y scherzoso facetico y dottor.

Tedeschino
Moresco ciurmatore,
Buon giorno al gran dottor de la bravura.
Che va facendo così scompagnato?

Baldassarre
Vostaiste benvenido puor aglià.
Che tien che hazer voiste de mis cosas?

to only exile me from her walls;
much like a pot put on to boil,
she is still is wont
to let the foam spill over her rim.
Oh, here's that blabbermouth Baldassarre.

Scene Twelve

Baldassarre, Tedeschino

Baldassarre
Don Baldassarre, *bravura del mundo*!
My principal merit is that I am *español*,
I am known in all of the *provincias*,
caballero del placer,[98]
escamberada[99] of princes,
amigo and counselor of kings,
purveyor of their *gustos*
and of their services,
for their *recreación*
and for my own fun,
and I am an indispensable part of *la corte.*
Médico, *astrólogo*, herbalist,
druggist, apothecary, *necromántico,*[100]
worthy surgeon and *matemático*,
filósofo, *teólogo*, buffoon,
right-hand *hombre* for kingly *conversaciónes*,
and virtuoso of the sciences,
royal *mapamundi*[101] of every *doctrina*,
poet, musician, and *improvisador*,
witty trickster and *doctor*.

Tedeschino
Morisco[102] swindler,
good day to the great doctor of bravura.
What are you up to all by your lonesome?

Baldassarre
Your Excellency is most welcome here.
What is your business with my affairs?

Tedeschino
Or che la vostra Ancroia
È del prencipe Meo
La pezzola del naso,
Lo scattolin del muschio,
La trappola de' topi,
De la sua acqua il vaso,
Non ti si può toccar la punta del naso.

Baldassarre
Los diavolo che te lieve, mentiroso,
Io non soi nada d'eglia; mi persona
Non viene a festegarla.
Io non son Tedeschiglio,
Che sovra todos mercantiera cuerna.
Infame piccarone,
E 'n ventiquattro lettras
De l'alfabedo eis vituperado.
Ma scuccia. A: asino,
Begliacco,
Cavezza,
Desvergonzado,
Eretico,
Farfaron
Y todo lo che dize la lettera.
Gangosso,
Lovo,
Marioldo, mierda, mangia,
Nada,
Papagaglio,
Tu te chieres comparare conmigho,
Piccaro, begliacco, desvergonzado,
Che te do quattros puntas des piè.
T'harò polve, puor hazer una lettras!
Tu nassido in Italia
T'hai faltado il nombre de la tierra,
Hazendoti gliamar il Tedeschiglio!
Comunitad zivil,
Baghezza de la tierra,
Infamia de los mundo,
Bravura de las pas,
Poltroneria de la ghierra!

Tedeschino
Now that your Ancroia
is the handkerchief
for Prince Meo's nose,
the little box for his musk,
the trap for his mouse,
and for his water the vase,
no one can yank your chain 'round this place.

Baldassarre
May *los diavolos* drag you away, you liar,
I have *nada* to do with her.
This man here does not sing her praises.
I am no *Tedesquillo*
who traffics with *todos* in horns.
Detestable picaroon,
by all twenty-four *letras*
of the *alfabeto* you are reviled.
Listen up. A: Ass,
Bonehead,
Coward,
Delinquent,
Erring heretic,
Fanfaron,
and *todo* that the letter implies.
Garbler,
Lobo,
Mooch, *mierda*, muncher,
Nada,
Parrot.
If you want to compare yourself to me,
pícaro, coward, scoundrel,
you have some sharp kicks coming to you.
I'll turn you to dust with one *letra* more!
You, born in *Italia*,
you have insulted the name of your homeland
by calling yourself *Tedesquillo*!
Oh, civil *comunidad*!
Scourge of the land,
infamy of *el mundo*,
braggart in times of peace
and sloth in times of war!

Tedeschino
Adagio, ciormatore de la corte,
Vantatore de l'orina,
Becchin degli ammalati,
Vituperio de l'arte medicina.

Baldassarre
Io? Dize a mi? Oh puerco, infame, locco,
Io, ch'en tanta bravura
Puerto mi medisina,
Mi gliami buffonaccio?
Vantator de l'orina?
Lo che toma la mia polvere,
Ia, ia devienta polvere.
Lo che toma el lattuario,
De' vivienti non es nel calendario.
Así mi medisina
Il vegho matta e 'l ghovane deglhina.

Tedeschino
Non mai tanto dicesti e così sano
Parlasti, Baldassarre! Fa' a mio modo:
Fuggi l'infermo e scherza con il sano.

Baldassarre
Caglia desvergonzado, cavronasso!
Scuccia lo che ti dize Baldassarre.
Io puor todos los mundo
Soi miedigho valiente conossido,
Muccio mas de ti estimados;
Y puor mio merecimento
Il cuente di Condé ia mi dio
Unas cadena d'oro.
Da la Reghina madres
Reghebbei sientos dobles de cadena,
Dal Rei un vestimiento
Des dumila dughados
Y cadena dal Duque di Navarres,
El Duque Bocchincan una cogliana,
Spignola una cadena,
Mantua una cadena,

Tedeschino

Careful now, swindler of the court,
vaunter of urine,
undertaker of the ill,
disgrace to the art of medicine.

Baldassarre

Me? Are you talking to me? Oh *puerco*, disgrace, *loco*.
Me, who with so much bravura
dispenses my *medicina*,
you call me a two-bit clown?
Vaunter of urine?
Whoever takes my powders
soon enough becomes a powder too.
Whoever ingests my brew
no longer counts among the living.
And so my *medicina*
kills off the old and saps the young.

Tedeschino

You've never said so much and spoken
so soundly, Baldassarre. Do it my way:
flee the sick and play with the sound.

Baldassarre

Quiet you scoundrel, you ass!
Listen to what Baldassarre tells you.
Throughout *el mundo*
I am a *médico* of virtue and reputation,
mucho más esteemed than you,
and for my merits
the count of Condé[103] has already given me
a chain of gold.
From the queen *madre*
I received a chain worth one-hundred *doblas*,[104]
from the king a vestment
worth two-thousand *ducados*,
and from the *duque de Navarra* a chain,
the *duque de Buckingham*[105] a neck-chain,
Spinola[106] a chain,
Mantua a chain,

D'Osson una cadena,
Conches una cadena,
Su igho un cavaglio,
Filiberto una cadena,
Il Rei una cadena,
Da la Reghina d'Espagna otra cadena.

Tedeschino
E nessun ti seppe incatenare
Con una corda da farti appiccare.

Baldassarre
Caglia, begliacco, che ti chiero dalde,
Se non te chitti, sientos palos! Caglia!

Tedeschino
Oh razza di gentaglia senza fede,
Moresco, infame, vantator di niente,
Mangia entragne di sabato e di venere,
Rinegato, imbriaco, impertinente.
Chi mi tien che non ti storci il collo,
E ti facci calar cotanta gala,
Nemico de la carne che si sala?
Dottor senza dottrina,
Medico senza scienzia,
Buffon senza politica,
Ciarlon senza materia,
Ebreo razza di mulo,
Con quello che ci va per condicillo.

Baldassarre
Oh piccaro, begliacco, piccherone,
Cara de verdugo y adorcado,
Tiengo vergonza di ablar contigho.

Tedeschino
Oh spagnol rinegato,
A me dici appiccato?

Baldassarre
Oh mui vituperio

De Osuna[107] a chain,
Conques a chain,
a horse from his son,
Filiberto a chain,
the king a neck-chain,
from the queen of *España* another chain.

Tedeschino
And yet no one figured out how to chain you up
with a rope long enough for you to hang.

Baldassarre
Be quiet, you coward. I'm going to give you
a hundred licks of my cane if you don't shut up! Quiet!

Tedeschino
Oh faithless breed of riffraff,
morisco, lowlife, vaunter of nothing,
Friday and Saturday eater of entrails,[108]
heretic, drunkard, smart-ass.
Who'll hold me back so I don't wring your neck
and put an end to your great conceit,
you enemy of the salted meat?[109]
Doctor without doctrine,
physician without science,
buffoon without diplomacy,
windbag without material,
Jewish mule,
with all that's on your codicil.

Baldassarre
Oh you *pícaro*, coward, picaroon,
face of the executioner and the dead,
I am ashamed to speak with you.

Tedeschino
Oh you Spanish heretic,
you call me a dead man?

Baldassarre
Whoever speaks with you, you dirty little *pícaro*,

De chi abla contigho, piccardiglio.
Ia, ia me chiero mattarmi contigo.

Tedeschino
Ogni volta che vuoi, su, metti mano.
Io ti vuò far in pezzi adesso adesso.
Spada fuora, oh poltrone.
Tu t'arrendi, marrano?

Baldassarre
Oh passicco, passicco, Tedeschiglia,
Assienta en la vaina la scuciglia.
Me pesa de mattar de la politica
Il maghior asino ch'haia nel mundo.

Tedeschino
Caccia mano, forfante! Hai tu paura?
Io non temo boccaccie, caccia mano,
Ch'io non voglio ammazzarti con vantaggio!
Ah tu non vuoi, poltrone, cacciar mano?
Che? Tu ti arrendi? Vittoria, vittoria!
Voglio ch'in questo loco
Si metta la mia statua,
E le tue spoglie appese per memoria.
Vittoria, vittoria.

Scena decimaterza

Tedeschino, Baldassarre, Michelino, Mantuano

Michelino
Fermare, olà, cacciatevi giù in terre.
Baldassarre son qui, non sciè paure.
Oh ve' che gran rumore e che gran guerre,
Tornare indietre per le più secure.
Fermate, olà; fermate, bricconascie!
Non fasciete custione
Che queste son le strade de le rescie.
Trandira, trandira trà.

comes away much disgraced.
I want to kill myself when I'm with you.

Tedeschino
Whenever you want, go ahead, en garde.
I'm going to hack you to pieces right now.
Out with your sword, you slouch.
Do you surrender, *marrano*?[110]

Baldassarre
Oh enough, enough, *Tedesquilla*,
put your sword back in its sheath.
It weighs on me to kill the greatest
political ass in *el mundo.*

Tedeschino
Hand on your sword, bigshot! What, are you scared?
I'm not afraid of loudmouths, hand on your sword,
I don't want to kill you by unfair advantage!
What, you slouch, you don't want to draw your sword?
What? Do you surrender? Victory! Victory!
I'd like my statue
to be erected in this spot
and your spoils hung in memory.
Victory! Victory!

Scene Thirteen

Tedeschino, Baldassarre, Michelino, Mantuano

Michelino
Hey *zere*, stop, drop to *zee* floor.
Baldassarre, I'm here, don't you fear.
Oh look *v*at a big struggle *und v*at a big uproar.
Get back, stay clear.
Stop it! Hey *zere*, stop it, you sleaze!
Do not brawl,
for *zese* are royal streets.
Tra-la-la, tra-la-lee.

Mantuano
Padrone, olà, spartiamo, che rumore
È tra di voi? Fermare Baldassarre!
Tedeschine non far, fermare un poche!

Baldassarre
Oh piccaro, ladron, igho di nada,
Toma esto, cavron, toma esto otro.
Tomas esto otro, marmitto di cusina;
Mires se io son dottor di medisina.

Tedeschino
Ferma un po' Baldassarre, stamme a udire.
Lascia ch'io mi rileghi quel ch'ho sciolto,
E già che ci è chi sparte,
Lasciamoci spartire.

Baldassarre
Oh dislegado puerco, svergonzado.
Mena le man, ghitton, puerco e mattado.
To', toma esta, toma esta otra.

Tedeschino
E tu pigliati questa! Oh maledette
Sian le rotture e chi porta tai lacci.

Michelino
Mantuane, soccorri; olà fermare!
Non più tante custione, briccionascie;
Non vedete che voi siete ammassate,
E avete tutte rotte le mostascie?
Pascie, pascie, non più tante rumore,
Che scià che sete brave ognun lo sa.
Tarantan, tarantan, tarantan, ta ta.

Mantuano
Padrone, padrone, se non vuon spartirse,
Noi leviame le spade a l'une e l'altre,
A ciò che non si forene il ventrone,
E se non von finirla,
Finianla noi a suone di bastone.

Mantuano
Hey, Master, let us break*en* them up!
What is this commotion between you two?
Stopp*en*, Baldassarre! Tedeschino, don't, stopp*en* for a moment!

Baldassarre
You *pícaro*, crook, son of *nada*,
take this, you ass, and this. [*hits Tedeschino*]
Take this too, you scullion;
I'll show you just who's a doctor of medicine.

Tedeschino
Hold on there, Baldassarre, listen up.
Just let me tie back up what's come undone,[111]
and since someone's already splitting us up,[112]
let's split.

Baldassarre
Oh you riotous pig, you degenerate.
Put up your dukes, you scum, you pig, you dead man.
Take this, take that, take one more.

Tedeschino
And you take this!
Oh, curse these ruptures and whoever wears such straps.

Michelino
Mantuano, help! Hey, stop it!
No more brawls, you scoundrels!
Do you not see *z*at you've been thrashed,
and your mugs have all been bashed?
Peace, peace, enough *vis* all *zee* noise,
everyone already knows how brave you both are.
Taran-tan, taran-tan, taran-tan, ta-ta.

Mantuano
Master, Master, if they don't want*en* to break*en* it up
we will rais*en* our swords against them both,
so that they don't stabb*en* each other in the gut,
and if they don't want*en* to cut it out,
let's end*en* it with the sound of our club. [*they beat them*]

Michelino
Fermatevi, fermate. Pascie, pascie.

Mantuano
Fermar, fermar, non più! Dàlle, padrone.

Michelino
Ghiottonascie, barone, pascie, pascie.

Tedeschino
Ohimè, le mie spalle. Scappa, scappa.
M'han rotto tutta quanta la casacca.

Baldassarre
Ohi es las piernas, la cavezza y el brazos.

Michelino
Dascie, Mantuane, dascie, olà.
Tarantan, tarantan, tarantan, ta ta.

Michelino
Stop it, stop. Peace, peace!

Mantuano
You stopp*en*, stopp*en*! No more! Get 'em, Master!

Michelino
Scoundrels, cretins, peace, peace!

Tedeschino
Ouch, my shoulders. Run, run!
They've completely ripped up my cloak.

Baldassarre
Ow, my legs, my arms, and my *cabeza*!

Michelino
Get 'em, Mantuano, get 'em!
Taran-tan, taran-tan, taran-tan, ta-ta. [*they exit*]

Atto secondo

Scena prima

Baldassarre, Catorchia

Baldassarre
Disdicciado de mi? Che vi parez?
Baldassar è 'l dottor maghior del mundo,
Haes da un piccaron esser mattado?
Ghuro Marte cavron col nigno infante
De mattar Tedeschiglio.

Catorchia
Piano, pian, Baldassarre, e che v'ha fatto
Il Tedeschino, bestia irrazionale?
Ingiuriar un dottor non puol un matto.

Baldassarre
Benvenido Catorchio. La cavezza
Tiengo alterada puor il Tedeschiglio,
Gli chiero hazer dar da un mi laccaio
Doisientos palos il die,
Paraque mui me pesa
Puor aver anco io mismo recebido
Mas de doisientos palos.
Ch'es maghior l'affruente de mi,
Che 'l dagno d'eglio.

Catorchia
E non è nulla; non saran le prime,
Né l'ultime ch'abbiate ricevute.
Trattiam di cose allegre, e sia più gusto.
Come vi tratta amore in questi freddi?

Baldassarre
Como es l'ordinar de los espagnolos
Siempre trattado bien dal nigno elado.

Catorchia
Or che la vostra Ancroia
È lontana da voi, come la fate?

Act Two

Scene One

Baldassarre, Catorchia

Baldassarre
He calls me a disgrace? Can you believe it?
Baldassar is the greatest *doctor* of *el mundo.*
Must he be slaughtered by some *pícaro*?
I swear by that bastard *Marte* and his *niño*[113]
that I shall kill *Tedesquillo.*

Catorchia
Easy now, Baldassarre, easy. What did he do,
that irrational beast Tedeschino?
A doctor can't be harmed by a cuckoo.

Baldassarre
Bienvenido, Catorchio!
My head is a mess because of *Tedesquillo.*
I'd like to have one of my lackeys
give him two hundred canings a day,
since it weighs on me so
to have received myself
more than two hundred licks.
The affront to me is greater
than the harm done to him.

Catorchia
That's nothing!
They can't be the first you've received, nor the last.
Let's talk about happier things and set you at ease.
How is Love treating you in these cold times?

Baldassarre
As usual for us *españoles*:
always treated well by the winged *niño.*

Catorchia
Now that your Ancroia
is far from you, how are you faring?

Baldassarre
Ausente estoi animoso,
Muccio temo in presenzia,
Entro varios pensamientos
Muccio malinconoso.

Catorchia
Son più varii gli affetti ne l'amore
Che la puzza e l'odore.

Baldassarre
Varios es gli effetti
Como vario es el fuegho en todos peccios.
E voiste como passa
Con la sennora dogna Filippetta?
Che 'l verdadiero amore de l'amantes
Es la comunicacion
D'un verdadiero amigho.

Catorchia
È de l'Amor lo stato una gran torre,
Ove chi sale, scende,
E chi va pian più corre.
Io sono nella via quasi di mezzo:
La Filippetta m'ama,
O se non m'ama almen dice d'amarmi.

Baldassarre
Mi digha puor su vida,
Sennor Catorchio, como la tratta?

Catorchia
Sempre, ch'ella mi vede, con le mani
Mi piglia il ferraiolo, e vuol che dentro
La sua porta il mio piè cacci per forza.

Baldassarre
Bueno, por vida mia! Dicami il resto!

Catorchia
Mi piglia sotto il mento,

Baldassarre
When she is absent I am dauntless
yet *mucho* fearful in her presence,
between one varied thought and the next
I am *mucho melancólico.*

Catorchia
There are more varied affects in Love
than there are stenches and smells.

Baldassarre
The effects are as varied
as fires vary in so many a breast.
And how goes it with you
and *Señora Doña* Filippetta?
For the true love of lovers
is the special confidence
of a true *amigo*.

Catorchia
The state of love is like a great tower:
he who goes up comes down,
and he who goes slowly runs the farthest.
I'm somewhere in the middle:
Filippetta loves me,
and if she doesn't, at least she says she does.

Baldassarre
Upon your life, tell me
Señor Catorchio, how do you treat her?

Catorchia
Whenever she sees me, she tugs on my cape
with her hand and wants me to thrust
my foot in her door at all costs.

Baldassarre
Bueno, upon my life! Tell me more!

Catorchia
She grabs me by the chin,

Mi mira, e poi me dice:
«Il mio bel cornacchione,
Sconciatura d'Orlando,
Viso scudo d'Alcide,
Occhi de la mia gatta,
Fronte de la mia monna,
Naso del mio bracchetto,
Scatolino al rovescio del zibetto.»

Baldassarre
Y a mi dize l'Ancroia:
«Viso de la mia fuente,
Occhos del mio seder,
Rostro de la mi buecca,
Frente de la mi flocca.»
Me digha puor su vida: donde piensa
Voiste veder su dama?
Io me creo che con la Sennora Ancroia
Eglia sarà puor sierto a la ventana.

Catorchia
Andianne, se vi pare, a ritrovarle.

Baldassarre
Bamus puor aglià, vosignoria.

Scena seconda

Marmotta ***su la finestra***

Marmotta
Deh, quanto sta Masino?
Quanto ritarda Tordo?
L'uno è inesperto, e l'altro fa il balordo!
Oh povera Marmotta, e pur è vero
Che Meo mio bel Cupido,
Meo mio candido foco,
Meo mia luce notturna,
Meo mio sole in Aquario,
M'ha cancellata dal suo calendario?

she looks at me, and then she says:
"My beautiful old crow,
miscarriage of Orlando,
face like Alcides' shield,[114]
eyes of my cat,
brow of my monkey,
nose of my hound dog,
overturned little civet-box."[115]

Baldassarre
And to me Ancroia says:
"Face of my fountain,
eyes of my behind,
semblance of my kisser
brow of my pisser."
Tell me upon your *vida*,
where do you think you'll see your *dama*?
I myself think that she'll surely be
with *Señora* Ancroia at the window.

Catorchia
If you like, let's go and find them.

Baldassarre
Vamos, Your Lordship! [*they exit*]

Scene Two

Marmotta *at the window*

Marmotta
Oh, how long will Masino be?
How long must Tordo dally?
The one lacks experience, the other's a halfwit!
Oh, poor Marmotta. Is it really true
that Meo, my beautiful Cupid,
Meo, my pure white flame,
Meo, my evening light,
my sun in Aquarius,[116]
has struck me from his memory?[117]

E chi potrà già mai darti maggiori
I godimenti che ti diede Fessa,
In farti di Marmotta aio e signore?
Fessa, ch'a te in tributo
Diede le mie bellezze?
Fessa, ch'a te già porse
De le gioie d'amore ogni ricetto?
Fessa, che ti fé prence
Di Marmotta sua erede,
Dovrà vedere Ancroia
Di me fatta agozzino, e di te boia?
Ah cieco più d'un orbo,
Orbo più d'un senz'occhi,
Rospo tra li ranocchi.
Possa ridurti Amore
Fame senza cibo,
Gelo senza foco,
Sete senza vino,
Ne gli affanni d'Amor sempre Zerbino.

Scena terza

Tedeschino, Marmotta

Tedeschino
Che le caschin le braccia. Oh ve' pensiere!
Per levarci dagl' urti e da' sgrugnoni,
N'hanno spartiti a suono di bastoni.
Ma ve', ecco Marmotta sui balconi!
Oh mio sol di gennaio,
Mia luna quando piove,
Mia porta senza cardini,
Oh cigli archi africani,
Belle carni da cani,
Mio fecado, polmone, oh milza mia,
Foss'io del suo balcon la gelosia.
Io la vuò salutar con verso sdrucciolo:
Vago allievo di Venere,
Ove le brine accendere
Suol lo dio de la cenere

Who will ever be able to give you
greater pleasures than Fessa
when it made you Marmotta's lord and master?
Fessa, that granted you
my beauties in tribute?
Fessa, that already gave you
every possible shelter for love's joys?
Fessa, that made you,
Marmotta's prince, its heir?
Must it see Ancroia become
my jailor and your executioner?
More unseeing than a blind man,
more blind than one without eyes,
a toad amongst the frogs he lies.
May love strike you down,
hunger without food,
frost without a fire,
thirst without vino,
in the anguishes of love forever a Zerbino.[118]

Scene Three

Tedeschino, Marmotta

Tedeschino

I wish they would knock it off!
Oh, just think—to keep us from thrusts and blows,
they separated us to the beat of their clubs.
But look, here is Marmotta at her balcony!
Oh, my January sun,
my moon in the rain,
my open door,
oh arched African brows,
lovely flesh fit for dogs,
oh my liver, my lung, oh my spleen,
would that I were her balcony's screen.
I shall greet her in verse:[119]
A pupil of Venus I wander
where the god of ash
oft burns the frost

E i cori a l'amo prendere,
A me volgete il lampolo
Belle faci lucifere,
Da voi non trovo scampolo,
Né frasi o contracifere.
Ombra risplendidissima,
Luna d'oscure nottole,
Alfana mia bellissima
Più bianca de le grottole.
A te ne vengo debile,
Irrobustito e flebile,
E pria che venga polvere,
Vuò il sì o 'l no risolvere!

Marmotta
Ben venga il Tedeschino. A punto, a punto,
Tu giungi a tempo, come suole il porco
Venir di carnevale, col pan unto.
Vien qua, fatti più sotto. Vuoi tu farmi,
Tedeschino, un piacer per vita tua?
Ho in capo molti grilli, ed il cervello
Mi va girando più d'un arcolaio,
Onde vorrei da te qualche bel gioco
Per traviarmi un poco.

Tedeschino
Eccomi pronto a ciò che mi comandi.
Farò, dirò, darò quanto domandi.

Marmotta
O' via, alle mani!

Tedeschino
Che volete ch'io faccia? Eccomi pronto.

Marmotta
Quattro botte di ballo, una ciaccona,
Cavalcare una canna a la disdossa,
Far quattro capitomboli in persona.

and hooks the heart.
Turn your blaze upon me,
beautiful firebrands so bright,
from you I find no escape,
not even with fine words or secret signs.
Shade most resplendent,
moon of darkened nights,
my most beautiful Arabian mare,[120]
more than any grotto white.
I come to you so weak,
enfeebled and effete,
but before I'm turned to dust,
learn your 'yes' or 'no' I must!

Marmotta
Welcome, Tedeschino.
You've arrived just in the nick of time,
like a pig served up at carnival, with all the trimmings.
Come here, a little bit closer.
Tedeschino, I beg of you, would you do me a favor?
I have a chorus of crickets in my head,
and my brain is spinning faster than a spindle,
and so I'd like some amusement from you
to help distract me a minute or two.

Tedeschino
Here I am, at your bidding.
I shall do, say, give whatever you ask.

Marmotta
Go on now! Hop to it!

Tedeschino
What would you like me to do? I stand ready.

Marmotta
A few dance steps, one *ciaccona*,[121]
ride bareback on a stick,
and why don't you do a couple flips?

Tedeschino

Voi mi pigliate in cambio, non son io
Un buffonaccio da tutti mistieri.
Son buon trattenitore, omo scaltrito,
Né in corte i pari miei sono un pan perso.
Ah Marmotta, Marmotta, voi scherzate,
E mi vorreste con tai giochi fare
Diventare il cucù de le minchiate.
Io non fo capitomboli, né salto
Il caval su la canna, o ballo, o scherzo.
Son politico accorto, e degli stati
So mescolar le carte quanto ogni altro.
Oh ve' che fantasia! Guarda pensiero!
Bench'io faccia il buffone,
Ne la mia villa nacqui cavaliero.

Marmotta

Orsù, l'ho intesa.
Va' e fa' che ti pare,
Né più ti venga umore
Di far meco il garbato e 'l bello umore.
Non mi venir più avante,
Ch'il negar grazie è proprio da furfante.

Tedeschino

Oh Amor, cervel di bestia,
Pur, pur mi farai fare
Corvette, capitomboli, e ballare.
Ma sia che vuole, io voglio
Compiacere il mio ventre,
Sodisfar la mia vista,
Obedir il mio mastro,
E, se non basta i salti su la canna,
Vuò saltare un balcone.
Ma che dico un balcone? Anzi una forca
Pure ch'io cada ne la sua capanna.
Bocca, porta d'Amore
Labra, poggi di Venere,
Occhi, stelle del suolo,
Fronte, piazza di Marte,
Cigli, archi moreschi,

Tedeschino

You've got it all wrong,
I'm no jack-of-all-trades clown.[122]
I am a performer of quality, a man of skill,
and my courtly peers are no chopped liver either.
Oh, Marmotta, Marmotta, you must be kidding,
with such games you'd like me to become
the joker in your deck.[123]
I don't do cartwheels,
nor do I prance on stick horses or dance or jest.
I am a shrewd statesman, and in the affairs of state
I know how to shuffle the deck as well as anyone.
Oh, what a crazy idea!
Even though I play the buffoon,
I came into this world a cavalier.

Marmotta

Oh, I see! I get it.
Go and do whatever you want,
but don't get any more ideas
about assuming fine and pleasing airs.
No longer show your face before me,
since denying one's favors is pure villainy.

Tedeschino

[*aside*] (Oh Love, you loon,
soon you'll even have me doing
courbettes,[124] somersaults, and dances.
But let it be as she wishes,
I want to gratify my belly,
satisfy my eyes,
obey my master,
and if jumping about on a stick isn't enough,
I'll jump onto her balcony.
But what am I saying, her balcony? Her trapdoor, rather,
so that I might fall straight down into her shack.)
Mouth, gateway of love,
lips, knolls of Venus,
eyes, stars of the earth,
forehead, piazza of Mars,
lashes, Moorish arches,

Mento, mescol di Febo,
Gola, corno d'Astolfo,
Petto, scala di Giove,
Poppe, zucche toscane,
Ventre, orcio di miele,
Cosce, travi di volta,
Gambe, d'Ercol colonne,
Piedi, base di torre,
Ov'il mio capo vorrei poter porre. [*qui il Tedeschino balla*]
Ecco, ch'io per te formo in vago giro
La dislegata vita, e a te ballando
Me ne vengo saltando.

Marmotta
Oh bene, oh bene, così,
Oh così, Tedeschino, in capriole.
Eccoti un chitarrino:
Accompagna col ballo
Quattro colpi di canto, Tedeschino.

Tedeschino [*qui canta*]
Si balli,
Si salti,
Si faccia per terra
Col capo a' mattoni perpetua la guerra,
Saltello
E snello
Corvetto,
Passeggio
Qual sotto il cozzone
Somaro a maneggio.

Marmotta
Orsù, via quattro salti su la canna.
A cavallo, a cavallo, Tedeschino,
Ecco a punto un caval pel tuo bisogno.

Tedeschino
Ap, ap, ap, ga, ga, ga, ga. [*a cavallo su la canna*]
Oh garbato cavallo, oh bella groppa.
Ei pare una rombata di galea.

chin, cauldron of Phoebus,[125]
throat, horn of Astolfo[126]
chest, stairway of Jove,
breasts, Tuscan pumpkins,
womb, pot of honey,
thighs, vaulted beams
legs, columns of Hercules,
feet, base of a tower
where I'd like to rest my head.
Here, for you I gracefully gyrate
my unbound hips, and dancing
I come towards you in leaps. [*here Tedeschino dances*]

Marmotta
Oh yes, oh yes, just like that,
oh yes, Tedeschino, some caprioles![127]
Here's a little *chitarrino*:[128]
accompany your dance
with a few bars of song, Tedeschino.

Tedeschino [*singing*]
I shall dance,
I shall jump,
and, beating my head against the bricks,
I shall wage perpetual war on the floor.
With a jump
and a nimble
courbette,
I promenade
before the horse tamer
like an ass at the manège.[129]

Marmotta
Come on! Hup hup! Let's see you hop up on that stick.
Giddy up, giddy up, Tedeschino,
I've got just the right hobby horse for you.

Tedeschino
Ya, ya, ya, whoa, whoa, whoa. [*riding on the stick*]
Oh what a handsome horse, what a fine crupper!
It looks like a galley rambade.[130]

Ga, ga, ga, non mi far più il bizzarro,
Non hai sopra qualche oca o pappagallo;
V'hai chi cavalcar seppe
Prima che tu tra noi fossi cavallo.
Come ben su le volte
Gli do le giravolte.
Come bene a la mano
Lo fo voltar su l'una e l'altra mano.
E come lo speron fra capo e collo
Gli fa tagliar per terra il caracollo.
Questa è botta maestra. [*qui dà una speronata al cavallo*]
Ma ve' come la bestia vi s'addestra!
Oh garbato animale!
Voleria su le volte s'avesse ale.
Quattro curvette su, brunel d'Argante.

Marmotta
Ah così, Tedeschino, oh buono, oh buono!

Tedeschino
Ga, ga, ga, ap, ap, ap, ap.
Oh come ben la trita. Oh ve' ch'a l'aria
Ei si rivolta, e par che fin le stelle
Calcitrar voglia co' castelli in aria. [*tira calci*]
Oh maladetto tempo, io son caduto. [*qui casca*]
Ma con quatro sferzate
Ti vuò, bestia, imparare
A farmi dar sì fatte crepacciate.
To', bestia maledetta,
Che ti pensavi, che foss'io civetta?

Marmotta
Tedeschin, manco furia; ei non sapea
Che tu al suolo volessi mover guerra.
Il povero animale si credea
Che l'avessi col ciel, non con la terra.
Orsù, per minor briga,
Fa' quattro capitomboli garbati,
Ch'io avrò più gusto, e tu minor fatiga.

Whoa, whoa, stop acting bizarrely,
you don't have some goose or parrot astride;
you have one who knew how to ride
before you even were a horse.
Look how well I lead him
through his voltes in pirouettes.
Look how well I turn him
this way and that with a touch,
and how a crop between his head and neck
makes him cut a caracole[131] across the ground.
This here is an expert blow. [*here he spurs the horse*]
Do you see how the animal is tamed?
Oh handsome beast,
he would fly on the voltes if he had wings!
A few more courbettes, Argante's[132] tawny steed!

Marmotta
Just like that, Tedeschino! Oh yes, oh yes!

Tedeschino
Whoa, whoa, whoa, ya, ya, ya, ya.
Oh, how he prances! Look how he defies the air.
He seems to want to kick up to the stars
with their castles in the air. [*he kicks*]
Blast it, I've fallen. [*here he tumbles*]
With one lash after another
I'll teach you, you brute,
to send me tumbling.[133]
Take that, you beast so foul,
did you think I was some kind of little owl?

Marmotta
Tedeschino, don't be so angry, he didn't know
that you wanted to start a war with the floor.
The poor beast was under the impression
that you'd teach the heavens, not the earth, a fine lesson.
Up now, no more brawls.
Let's have some nice flips instead.
I'll be more entertained, and you less strained.

Tedeschino
Oh bellezze cornute!
Il Tedeschin il savio,
Lo statista de' prenci,
Il politico altier di tutto il mondo,
L'inventor de l'archimia,
Il fondator de l'oro, il soffiatore
Del fornello alchemistico,
Per amor si riduce,
Mirabilmente snello,
A far i capitomboli, a ballare,
E su la canna fare il saltarello.
Oh di Fessa, di Fessa
Regia prole nudrita,
Quanto puon far tuoi occhi,
Quanto può la tua bocca.
Quanto vale il tuo naso,
Quanto, quanto bram'io
Diventar farfallone,
Per ragirarmi al lume
De' tuoi occhi lucenti
Ch'a me di notte sono (oh mio contento)
Le fiaccole d'Amore,
Mie belle torcie a vento.

Marmotta
E per che farne poi?
Benché di Fessa io sia,
D'altro che farfalloni ho fantasia.

Tedeschino
Ah mia verdea frizzante,
Ancor non hai provato
Quel ch'io provo per te d'amor piagato.
Ancor non sai Marmotta,
Quai siano i vezzi cari
Del Tedeschino amante.
Vuoi tu ch'io te l'impari?

Marmotta
E di che sorte sono? Io crederei

Tedeschino
Oh barbed beauties!
Tedeschino the wise,
the statesman of princes,
the eminent politico of the whole world,
the inventor of alchemy,
the founder of gold,
the blower of the alchemist furnace,
for love is reduced
to doing flips, to prancing,
and, astride a stick with admirable dexterity,
the *saltarello*[134] dancing.
Oh royal progeny born and raised
in Fessa, oh Fessa,
how potent are your eyes,
how able is your mouth,
how precious is your nose,
oh how I yearn
to become a great moth[135]
circling the flame
of your bright eyes,
which, oh joy of mine, in my dreams
are like lanterns of love,
my radiant beams.

Marmotta
And to do what with them?
Though I am indeed from Fessa,
I fancy more than some pest.

Tedeschino
Ah, my bubbly Verdea,
you still don't feel
what I, wounded by love, feel for you.
You still don't know, Marmotta,
the fine charms that are the purview
of your lover Tedeschino.
Do you want me to teach them to you?

Marmotta
And of what sort are they?

Che tu né men valessi
A vezzeggiar le monne.
Tu pai un scacciadonne. Io non t'ho fede,
E s'ho da dirte il vero,
T'ho per Cillenio e non per Ganimede.

Tedeschino
Più tosto potei dire
Ch'io ti paia uno Adone.
Io ho più tosto cera
Del drudo di Ciprigna
Che d'esser di Vulcan voltastidione.

Marmotta
Al fare i capitomboli, che poi
Discorrerem di quel che tu m'hai cera.

Tedeschino
Eccone uno. Oh garbato!
Eccone un altro, or vedi,
S'io so levarmi in aria senza i piedi.
Oh bella forza! A fé, che, se s'usasse
Di fare i capitomboli in la corte
Io v'avrei più d'ogni altro bella sorte.

Marmotta
Tedeschin, Tedeschin, ve' che ti cade?
L'è una cigna, una fune, o che cos'è?
È una cigna, a la fé.
Oh che ti venga d'ogni cosa sette,
Almen, se rotto sei,
Porta l'allacciature un po' più strette.

Tedeschino
Che rotture, che lacci?
Amor l'altrier per gioco
Mi prestò la sua benda,
Mi disse ch'io d'intorno
A la regione de' rognioni in cura
Quella stretta legassi,
Ch'avrei d'amor sentito

I'm inclined to think
you don't know the first thing about charming the ladies;
you seem more likely to send them running.
I don't trust you, and if truth be told,
I peg you more as a Cyllian[136] than a Ganymede.

Tedeschino
I'd rather say
that I come off as an Adonis.[137]
I look more like
Ciprigna's paramour
than Vulcan's turnspit.[138]

Marmotta
Let's get to those somersaults, and then we'll see
about the look you have for me.

Tedeschino
Here's one. Oh, how fine! [*performs acrobatics*]
Here's another. Now you see how
I can fly through the air without touching the ground.
Oh, what might! I swear, if it were common
to do flips at court
next to me all others would fall short.

Marmotta
Oh Tedeschino, Tedeschino, what's that falling off you?[139]
Is that a girth, a halter,[140] what is it?
Oh my word, it's a girth.
May you be repaid ten-fold for your pains,
or at least, if you are truly hurt,
wear your bandages more tightly girt.

Tedeschino
What? Hurt?[141] What bandage?
On a lark the other day
Love lent me his blindfold,
told me that I should
tie it snugly down there
around my two kidneys[142] for relief,
that I'd feel less of a singe

Meno ardente l'arsura.
Amor mi diè quel laccio,
Acciò che stretto il ventre,
Mirando tue facelle,
Vacuar non mi fesse le budelle.
Amor mi diè quel ferro
Acciò dei dardi tuoi
Fosse coperta al core,
E, qual egli è bendato,
Allacciato foss'io, novello Amore.
Onde cigna non è, ma ben è benda;
Ove fia, che Marmotta
Dal Tedeschin si prenda.

Marmotta
Son sodisfatta a pieno
De le tue ritrovate. Or vedi s'altro
Sai far per travviarmi un po' l'umore.

Tedeschino
Oh mio verno d'estate,
Primavera d'inverno,
Mia rosa d'ogni mese,
Mia stella fuor del cielo,
Mio sole di campagna,
Trappola del mio core, e di me ragna.
Dimmi, dimmi burlando,
Ch'io del tuo amor altero
Ne andrò, mio lume oscuro!
Dimmi, dimmi, sdegnata,
Ch'io sarò il tuo Cupido,
Tu del mio core il nido;
Che già di me invaghita
Hai per mano d'Amore
Una larga ferita.
Io ardo, o principessa,
E sol brama il mio seno
In Marocco goder Marocco, e Fessa.
Io ardo, o mio tesoro,
E sol brama mia voglia,
Che tu sii la mia terra di lavoro.

from love's fire.
Love gave me this bandage
so that, with tummy held tight,
gazing on your bright torches
wouldn't make me crap my britches.
Love gave me this iron plate[143]
so that from your arrows
my heart would be shielded.
And just as he is blindfolded,
so too am I bound, new Love.
It is not by the girth but by the blindfold
that Tedeschino shall thus
of Marmotta take hold.

Marmotta
I am fully satisfied by your reasoning.
Now let's see what else you can do
to lift my spirits.

Tedeschino
Oh Tedeschino summer's winter,
winter's spring,
my monthly rose,
my heavenly star,
my country sun,
my heart's trap, and my entanglement.
Tell me, tell me in jest,
that I shall be able to boast
of your love, my dark light.
Tell me, tell me, oh scornful one,
that I shall be your Cupid,
and you my heart's abode,
and that you, already spellbound,
have by Love's hand
a deep wound.
I burn, oh *principessa*,
and my heart yearns only
to enjoy in Morocco both Morocco and Fessa.
I burn, my darling,
and my desire yearns only
that you become my land for milling.

Infine nel tuo mare
Vorrei poter vogare,
E tra le sponde, onde il mio cor s'aggela,
Esser io timonier, vogante, e vela.

Marmotta
Oh bel modo di dire!
Certo ch'io non t'avea
Per sì bravo ciarlone.
Ma dimmi, e che vuoi fare?
Io non son mare, e tu non sai vogare.

Tedeschino
Ah che purtroppo sei
Per me mutabil onda,
Ov' Amor mi sguazzuglia, e non m'affonda.
Ah che tu il mare sei, ed io son legno;
L'un senza approdo, e l'altro senza segno.

Marmotta
Orsù, dimmi che vuoi!
Ch'a fé da principessa io ti prometto
Fartene or or l'effetto.

Tedeschino
Or ora, oh me felice.
Amore, e sarà vero
Ch'io sia de la tua targa asta e brocchiero?
Sarà vero, Marmotta,
Che dopo tanti affanni
Io finisca le pene, abbia i malanni?

Marmotta
Io ti prometto, e giuro
Il presente non darti col futuro.
Or a Dio Tedeschino, a rivederci.

Tedeschino
Oh felice ballare,
Oh beato saltare!
Oh bel far capitomboli.
Altri stia su le sue, arrabbi e sfondoli.

In your sea, to put it so,
I should like to row,
and between your shores, where a chill my heart assails,
to be helmsman, oarsman, and the sails.

Marmotta
Oh, what fine words!
I certainly did not have you pegged
for such a big gasbag!
But tell me, what do you want to do?
I'm no open sea, and you don't know how to row.

Tedeschino
Ah, sadly for me you are like
Love's changing wave,
which splashes but does not submerge.
Oh, for you are like the sea, and I a bark,
the one without a dock, the other with no landmark.

Marmotta
Come now, tell me what you desire!
Upon my word as a princess,
I pledge you will soon meet with success.

Tedeschino
Soon? Oh my, what joy!
Love, can it be true
that I might be the rapier and buckler to your shield?[144]
Can it be true, Marmotta,
that after so much grief
my pain and suffering will find relief?

Marmotta
I swear to you, I'll grant your wish,
I will not pull a bait-and-switch.
Now, farewell, Tedeschino. Until we meet again. [*exits*]

Tedeschino
Oh, joyous dancing!
Oh, jubilant jumping!
Oh, how wonderful to do flips!
Let others sulk, grow angry, and screw themselves. [*exits*]

Scena quarta

Meo, Ancroia, Filippetta, Pedina, Gobbo, Cacciatori

Meo
Oh che gran gusto è di cacciare, Ancroia.
Quanti sono i diletti de la caccia.
Dimmi, come ti piace andare a caccia?

Ancroia
A me mi piace assai veder cacciare,
Ma quel correr di dietro agli animali
Mi pare una fatica da crepare.

Meo
Gobbo, da' qua quel gatto! Oh com'è grasso!
E pur come correa dietro quel topo!
Non credo che vi sia
Animal che più corra di costoro.
Come per quella china
Correva quella cutta!
Si vedeva ch'avevano gran fretta.

Gobbo
Credimi, signor, ch'io ho tanto gusto,
Che dopo che cacciamo,
Non ho con maggior spasso fatto presa.
Giù per quel monterozzo
So che ci feron correre.
Vi giuro per la madre d'una cutta
Ch'ella m'ebbe andar brutta.

Meo
E che t'è intravenuto?

Gobbo
Mentre correvo in posta,
Il somaro inciampò
In un piede di pino,
E mi fe' dare in terra
Così gran stramazzone
Che mi strappò la stringa del calzone.

Scene Four

Meo, Ancroia, Filippetta, Pedina, Gobbo, Huntsmen

Meo
Oh, there is such great pleasure in hunting, Ancroia.
Many are the joys of the hunt.
Tell me, how do you like to hunt?

Ancroia
I do so love to watch the hunt,
but all this chasing after animals
is enough to make you want to croak.

Meo
Gobbo, bring over that cat! Oh, it's so fat!
And yet, how it ran after that rat!
I don't think that any animal
runs more than those two.
How fast across the slope
did that wagtail[145] scurry?
You could see they were in a big hurry.

Gobbo
Believe me, sir, I take such great pleasure
when we hunt together
that bagging our prey has never been more fun.
They sure did make us run
down that damn hill.
I swear, by that mother of a wagtail,
it gave me one hell of a time.

Meo
And what happened to you?

Gobbo
While I was racing along,
the packhorse tripped
on the foot of a pine
and threw me to the ground
with so great a blow
that it ripped the stitches right out of my hose.

Meo
Eh non è nulla! E a te Messer Pedina,
Come t'è andata, bene?

Pedina
Io porto ancora il dito
Fasciato per il morso che mi diede
Quel topo maladetto nel pigliarlo.

Meo
Eh che? Non gli lasciasti il can, balordo?

Pedina
Glielo lasciai, ma il sciocco
Smarrì la via, e lo perdè di vista.

Meo
E i bracchi, che facevan? Bisognava
Pigliar un bracco a lassa,
Ch'al topo è sufficiente simil lassa.

Pedina
Io gli le lasciai tutti, ma che vale
Tutta una braccheria
Dietro un topo che corre per la via?

Gobbo
S'aveva a far con me, non gli riuscia.
Questa cutta maligna
Mi diè ne lo speron un morso tale
Che si riempì di sangue lo stivale.
Ma che gli feci a lei?
Tosto la gettai in terra, e con le reti
Gli fui sopra sì lesto
Ch'ella fe' d'esser mia il manifesto.

Meo
A me solo quel corvo
Mi s'avventò negli occhi, e se non era
Ancroia con il guanto
Di mezzogiorno mi facea far sera.

Meo
But that's nothing!
And for you, Master Pedina, how did it go? Well?

Pedina
My finger is still
bandaged up from the bite I got
from that damned rat I caught.

Meo
And what, you didn't sic the dog on it, you oaf?

Pedina
I did sic him on it, but the stupid thing
got off course and lost sight of it.

Meo
And what were the bloodhounds doing?
You should have grabbed a hound on a leash,
since such a pack can handle a rat.

Pedina
I sicked all of them on it,
but what good is an entire pack of hounds
after a rat that runs away?

Gobbo
If it had messed with me, it wouldn't have gotten away.
That dirty wagtail
bit down on my spur so hard
that my boot filled up with blood.
But what did I do to her?
I threw her to the ground, and with my nets
I swooped down on her so swiftly
that she became mine manifestly.

Meo
I only had that raven
dive for my eyes,
and had Ancroia not been there with her glove
I'd never again see the sun above.

Ancroia
A fé, a fé, ch'a me quella cornacchia,
Se non era Pedina con lo spiedo
La mi guastava tutti i ricciolini.

Filippetta
E quel gatto, padrona,
Ch'a torno a me parea
Che far volessi la caccia de' topi?
Ma che! Subito questi cacciatori
Gli si cacciorno sotto,
E 'l gatto v'infilzarono di botto.

Meo
Orsù, Gobbo, vogliam noi far banchetto.

Gobbo
Vostra Eccellanzia sì, adesso, adesso
Vuò a chiamar Grasso, e tosto
Gli fo far guazzapugli, fritto, e arrosto.

Meo
Chiamalo, e fa' la caccia
Ben cucinare al Grasso;
E di' ch'abbia buon sito e brodo grasso.

Gobbo
Farò quanto comandi. Or ora vado.

Meo
Ancroia, e voi partite
Verso la vostra stanza,
E ripulita meglio
Ritornate a la regia, o lì vicino
Spedite Filippetta,
Ch'io vi vuò pasteggiare nel giardino.

Ancroia
Io vado, e tosto torno.

Ancroia
I swear, I swear, that old crow sure came at me.
If Pedina hadn't been there with that spit,
it might have ruined my little ringlets.

Filippetta
And what about that cat, Mistress,
that seemed to want to go
mousing all around me?
These hunters made a sneak attack
and in one fell swoop
they skewered that cat.

Meo
Come now, Gobbo, we have a feast[146] to put on.

Gobbo
Right away, Your Excellency, I'll summon Grasso
and get him to whip up a mess
of fried and roasted meats.

Meo
Summon him, and make sure Grasso
cooks the game carefully
and makes the stew rich and savory.

Gobbo
I'll do as you command. Off I go. [*exits*]

Meo
And Ancroia, you head back
to your room
and once you have freshened up a bit,
come back to the palace
or send Filippetta around first,
for in the garden I want to give you a feast.

Ancroia
I'm off and will return in a jiff.

Filippetta
Principe, a Dio, anch'io mi vuò pulire,
Mi vuò lavar le scarpe e la gonnella,
Ch'oggi con questa caccia
Mi ci son fatto più d'una frittella.

Meo
A Dio, Ancroia, a Dio.
Vattene ch'io Marmotta
Intanto ritirar farò di sopra.

Scena quinta

Grasso, Gobbo, Cacciatori

Grasso
Oh quanta robba! oh ve' uccellatori!
Oh queste son le cacce e cacciatori!

Gobbo
Senti Grasso, vien qua. Vuol far banchetto
A la sua bella Ancroia il nostro prence,
Però tutta la caccia
Condur fatti in cucina,
E mostra il tuo saper questa mattina.

Grasso
Lasciate fare a me, quest'arte mia
L'ho fatta mille volte a l'osteria.

Gobbo
Grasso, fa' quella cutta a la lombarda
Con una zuppa sopra senza cascio;
Quella civetta falla in gelatina,
Il corbo fallo arrosto con la gatta,
La cornacchia in guazzetto con il topo:
Tu sai meglio di me l'arte del coco.

Grasso
Lascia pur fare a me,
Che so mangiar la roba quando ci è.

Filippetta
Prince, farewell. I also want to get cleaned up
and give my shoes and skirts a scrub
since over the course of today's hunt
I've given myself more than one greasy spot.

Meo
Farewell, Ancroia, farewell.
Go, and in the meantime I'll go
and get Marmotta to retire upstairs. [*they exit*]

Scene Five

Grasso, Gobbo, Huntsmen

Grasso
Look at all this stuff! And the fowlers!
Look at these hunters and their game!

Gobbo
Listen, Grasso, come here.
Our prince wants to feast with his beautiful Ancroia.
Have all of the game
brought to the kitchen for you,
and show us just what you can do.

Grasso
I know my art, just leave it to me,
I did this a thousand times at the hostelry.

Gobbo
Prepare that wagtail Lombard-style,[147]
with sauce on top but hold the cheese.
Prepare the owlet in gelatin,
roast the raven with the cat,
the old crow in gravy with the rat.
But you know better than me the art of cookery.

Grasso
Just leave it all to me,
I know what eating ought to be.

Gobbo
Lascio la cura a te, ed io me n' vado
Verso la regia a ritrovare il prence.

Cacciatori
Ecco qui tutta la caccia,
Cucinate e pappate!
Quanto a voi
Non a noi
Ella piaccia.
Non ne tocca a chi la caccia.

Scena sesta

Grasso, Tedeschino

Grasso
Oh com'è grasso questo topo ghiotto!
Ei pare una lanterna di galea.
E questa cutta, oh l'ha la bella coda.
Oh gatto maledetto, so ch'il ventre
Ti sei ripieno per quella verdura,
E tu corvo ciarlone,
Avrai finito il presagir novelle?
Ah civetta, frugnolo degli augelli,
Vuò far degli uni e gli altri pappardelle;
Del foco avrete ne la mia cucina:
Chi allesso, chi rifritto, e 'n gelatina.

Tedeschino
Grasso, che nova ci è? Che cosa è questa?
Che fai di tante cutte, gatte e topi?

Grasso
Oh, buongiorno, padrone. Non sapete
Ch'il prence è stato a caccia e ch'ha predato
Co' bracchi e i cacciator quel che vedete?

Tedeschino
So ch'egli è stato a caccia, ma perché
Hai tanta roba tu da cucinare?

Gobbo
I leave it in your hands,
and head back to the palace to find the prince. [*exits*]

Huntsmen
Here you go, all of our game.
Cook it up and scarf it down.
It is for your,
not our,
great delight,
for those who hunt don't get a bite. [*they exit*]

Scene Six

Grasso, Tedeschino

Grasso
Oh, this greedy rat is so fat!
It's as big as a galley lantern.
And this wagtail, oh what a very fine tail!
You damn cat, I know you've stuffed your belly
up in the meadows.
And you, you chatty raven,
you're quite done foretelling the future!
Ah, owlet, lure of all fowl!
I want to make pappardelle out of you all.
You'll all taste your share of the flames in my kitchen:
some I'll boil, some I'll fry, some I'll set in gelatin.

Tedeschino [*enters*]
Grasso, what news have you? What is all this?
What are you doing with so many wagtails, cats, and rats?

Grasso
Oh, good morning, Master.
Don't you know that the prince went hunting,
and with his hounds and hunters bagged all that you see?

Tedeschino
I know that he's been on a hunt,
but why do you have so much stuff to cook?

Grasso
Oh non sapete niente. Egli banchetta
Ancroia: quella Ancroia, Ancroia usata
Di trattenere Baldassare amante.

Tedeschino
Ancroia? E che vuol seco
Il nostro prence gracchiolar d'amore?

Grasso
Sì, sì, pur egli seco è stato a caccia
Ed ora la banchetta nel giardino.

Tedeschino
Oh povera Marmotta! Ma che dico?
È questa, è questa a punto
L'origin vera de le mie fortune.
Va' Grasso, va' in cucina,
Ch'Amor per vie inusate
Sa cuocer senza foco le frittate.

Grasso
A Dio padrone, a Dio. Oh quanta robba!
Almen cotta ne fuss'io guardarobba!

Tedeschino
Oh Amor del ventre mio cibo soave!
Mia vitella di latte,
Ortolano bramato,
Staggionato mio bue, starna mia buona,
Mio piatto di lasagne col formaggio,
Ravagiolo d'april, latte di maggio,
Fiasco mio di Trebiano,
Vin de Montepulciano,
Mio liquor di Genzano,
Verdea, ch'il duol mi molce,
Mio bel fico brusciotto grosso e dolce;
E tu madre di quel ch'innesta i putti,
Bella madre d'Amore,
Ben ver me spalancate
Hai di pietà le porte;

Grasso
Oh, you don't know a thing: he's feasting Ancroia,
yes, that Ancroia, the same Ancroia who used to
keep Baldassarre as her lover.

Tedeschino
Ancroia? And why should our prince
want to prattle about love with her?

Grasso
Yes, yes, he even went hunting with her,
and now he's feasting her in the garden.

Tedeschino
Oh, poor Marmotta! But what am I saying?
This, this right here will be
the beginning of my good fortune.
Go, Grasso, go back to the kitchen,
since Love through his mysterious ways
knows how to fry up an omelet without a fire's blaze.

Grasso
Farewell, Master, farewell. There's just so much stuff!
But sadly for this steward it's look but don't touch! [*exits*]

Tedeschino
Oh Love, my belly's sweet fare!
My suckling calf,
my hungered-for finch,
my seasoned ox, my tasty partridge,
my plate of lasagna with cheese,
raviggiolo[148] of April, milk of May,
my flask of Trebbiano,
wine of Montepulciano,
my liquor of Genzano,
Verdea that makes my pain obsolete,
my beautiful black fig, large and sweet.
And you, mother of he who grafts putti,[149]
fair mother of Love,
truly for me you have left
the doors of compassion wide open.

Non si dee fuggir mai benché si tema.
Il dimostrar la fronte,
Il fare il viso d'arme
E l'intrepido stare a le batoste
Fa che si mangi senza pagar l'oste.
Quanto ha potuto far la mia politica:
L'importuno talor vince l'avaro.
Or ch'io mi disperavo, e con Amore
Non mi credevo più saldare i conti,
Ei mi porge a la penna il calamaro.
Infine gli è un fanciullo incanutito,
Orbo, che piè degli altri il tutto vede,
Un savio tra i balordi, uno scaltrito
Fra gente ch'usan far le trufferie.
Vuò chiamar la Bertuccia di Marmotta,
E far ch'ella da me sappia ch'il prence
Con Ancroia vuol far a la campagna
Un banchetto real entro la grotta.

Scena settima

Bertuccia, Tedeschino

Tedeschino
Bertuccia, a punto adesso io ti cercavo.

Bertuccia
Oh mi maravigliavo. E che tu vuoi?
Io ho altro che far che le tue ciance!

Tedeschino
E vien qua, se tu vuoi, stammi a sentire!

Bertuccia
Che cosa m'hai che dire?
Forse de li tuoi soliti precetti
Di politica sciocca, farfallone?

Tedeschino
E non star su le burle! Senti, dico!

One must never flee, though one may falter.
By showing one's brow,
by looking daggers,
and by intrepidly withstanding blows,
one can eat without paying the innkeeper.
I've accomplished so much with my politicking:
the squeaky wheel gets the grease.
Just as I was losing heart
and felt I could never settle up with Love,
he supplied an inkwell for my pen.
In short, he is a white-haired lad,
blind but sees more than others,
a sage among fools,
a cynic among swindlers.
I'd like to call Marmotta's Bertuccia
and tell her that the prince
plans to throw Ancroia a royal banquet
inside a rustic grotto.

Scene Seven

Bertuccia, Tedeschino

Tedeschino
Bertuccia, I was just looking for you this very moment.

Bertuccia
Surprise, surprise. What do you want?
I don't have time for your jabbering!

Tedeschino
Then come here, if you don't mind, and listen to me!

Bertuccia
What do you have to tell me?
More of your idiotic
rules of politics, you nitwit?

Tedeschino
Lay off the jokes! Listen up!

Va', di' a la principessa,
Ch'io ho da dirle cose di gran conto.

Bertuccia
Sopra di che? Che forse gli vuoi fare
Quattro altri capitomboli, o saltare?

Tedeschino
Che salti e capitomboli? Io vuò dirle
Quai torti gli prepara il suo buon Meo.

Bertuccia
Il prence, il prence; adesso, adesso vado.

Tedeschino
Ora è tempo ch'io tutta versi fuori
La politica mia dal bussolotto.
Lingua aiutati pur, che ti bisogna?
Questo è pur il bel modo
Di grattar con l'altrui la propria rogna.

Scena ottava

Marmotta, Tedeschino

Marmotta
Tedeschino, che ci è? Che m'hai da dire?
Che mi ha fatto il mio prence?
Già, già ben le sue brame a me son note,
Ch'ei vagheggia un bel volto in crespe gote.

Tedeschino
O luna, ch'ad Apollo i raggi togli,
Sole ch'il sen m'aghiacci,
Fa' ch'io fra i cenci tuoi esca di stracci!
Sappi bella mia diva, ch'il tuo prence
Con Ancroia la brutta
Entro l'orto ridutto
Vuol cor fra due seponi
Il malcresciuto e maturato frutto;

Go tell the princess
that I have things of great import to tell her.

Bertuccia
About what? Maybe that you want to perform
some more cartwheels or jumps for her?

Tedeschino
Jumps and cartwheels? I want to tell her
what indignities her good Meo has in store for her.

Bertuccia
The prince, the prince! Now, I'll go right now. [*exits*]

Tedeschino
Now it is time for me to toss
all of my politics out from the tumbler.
Tongue, do your best. What more do you need?
This is the very best way to use another's sores
to scratch where it itches.[150]

Scene Eight

Marmotta, Tedeschino

Marmotta
Tedeschino, what is it? What do you want to tell me?
What has my prince done to me?
I already know all too well about his desires,
how he longingly perceives a pretty face on wrinkled cheeks.

Tedeschino
Oh moon, who robs Apollo of his rays,
sun that brings a chill to my chest,
grant that between your rags I may rise to riches.
Know, my beautiful goddess,
that within the nettle patch
between two large hedges
your prince wants to pluck
foul Ancroia's malformed and over-ripened fruit.

E zappator novello
D'allagato terreno
Ad onta tua desia
L'arena coltivare in sua balìa.
Che ne dite, signora? Non vi pare,
Ch'egli ha finito affatto d'impazzare?

Marmotta
Io non so che ti dici, e ancor non posso
Saper che s'abbia fatto, o io m'abbia a dosso.

Tedeschino
Ah voi non m'intendete per enigma.
Vi parlerò più chiaro. Ei nel giardino
Vuole innaffiar il suolo, e sovra il sodo
Coltivar mescolanze d'ogni sorte.
M'avete inteso?
Il prence non di Fessa di Marocco
Vuol giocar con Ancroia a la staffetta,
E vuol ch'il tutto attesti Filippetta.

Marmotta
Che Filippetta, che Fessa, che Marocco?
Oh tu m'hai de lo sciocco?

Tedeschino
Orsù, l'ho intesa: la dirò volgare.
Il prence con Ancroia a la verdura
Vuol ratemprar l'arsura.
Egli vuol farvi un cornicion su l'arme,
Un vestito a la moda poiché s'usa
Quanto questo vestir simil lavoro.

Marmotta
Che vuol dare ad Ancroia la verdura,
E con un cornicion la vuò vestire?

Tedeschino
Sì, zucche infarinate! Egli sicuro
A voi dà il cornicione,
Da lei prende l'arsura, e le dà il verde.

Despite your wishes
the latest hoer of her sodden fields
wishes to cultivate
the sand under his command.
What say you to that, madam? Does it not seem to you
that he's gone mad through and through?

Marmotta
I do not know what you're saying, and I still cannot see
what he has done, or what's been heaped on me.

Tedeschino
Ah, you do not understand my riddle.
I shall speak more clearly.
In the garden he wishes to water the soil,
and in the hard ground sow a variety of seeds.
Now do you get it?
The prince, not of Fessa but of Morocco,
wants to engage Ancroia in a game of pass-the-baton
and for Filippetta to vouch that the whole thing went on.

Marmotta
What's this about Filippetta, about Fessa, about Morocco?
Oh, do you take me for a fool?

Tedeschino
Alright, now I've got it. I'll put it plainly.
The prince wants to quench his burning desire
in the green fields with Ancroia.
He wants to stick a cornice[151] on your coat of arms,
an embellishment much in vogue
since it's often used to dress up such handiwork.

Marmotta
So he wants to get his greens with Ancroia[152]
and dress her with his cornice?

Tedeschino
For the love of stuffed gourds, yes!
Without a doubt, he's sticking you with the cornice.
She makes him burn, and he gives her the greens.

Le vuol dar la marenda oggi ne l'orto
E di già in ordinanza
Ha messo de la caccia
Il mio Grasso l'insolita pietanza.

Marmotta
Ah dunque Meo, Meo vuole
Banchettar la sua druda nel giardino?
S'egli lo fa, mio danno!
Farò ben tanto, e tanto saprò fare
Che gli farà mal prode il merendare.
Ah prence, prence ingrato,
Ad altra fai banchetto
Di quello ch'a me fai star a stecchetto.
Altra fia che disfame
Di quello che a me fai morir di fame.
Ah quanto meglio fia
Saziar la voglia mia e non altrove
Il tetto racconciar, s'in casa piove.
Dunque ad altra il convito
Fai, mal dispensatore,
Di quel ch'a me non cavi l'appetito?
Ad altra la vivanda
Porgi, che non la chiede,
Per negarla a chi sempre la domanda?
Altrui co' cibi tuoi porgi fortuna,
E me senza cibar lasci digiuna?
Ah Meo, Meo t'arriverò ben io,
Se tu mangi, ch'io possa
Morir sempre di fame e roder l'ossa.

Tedeschino
Non dee la principessa
Col prencipe usar flemma,
Poiché questo saria darli licenza.
Ma con consiglio scaltro,
Per spaventarlo, anch'essa
Provedersi d'amanti,
Poich'un male talor discaccia l'altro
Ed è gentil costume
Di chi regna talor darne al comune,

In the garden he plans to give her a snack,
and following his wish,
from the day's hunt
Grasso has made an unusual dish.

Marmotta
Ah, so Meo, Meo wants
to feast with his hussy in the garden?
Over my dead body!
I'll get him good, I know how to get him yet
so that this evening's snack he'll soon regret.
Ah Prince, ungrateful Prince,
you'd have another dine,
starving me and giving her what's mine?
You'd let another have her fill
of what I starve for, unfulfilled?
Ah, how much better would it be
to satisfy the need in me,
and if at home the rain does pour,
not to plug the roof next door.
You misguided wastrel, you'd have another feast
on what from me you crave the least?
You'd bring another the viands,
though she wants not,
and still deny she who demands?
You'd feed another your riches
while I starve and taste none of your dishes?
Ah Meo, Meo, I'm going to get you.
If you eat, then I will famish,
gnawing on bones until I perish.

Tedeschino
The princess should not
lose her cool with the prince,
since this would give him free license.
Instead, with some shrewd advice
she too should acquire lovers
in order to scare him,
since sometimes two wrongs make a right.
And it is a fine custom for the sovereign
to sometimes share with the common:

Che non spuntano i torti
Le fronti che son grandi,
Né il sol, che chiaro splende,
Benché tra 'l fango sia, macchia v'apprende.
Orsù, spina traversa del mio core,
Febre maligna de la vita mia,
Petecchia del mio volto, mio dolore,
De la gola catarro, e schinanzia,
Lasciami omai fruire,
Lasciami omai godere,
Lasciami omai beare,
Non far, non far che mora
Chi per viver t'adora!
Lasciami nel tuo sen fare il mio letto,
Lascia ch'il petto tuo sia il mio coltrone,
Lascia ch'il matarazzo
De le mie stanche membra
Sia la tua bella imago,
Lasciami riposare in te mezzora,
Poi mandami in malora.

Marmotta
In malora, e in mal punto. Oh vé discorso
Di nudrito asinaccio ne la corte!

Tedeschino
Ah Marmotta, mia anguilla nel vivaio,
Mio pasticcio a l'inglese,
Mia ricotta sfiorita senza sale,
Fa' conto, mio tesoro,
Tu sii la paglia ed io sia l'animale;
Fa' conto ch'io m'annegri
A' rai del tuo bel sole;
Servimi per ombrello
Se non vuoi ch'io stia sempre
In piè senza cappello.

Marmotta
Che vorresti da me? Parlami chiaro.

Tedeschino
Vorrei, dirollo alfine,

since misdeeds cannot trouble
a noble brow,
nor does the brightly shining sun
pick up any stains when it strikes the mud.
Come now, thorn in my heart,
malignant fever of my life,
petechia[153] on my face, my anguish,
phlegm and quinsy[154] in my throat,
let me now take pleasure,
let me now delight,
let me now make merry,
don't let someone die
who lives to adore you!
Let your bosom be my bed,
let your breast be my quilt,
let the mattress
for my tired members
be your beautiful form,
let me rest in you for a spell,
and then tell me to go to hell.

Marmotta
Damn you and your bad timing.
Just listen to the speech of an ass reared at the court!

Tedeschino
Oh Marmotta, my eel in the pond,
my English meat pie,
my spoiled unsalted ricotta.
Just imagine, my darling,
that you're the hay and I the animal.
Just imagine that I'm drowning
in the rays of your beautiful sun.
Act as my umbrella instead
if you don't want me to stand erect
without a hat for my head.

Marmotta
What would you have from me? Speak clearly.

Tedeschino
I would like (at last let it be said!)

Esser del vostro letto le cortine.
Volete voi ch'il dica?
Vorrei da voi signora,
Che mi deste licenza
Ch'io con voi dimorasse una mezzora.

Marmotta
Orsù, taci, t'ho inteso.
Or non è tempo, ch'è tornato il prence.
Tu dici ch'oggi deve
Venire Ancroia in corte.
Vestiti come lei, muta sembiante,
E vien da me sì travestito amante.
Così senza sospetto
Ne la regia entrerai
E sarai la cortina del mio letto.

Tedeschino
Io vado, e travestito
Or or in corte a rivedervi io torno.

Marmotta
Va', ch'io di qua mi parto, e ne la regia
Ti sto attendendo or ora.
Per torlo da la noia
Il Tedeschino è diventato Ancroia.

Scena nona

Catorchia, Scatapocchio

Catorchia
Infine io Filippetta
Adoro, come adora il pesce l'amo,
La gatta il topo, il tordo il teso laccio,
Lo smeriglio la quaglia, il lepre il cane,
La volpe il cacciatore, il gufo il giorno,
L'acqua il villano, il cavalier lo scorno.
Filippetta è il mio letto ove non poso,
Il mio nido, il mio porto,
Ov'erro senza mai giungere in porto.

to be the curtains for your bed.
Do you want me to say it?
Mistress mine, I'd like for you
to give me free leave
to tarry with you a minute or two.

Marmotta
Okay, quiet, I get it.
Now is not the time, for the prince has returned.
You say that today
Ancroia is coming to court?
Dress yourself up like her, change your appearance,
and come to me as a lover so disguised.
And so without suspicion
you shall enter into my palace
and for my bed you'll be the curtain.

Tedeschino
Off I go, and in disguise
I shall hurry back to court to see you again.

Marmotta
Go, for I shall now take my leave
and soon will await you in the palace. [*Tedeschino exits*]
To put an end to this annoyance,
Tedeschino has become Ancroia. [*exits*]

Scene Nine

Catorchia, Scatapocchio

Catorchia
In the end I adore Filippetta
just as a fish adores the hook,
a rat the cat, a thrush the taut trap,
a quail the sparrow hawk, a hare the dog,
a fox the hunter, an owl the day,
a bumpkin water, a gentleman dishonor.
Filippetta is my bed where I do not rest,
my nest, my port,
where I drift and never dock.

Scatapocchio
Io sento, e nel sentir sento, e mi pare
Che tu tutto possiedi, e nulla godi.

Catorchia
Possiedo e non possiedo, amo e non amo.
Ah Filippetta, Filippetta cruda,
Mira dentro il mio seno,
Fatto d'amor la stalla,
Qual son de' lumi tuoi arsa farfalla
Scorgi dentro il mio core
Fatto d'amor lo scudo,
Il tuo ben fatto drudo!
Queste mie gambe arcate
Son di Marte novello
Sotto il peso incurvate
Di trattar some e di portar fardello.

Scatapocchio
Bisogna che l'amore
Sia un pazzo pizzicore.
Vuoi ch'io faccia qualcosa di mia mano?

Catorchia
E che ci vuoi tu fare?
Ella sta qui: chiamarla.
Tu batti Scatapocchio.

Scatapocchio
Tic toc, tic toc, olà di casa.
O la non sente, o ch'ella non è in casa.

Catorchia
Ribussa, Scatapocchio, bussa forte.

Scatapocchio
Tic toc, olà venite a basso,
Se non ch'io rompo l'uscio con un sasso.

Scatapocchio
I feel, and in feeling I sense, and it seems to me,
that you possess everything and enjoy nothing.

Catorchia
I possess and possess not, I love and love not.
Ah Filippetta, cruel Filippetta,
look within my breast,
transformed into love's stable,
at how by your lights I am a moth consumed!
See within my heart,
transformed into love's shield,
how I am your well-formed paramour!
These bowed legs of mine
are of a young Mars,
bent beneath the weight
of bearing his load and carrying his package.

Scatapocchio
Love must be a maddening itch.
Do you want me to take matters
into my own hands?

Catorchia
And what do you want to do about it?
She's here: call her.
Knock, Scatapocchio.

Scatapocchio
Knock, knock, knock. Hey, you at home!
Either she doesn't hear, or she isn't home.

Catorchia
Knock again, Scatapocchio, knock hard.

Scatapocchio
Knock, knock. Hey you, come down
or I'll bust open the door with a stone!

Scena decima

Catorchia, Scatapocchio, Filippetta, Gobbo del violino

Filippetta
Chi batte l'uscio?

Scatapocchio
Son io, che voglio entrare;
E se non apri, getterò per terra
La porta, il chiavistello col battocchio.

Catorchia
Fermati Scatapocchio!

Filippetta
Oh, ve' chi vuol bravare,
Razza di tartaruca.
Se ci calo da basso
Ti ficco con un calce in una buca.

Catorchia
Filippetta, son io, lascialo dire.

Filippetta
Catorchia tu sei tu, or vengo a basso.

Catorchia
Oh come ha fatto Amore
Destarsi in me la febre a la sua vista.

Filippetta
Dov'e questo bravaccio? Oh ve' Catorchio,
Che gran gigante che tu porti teco.

Scatapocchio
Così, come mi vedi,
Non ho bisogno di banchetto a' piedi.

Catorchia
Com'hai sì lungo tempo, Filippetta,

Scene Ten

Catorchia, Scatapocchio, Filippetta, Gobbo of the Violin

Filippetta
Who's knocking on the door? [*from the window*]

Scatapocchio
It's me, and I want to come in!
If you don't open up, I'll break down the door,
deadbolt, knocker, and all.[155]

Catorchia
Cut it out, Scatapocchio.

Filippetta
Oh, look who's grandstanding,
you turtle.
If I have to come down there,
I'm going to ram my heel up your hole.

Catorchia
Filippetta, it's me. Let him speak.

Filippetta
Catorchia, it's you. I'm coming down now.

Catorchia
Oh how Love has aroused
a fever in me at just the sight of her.

Filippetta [*at the door*]
Where is that hotshot? Oh look, Catorchio,
what a great big giant you've brought with you.[156]

Scatapocchio
Indeed, as you can see,
I have no need for a stool beneath me.

Catorchia
How have you gone so long, Filippetta,

Sofferto a non vedere il tuo Catorchio?
Deh, per tua fé, mia Filippetta bella,
Fa' conto ch'io sia un soldo,
E mettimi pian piano
Con le tue belle mani a la scarsella.

Scatapocchio
Fa' conto, Filippetta,
Ch'egli sia il tordo, e tu sii la civetta.

Filippetta
Catorchio, vuoi tu nulla, io ho che fare?

Catorchia
Deh Filippetta cara,
Non lasciar che si perda la semente
De' Catorchi nel mondo.

Filippetta
Che vorresti da me?

Catorchia
Vorrei, se ti contenti, starmi teco
A magniar un cantuccio, e ber del greco.

Filippetta
Va' torna, come Ancroia
Va' a desinar da Meo, e Scatapocchio
Conduci teco, che con l'uno e l'altro
Vuò che giochiamo al tiro nel giardino.
A Dio, mio Catorchino.

Gobbo del violino
Oh ve' che bella coppia!
Filippetta, che forse hai nimicizia
Che si ben sei provista di giganti?

Catorchia
Che fa quivi il Trafedi?
Oh Gobbo sciagurato.
Che forse, Filippetta,

without seeing your Catorchia?
Oh, by your faith, Filippetta my pretty,
just pretend that I am a coin
and with your lovely hands
slip me nice and slow into your satchel.

Scatapocchio
Pretend, Filippetta,
that he is the blackbird and you the owlet.

Filippetta
Catorchia, what do you want from me?

Catorchia
Oh dear Filippetta,
do not allow the seed of the Catorchi
to go lost in the world.

Filippetta
What would you like from me?

Catorchia
I would like, if you please, for you to stay with me
to nibble on a cantuccio[157] and sip some Greco.

Filippetta
Go on ahead and take Scatapocchio with you,
for Ancroia is going to dine with Meo,
and I'd like to play tug-o-war
with you both in the garden.
Farewell, my lil' Catorchin.

Gobbo of the Violin [*enters*]
Oh, look what a nice couple!
Filippetta, perhaps you're involved in some feud,
since you're so well-stocked in giants?

Catorchia
What is Trafedi[158] doing here?
Oh Gobbo, you wretch!
Perhaps, Filippetta,

Apprendi da costui
A portar polli fuori del mercato?

Scatapocchio
Oh l'è il Gobbo Trafila
Che torce senza fuso l'altrui fila.

Gobbo del violino
Che dici, sconciatura d'una botta?
Nanaccio male in piedi,
Se ti piglio co' calci,
Ti fo levar di qui senza i tuoi piedi.

Catorchia
A chi dici, Gobbaccio?
Qui tu non hai che fare.
Non v'è nessun che si voglia arruffare.
Oh bell'uomo di corte,
Spacciare il sonator di violino
E senza morti fare altrui becchino.

Gobbo del violino
Oh malfatto gigante,
Va', va', va', fa' l'amore con la fante.
Oh ve' chi fa l'Adone,
Balordo animaletto da stidone!

Filippetta
Catorchia, oh via, non più, lascialo dire!
Ogniun deve adattarsi
Per poter sostentarsi,
E poi non è difetto
In un che sa sonare
Il saper dar lezione di cornetto.

Catorchia
A Dio, Filippetta, adesso, adesso,
Ritorniamo da te, mettiti in punto.
Va', va', Gobbaccio, va',
Va', porta i polli in là.

you're learning from him
how to peddle chicks at the market?[159]

Scatapocchio
Oh, that is Gobbo Trafila[160]
who, without a spindle of his own, twists together others' threads.

Gobbo of the Violin
What are you trying to say, you misshapen toad,
you bumbling little dwarf?
With one good kick
I'll send you flying right off your feet.

Catorchia
Who are you talking to, you damned hunchback?
You have no business here.
None of us wants to be pimped out.
Get rid of this violin player,
my fine courtier,
and bury him alive.

Gobbo of the Violin
Oh, you deformed giant,
go on, go make love with that servant.
Oh, just look who's acting like an Adonis,
silly little animal fit to be skewered!

Filippetta
That's enough, Catorchia, let him speak!
We must all adapt
in order to support ourselves.
And besides, it's hardly worthy of scorn
if one who knows how to play
can give lessons on the horn.[161]

Catorchia
Farewell, Filippetta, and get ready,
for we will return to you quickly.
Go, go, you nasty hunchback, vamoose,
go on, bring the chickens home to roost. [*exits*]

Scatapocchio
Io no, non vuò tornare,
Che non vuò che vi sia qualche pantano
Ov'io portassi rischio d'affogare.

Filippetta
A Dio tutti, a Dio tutti, a Dio Trafedi,
A rivederci poi:
Lor non san quel che passa fra di noi.

Gobbo del violino
A Dio, Filippetta,
Non ti scordar del gioco di civetta.

Scena undecima

Tedeschino ***vestito d'Ancroia***

Tedeschino
Ve' come per l'appunto
Il vestito d'Ancroia mi s'adatta.
Infine Amore è quello
Che fa fare ogni cosa,
E a' matti, e a' savi toglie anco il cervello.
Un che sia innamorato
Per aver quel che brama
Ad ogni atto più vile accomodato
Ha l'animo il pensiero, e per amore
Farebbe il birro, il boia, e l'appiccato.
In me ecco l'effetto più d'ogni altro.
Io, che sempre sul grave
Da cavalier di scherzo ne la corte
Mi trattenni famoso!
Io, che di maggior prenci lo statista
Fui con tanto mio vanto,
E ad ogni potentato
Imparai di politica il donato!
Or per man d'un arciero
Muto voce, sembiante, opra, e mestiero.
D'Ancroia invece or ora

Scatapocchio
Not I, I don't want to return,
for I don't want to plunge into some morass
in which I might drown. [*exits*]

Filippetta
Farewell to all, farewell to all. Farewell Trafedi,
until we meet again.
They don't know what goes on between us.

Gobbo of the Violin
Farewell, Filippetta,
don't forget our little game of hide-and-seek.[162] [*they exit*]

Scene Eleven

Tedeschino *dressed as Ancroia*

Tedeschino
Yes indeed, look how well
Ancroia's dress suits me.
In the end, love makes us
willing to do anything,
and robs both the mad and the wise of their wits.
To obtain that for which he yearns,
a man in love
is willing to perform
even the vilest of acts,
and for love would be the bailiff, the executioner, and the hanged.
I am more affected than any other.
I, who in the solemn affair
of being the cavalier of jest at court
have always maintained my fame!
I, who, much to my credit,
was to the greatest princes a statesman,
and to every potentate
taught the ABC's of politics![163]
And now by the archer's[164] hand,
of voice, appearance, craft, and deed I've lost all command.
In the guise of Ancroia instead I wish

Entrar io voglio in corte
E con la principessa
Per questa via tentare
Di languir sempre per non più penare.
E s'io donna pur fossi,
Quanti, quanti merlotti
Avrei pigliato nel mio serbatoio.
In mia fé, ch'in tal'abito
Mi par più grazioso comparire.
Con questi occhi furbeschi
Sembro dardo de' cori;
Con queste labra orlate
Sembro de la mezzina di Cupido
La più sdrucita bocca.
Con questo curvo naso
Di Vener sono il naspo;
La diradata fronte
Gallinaio è d'amore;
Infin questa mia vita sì ben fatta,
Se, qual'uom son io, fossi una donna
De le gioie amorose
Sarei la più ben fatta e bella gonna.
Ah Marmotta, Marmotta, quanto meglio
T'era non così farmi a te venire.
Forse, se m'aspettavi a te davante
Di Tedeschino in forma,
Non così tosto divenivi amante.
Ma in questo abito a fé,
Che tu ci cadi affatto,
Ed io son di Marmotta fatto il re.
In Licia ancor Achille
Portò fra le donzelle
Abiti femminili,
E pur alfin mandò Troia in faville.
Ed Ercole con Iole
E con Onfale stette
A tessere, e filare
Or un manto, or un velo,
E pur con le sue spalle
Fu buon fachino a sostenere il cielo.

to enter the court right away
and with the princess
endeavor in this way
to languish evermore so as to not suffer anymore.
And if I really were a woman,
just think how many gulls
I would have trapped in my pantry!
Upon my word, in such a dress
I think I cut an even finer figure.
With these sly eyes,
I look like a dart of the heart;
with these lined lips,
I look like the glazed mouth
of Cupid's pitcher;
with this curved nose,
I am Venus's spinning wheel;
my plucked brow
is the roost of Love;
and finally, my waist is so well-shaped
that if I were a woman of amorous delights,
instead of the man that I am,
I would be the prettiest and most well-made skirt of them all.
Oh Marmotta, Marmotta, it would have been better
if you hadn't made me come to you like this.
If you were to see me before you
in the guise of Tedeschino,
perhaps you wouldn't so readily become my lover.
But with me in this dress, I swear,
you will fall head over heels,
and I of Marmotta will be the king.
In Lycia even Achilles
amongst the ladies
wore women's dresses
and in the end still set Troy ablaze.[165]
And with Iole and Omphale
Hercules stayed,
weaving and spinning,
now a mantle, now a veil,[166]
and yet upon his own shoulders
held up the heavens like a fine porter.[167]

Scena duodecima

Meo, Tedeschino ***d'Ancroia***

Meo
Oh ecco a punto la mia bella Ancroia.

Tedeschino
Oh fortuna malvaggia, che sarà?
Amore, aiuto, Amore, io son già perso.

Meo
Ancroia, anima mia, come cotanto
Sei tardata a venir dal tuo bel Meo?

Tedeschino
Ah Cupido cornuto, e che farò?

Meo
Ancroia, a che così? Con chi raggioni?
Perché da me ti scosti, e par che fuggi?
Vien qua, vien qua cattiva. Ah tu conosci
Ch'è dato il fringuellone ne la ragna.
Fatti più qua, che fai? Oh via, non più!
Traditora sì sì; così si fa?
Adesso che tu vedi
Ch'io non ti voglio male
Mi fai il grugno di porco, e 'l pelapiedi.

Tedeschino
Eh lasciatimi stare! Ho altro umore.
Nel venire a la reggia a me qui presso
S'è sciolta de la testa la correggia.

Meo
Che correggia? Vien qua, vien qua balorda,
Ch'io ti darò 'na stringa d'allacciarti.

Tedeschino
Sì, buono, buono, mi è successo peggio.

Scene Twelve

Meo, Tedeschino *dressed as Ancroia*

Meo
Ah, here now is my lovely Ancroia.

Tedeschino [*aside*]
Oh cursed luck, what does he want?
Love, help me. Love, I'm finished.

Meo
Ancroia, my soul, why did you tarry so
to come to your handsome Meo?

Tedeschino [*aside*]
Ah you cuckold Cupid, what am I going to do?

Meo
Ancroia, what's this? Who are you talking to?
Why do you pull away from me and seem to flee?
Come here, come here, naughty girl.
Ah, you know who's getting a big fat finch in her net.
Come a bit closer, what are you doing? Oh, come on, cut it out!
Oh, I see, you little tease,
so this is how it's going to be?
Now that you see that I wish you no ill,
you scowl and treat me like a scoundrel.

Tedeschino
Hey, leave me alone! I'm not in the mood.
While I was coming here to the palace,
the band around my head came undone.

Meo
What band? Come here, come here, silly girl,
I'll give you a rope you can wrap yourself up with.

Tedeschino
Yes, fine, fine. It got even worse.

Meo
E che mai t'è successo? Dillo a Meo!

Tedeschino
Lingua aiuitati, a fé, che n'hai bisogno!
Quando che serrai l'uscio de la porta
Vi serrai dentro mezza la gonnella.
Guardate, l'è stracciata, e senza coda!

Meo
E questo ancora è nulla; se non vuoi
Altro che far la coda a la gonnella,
Io te ne voglio fare una più bella.

Tedeschino
E pur lì ci vuol altro.
Se tu sapessi quel che m'è accaduto
Non scherzeresti meco così franco!

Meo
Che diavolo mai t'è succeduto?

Tedeschino
Tra via diedi in un sasso, e caddi in terra
Con tutta la persona,
E mi squarciò la bocca la pianella.

Meo
Mostra dove l'hai rotta. Ancroia, Ancroia,
Dove fuggi? Vien qua, mostra la bocca.
Oh ve' che ritrovata!
Tu non vuoi esser tocca?

Tedeschino
Deh, prence, per tua fé, lasciami stare.
Chi cerca, talor trova
Quel che forse non brama di trovare.

Meo
Io son fuor di me stesso. Ingrata, è forse
Questo tuo tiro per strapazzar Meo?

Meo
And what happened to you? Tell Meo everything!

Tedeschino
[*aside*] (Tongue, do your best, since I swear you'll need it!)
When I shut the door of the gate
half of my skirt got caught inside.
Look, here it is, torn and with no train!

Meo
But that's still no big deal.
If all you want is to stick a tail on that dress,
I can give you an even finer one.

Tedeschino
[*aside*] (And yet it will take more than that!)
If you only knew what happened to me,
you wouldn't tease me so freely!

Meo
What the devil happened to you?

Tedeschino
On the way over I tripped on a rock
and fell flat on the ground
and busted my mouth with my shoe.

Meo
Show me where you split it open. Ancroia, Ancroia!
Where are you going? Come here, show us your mouth.
I swear, what a faker!
You don't want be touched?

Tedeschino
Oh, Prince, for the love of God, leave me alone.
He who seeks shall sometimes find
things he'd rather not.

Meo
I'm losing my mind. You ungrateful woman,
is this perhaps a trick of yours to injure Meo?

Io, che tanto t'ho amata,
Io, che ti diedi tanto gusto a caccia,
Io, che meco a banchetto t'ho invitata,
Devi trattar così? Va' via vaccaccia,
Che forse fra quei corni
A me più mansueta fia che torni!

Scena decimaterza

Baldassarre, Meo, Tedeschino, Croatto

Croatto
Badrona, mirar Ancroia e 'l brincipo!
Che voltar, che fuggire?
Fermare, non partire!

Baldassarre
Non es possibiles,
Sì pares, non creo di veser:
Creo m'aglegar mas erea.
Eglia has como fusse queglia.
Infame, mal nassida,
Piccherona, hoi mui tiempo granchiado
Puor hazerte bien.
Mandil de la cuerte,
Lavandiera de la comunitades,
Glievares quattros cosses y dos buffettas.

Tedeschino
Piano, piano, col dare! Oh ve' spagnolo!
Insolentaccio! Oh ve' quanta superbia!

Croatto
Risbettar veramente
Per ti dover la brincipessa Ancroia,
Che de l'onora e de la nobiltata
Un quarta ha boste in Fessa, e l'adra in Troia.

Tedeschino
Infin questi don Corni,

This is how you treat me? Me, who have loved you so,
me, who during the hunt gave you such delight,
me, who invited you to feast in my company?
Get out of here, you filthy cow,
maybe once you're between those other horns
you'll come back to me a little tamer!

Scene Thirteen

Baldassarre, Meo, Tedeschino, Croatto

Croatto
Master, look at Ancroia and the *b*rince!
Why turn away, why flee?
Stop, don't leave!

Baldassarre
No es posible!
It looks like her, though I can't believe my eyes.
I think I'll go in for a closer look.[168]
She sure acts like her.
You hussy, you tramp, you *picarona*!
For too long I've clawed away
to treat you *bien*.
Curse of fortune,
lowly washing wench,
now you'll get my fist and foot! [*beats Tedeschino*]

Tedeschino
Watch it with those blows! Look here, Spaniard!
Insolent wretch! Oh, look what arrogance!

Croatto
Truly you must be res*b*ected
by *b*rincess Ancroia,
whose honor and nobility
comes one fourth from Fessa, the rest from Troy.[169]

Tedeschino
At the end of the day, if you give these Don Hornies

Come che se le da tantin di dito,
Si pigliano la man con tutto il braccio.
Smerdarol d'Avicenna,
Più non son calamar de la tua penna.

Meo
Guarda come tu tratti!
Non hai a far con matti!
Oh ve' ch'impertinenza!
Sfacciato, hai tanto ardir in mia presenza?

Baldassarre
Y tu, principe de cuerno,
Borroccio, cuero, cavronasso,
Tales pagas havereis,
Como eglia ha recebido.
Toma esta a buena cuenta, [*fa finta di darli*]
A memoria de los servisios.
Toma esta otra, begliacco, begliaccone,
Prencipe de mierda.

Meo
A me, a me, forfante, a me si dà?
Oh guardia, oh guardia, corri,
Corri, oh guardia! Che fai? Corri, vien qua!

Baldassarre
A ti, a ti, a ti,
Puerco, picaro, lovo.

Meo
Ah, spagnolo marrano,
Ti vuò far appiccar per una mano.

Scena decimaquarta

Michelino, Gobbo, Pedina, e li medesimi

Michelino
Ferme, ferme, fermate furfantascie.

so much as an inch,
they'll take a mile.
Avicenna's shit-scraper,[170]
I'm no longer the inkwell for your pen.

Meo
Watch what you're saying!
You're not dealing with some stooge!
Oh, what impertinence!
You fraud, how dare you have such nerve in my presence?

Baldassarre
And you, *príncipe* of horns,
you drunk, you sot, you son-of-a-bitch,
the payment you'll receive
will be equal to hers.
Take this fine bill [*pretends to give it to him*]
for services rendered.
Take this one too, you bum, you good-for-nothing,
you *príncipe de mierda.*

Meo
To me, to me, you thug, you're giving it to me?
Guards, oh guards, come quick!
Hurry, guards! What are you doing? Run quick, come here!

Baldassarre
Take this, take this, take that,
puerco, pícaro, lobo.

Meo
Ah, you *marrano* from Spain,
I'll have you strung up by one hand.[171]

Scene Fourteen

Michelino, Gobbo, Pedina and the same

Michelino
Stop *zis*, stop *zis*, stop, you thugs!

Baldassarre
Mi has faltado mi dama.
Toma esta, toma est'otra.

Michelino
Voler al nostre prenscie
Rompere le mostascie.

Pedina
Oh spagnol senza fede,
Questa è la riverenza
Che verso il signor nostra si richiede?

Gobbo
Oh ve' questo nemico
De la carne di porco!
Schernir così Marocco?
Fermati, morescaccio senza fede,
Ti vuò far strangolare per un piede.

Michelino
Pedina, dascie. Dascie, Gobbo, dascie.
Spasciacamine de la merdarole,
Ti vuò far impiccare per le gole.

Tedeschino
Oh che venga la peste
A chi mi diè tal veste.
Oh pover Tedeschino:
Fermati Michelino!

Michelino
Oh questo non è Ancroia, è Tedeschine.
Oh brutte furfantascie, come sta?
Tarantan tarantan, tarantan, ta, ta.

Gobbo
Oh brutta Ancroia, oh fetido barone.
Oh guarda il bel politico buffone.

Baldassarre
You have taken my *dama* from me.
Take this, and that! [*beats Meo*]

Michelino
You *v*ant to smash in
zee snout of our prince?

Pedina
Oh you godless Spaniard,
is this the kind of reverence
our lord is due? [*beats Baldassarre*]

Gobbo
Oh look at this enemy
of pig's meat!
Mock Morocco in this way?
Stop, you lousy godless Moor.
I'll have you hanged by one foot.[172] [*beats Baldassarre*]

Michelino
Give it to 'em, Pedina! Let 'em have it, Gobbo!
You shit packer,
I'll have you hanged by *zee* *z*roat.

Tedeschino
A plague upon the one
who gave me such a gown.
Oh, poor Tedeschino!
Cut it out, Michelino!

Michelino
Oh, but *z*is is not Ancroia, *z*is is Tedeschino!
Ugly *v*retch, how can *z*is be?
Taran-tan-ta, taran-tan-tee.

Gobbo
Oh ugly Ancroia, oh stinking idiot.
Check out this fine political buffoon!

Baldassarre
Mires che linda Ancroia,
Puerco desvergonzado.

Croatto
Oh quanta per ti degna di star fatta.
Vere donne per ti per man d'un gatta.

Meo
Oh Tedeschin statista,
Tu fai la bella vista?

Pedina
Oh proprii di barone,
Oh degni di castigo,
Sciocchi andamenti, ed insolenti fatti:
Convengon piattonate a leccapiatti.

Tedeschino
Io me ne vuò fuggire.
Maladetta Marmotta e 'l travestire.

Michelino
Toffi, taffe, briccone.

Gobbo
Gli sian le scosse a furia radoppiate,
Seguitiamolo a suon di piattonate.

Croatto
Badrona, a chisda mala,
Per ti e per mi fuggire la malora.

Baldassarre
Un bel fuggir toda la vida onora.

Baldassarre
Look, what a lovely Ancroia,
you shameless *puerco*.

Croatto
How *b*erfect this is for you.
A real woman by your own cat's *b*aw.[173]

Meo
Oh statesman Tedeschino,
you're the good-looker?

Pedina
Oh, what a bunch of idiots,
oh, they deserve to be punished
such foolish deeds and insolent acts:
these moochers need a good smack.

Tedeschino
I'm going to make a break for it!
Damn Marmotta and this disguise.

Michelino
Wham! Bam! You rascal!

Gobbo
Let our fury rain down upon him,
let's chase him away to the sounds of our blows. [*they exit*]

Croatto
Master, this is quite a jam.
Best for you and me to scram.

Baldassarre
A good escape honors one's whole life.[174] [*they exit*]

Atto terzo

Scena prima

Michelino, Mantuano

Michelino [*uscirà cantando queste parole*]
Oh calde pasticcie uscite dal forne
Con dieci fiaschi de vin del miglior,
Acciò ch'a l'odor il mi nase s'arriccie.
Oh calde pasticcie, oh calde pasticcie.
Trandira, trandira, trandira trà trà.
Buone piscione arroste, arroste allesse,
Vitelle, fegatelle, e buon pulpette,
Sanguinascie, salciscie, e scervellate,
Quattre pollastre fritte a la padelle,
Un buon fiasche di Greghe, e du frittate;
Andare a trovar grasse coche, e coche grasse,
E dir che cutte in stufe, e corve allesse,
Gatti in le padelle, e tope arroste,
Cornacchioni in teame, e 'n gelatine,
Le civette col grasse de cucine.

Mantuano
Padrone, andiame, che fra di mezzora
Meo vuol desinar con la signora.

Michelino
Andiame Mantuane,
Marmotte sta disciune
E Ancroia nel sciardine
Con le sue belle trude pranserà.
Ancroia ha 'l tope, e Marmotte non l'ha.
Trandirà, trandirà, trandirà trà.

Mantuano
Padrone, andiame via.
Troppe il principe nostre
Di giocare a civette ha fantasie.

Act Three

Scene One

Michelino, Mantuano

Michelino [*comes out singing these words*]
Oh, varm *pies straight from* zee *oven*
vis *ten flasks of* zee *best* vine,
such zat *my nose perks up at* zee *smell.*
Oh varm *pies, oh* varm *pies,*
tra-la-la, tra-la-la.
Good roasted pigeons, roasted boiled meats,
veal, liver, *und* good meatballs,
black pudding, sausage, *und* hare-brains,
four pan-fried hens,
a good flask of Greco *und* two fritters.
Go find some big *und* juicy eggs,
und say *zat* zere are fricasseed *v*agtails *und* boiled crows,
cats in *zee* pans, *und* roasted rats,
crows in the fryer *und* in gelatin,
zee owlettes in grease from *zee* kitchen.

Mantuano
Master, let's go, for in half an hour
Meo wants to dine with the lady.

Michelino
Let's go, Mantuano,
Marmotta is fasting
but Ancroia *v*ill soon be dining
vis her handsome lover in *zee* garden.
Ancroia has *zee* mouse, *und* Marmotta has none.
Tra-la-la, tra-la-la, tra-la-la, dum-dum.

Mantuano
Master, let us be gone.
Our prince has big plans to play
a game of hide-*und*-go-seek.[175] [*they exit*]

Scena seconda

Masino, Tordo

Masino
Tordo, vedesti tu con qual rispetto
Al nome di Marmotta Baldassarre
Si mostrò riverente ad ubedire?
È un garbato par suo, per vita mia.
E par che fra di loro
Vi sia di sangue qualche simpatia.

Tordo
Certo, ch'io ne restai tutto confuso,
Credevo che 'sta bestia
Non servissi per altro che per smorfie,
E che sol ne la corte
Egli sapessi fare
Una boccaccia, una risata a ufo,
Un dar nel ravanicco,
Uno star sempre teso col palicco,
Ma vedo ch'egli è buono in ogni cosa!
Vuoi ch'io ti dica? Stimo che costoro
Faccino il pazzo per far pazzo altrui.

Masino
Purtroppo è vero, Tordo;
Via, Baldassar da noi si lasci stare.
Ma il Tedeschin, che cosa serve in corte?

Tordo
A dir mal di qualcuno, et in tinello
Mangiar a ufo senza discrizione.

Masino
Gli è un pan perso da vero; ei non è buono
Se non a far lo sciocco di politica.

Tordo
Sicuro, che politica migliore
Non si può trovar di questa sua,

Scene Two

Masino, Tordo

Masino
Tordo, did you see how
at the mere mention of Marmotta's name
Baldassarre showed himself ready to obey?
Upon my life, he is as genteel as she,
it's almost as if they share in their blood
some kind of affinity.

Tordo
Indeed, it got me all confused.
I had thought that the damn beast
was only good for making faces,
and that at court
he only knew how to mock,
to laugh at another's expense,
to make an ass out of himself,
to live hand to mouth.
But now I see that he is good at everything!
Shall I tell you? I think that these guys
play the fool to make fools out of others.

Masino
Sadly it's true, Tordo.
Enough, let's leave Baldassarre be.
But what of Tedeschino? What use is he at court?

Tordo
To speak ill of others, and to shamelessly
mooch food in the servants' quarters.

Masino
He truly is a lost cause: he's only good at playing
the dimwit of diplomacy.

Tordo
Surely, for no better diplomacy
can be found than his:

Bere, mangiar, vestire, e a l'altrui spese
Fare il cavallerazzo pe'l paese.

Masino
E sai come si gonfia e come sbuffa?
Ei pare una gallina mantoana.
A fé, a fé, che s'avesse a far io
O vorrei che facesse da buffone,
O mandarlo al barone.

Tordo
Che vuoi fare? Oggidì questo mestiero
A segno s'è ridotto,
Che tanto val l'astuto che 'l balordo.

Masino
L'è una bell'arte, a fé.
Da Masino ti giuro
Ch'io cambierei il mio stato col buffone.

Tordo
Ed io prima di te lo cambierei:
Che fatica si sente
In fare una risata, in motteggiare,
Far con una boccaccia un viso arcigno,
Pigliare una chitarra, e schitarrare,
Dir quattro sfiondature a la spagnola,
Accomodarsi sempre a l'altrui voglie,
Se quegli dice sì, dir sì due volte,
Se no, non sia; e sempre su lo scherzo,
Mostrar di piccardia aver bei motti:
Questi son ne la corte i cortegiani,
Che fan gli altri merlotti.

Masino
Veramente l'è un'arte benedetta.
Ma sai cos'è, ch'io non vi ho quel talento
Che vi bisognerebbe, e tu ci avresti,
Che, se ciò fosse, a fé ch'il segretario
Altri farebbe in corte.

to drink, to eat, to dress, and at someone else's expense
to play the highfalutin cavalier about town.

Masino
And you know how he puffs himself up and struts around?
He looks like a Mantuan hen!
I swear, if it were up to me,
I'd either have him play the buffoon
or send him to the devil.

Tordo
What can you do? Nowadays this profession
has been reduced to the point
that a shrewd man is worth as much as a fool.

Masino
I say, it sure is a fine art.
Speaking as Masino, I swear
I'd gladly swap places with the buffoon.

Tordo
I'd be the first to swap places!
What's so hard about
getting laughs, cracking jokes,
twisting your face into a scowl,
grabbing a guitar and hacking away at it,
telling a couple tall tales in the Spanish style,
always bending to another's whims,
saying yes twice over if that one says yes,
letting it all go with a laugh if he says no,
and showing off your gallows humor?[176]
At court such are the courtiers
who make the others look like suckers.

Masino
Truly it is a blessed art.
But you know what the problem is?
I just don't have the talent, though you do.
But if I did, I swear that someone else
would be the secretary at court.

Tordo
Ed io, se qual hai tu la vista avessi,
Vorrei ch'il consigliero altri facesse.
Nel dir non ho paura. Io so sonare,
So ballar, so cantare, e mi s'avviene
Il far ridere altrui con belle botte.
Sai che cosa non ho? La complessione
Assuefatta a star sempre imbriaco,
Oltre che non so nulla in medicina,
Né saperei mai fare
Altri e me vacuare;
E ancor sono ignorante
De la ragion di stato, e non so come
Tratti de la politica il buario!
Non no, meglio è ch'io stia fra le due acque,
Così son consigliero, e appresso il prence
Nome ho di bell'umore e di faceto.

Masino
Eh Tordo, il star così non ti può dare
Quello che ti darebbe esser in tutto
Ne la corte buffone, e non a mezzo.
Tu dici che non sai far cosa alcuna?
Non sai tu far gli occhiali?
Io veggio pur che tu n'hai tanti attorno
Che pari l'occhialaio del comune.

Tordo
Sì, so fare una zucca.
Che credi, che gli occhiali
Ch'io vendo siano fatti di mia mano?

Masino
E chi dunque li fa? Io sempre tenni
Che tu di tal mestier fossi inventore!

Tordo
Oh buono. Masino, è questo mondo
Una palla, che chi non sa sbalzarla
La caccia perde, ed il suo colpo falla.
Sai tu sotto gli offici,

Tordo
And if I had your looks
I'd want someone else to be the advisor.
I have no fear of speaking, I know how to dance,
I know how to play music and to sing,
and I have a knack for making others laugh with a few good blows.
Say, you know what I don't have?
The strung-out constitution for always being drunk,
and, besides, I don't know a thing about medicine,
and I have no idea how to make
myself and others defecate.
I'm also ignorant about the reason of state,[177]
and I know as much about politics
as some country bumpkin!
No, no, better that I keep a foot in both camps.
This way I'm an advisor, and when I'm with the prince
I maintain my reputation for wit and good humor.

Masino
Hey, Tordo, this stance can't give you what you'd get
by being a complete buffoon at court
instead of a half-assed one.
You're saying you don't know how to do anything?
Don't you know how to make glasses?[178]
I see that you have so many of them lying about
that you look like the town optician.

Tordo
Oh, sure! I don't know how to make squat.
What do you think, that the glasses
that I sell are made by my own two hands?

Masino
So who makes them then?
I always thought you invented that trade!

Tordo
Oh, that's a good one! Masino, this world is a bullet,
and if you don't know how to shoot
you lose your prey and miss the mark.
You know those Armenians

Che vi son quelli armeni?
Da lor compro gli occhiali,
E poi per miei li vendo
A chi per miei li tiene. Oh ch'animali!

Masino
Infatti dice il vero.
Non luce senza truffa alcun mestiero.
Oh ve' come s'ingannan le persone!
Che tu sii per gli occhiali
Il primo uomo del mondo è l'opinione.

Tordo
L'opinion fa caso
Ed oggidì gli è sciocco
Colui ch'altrui non sa menar pe'l naso.

Masino
Or tira dunque avante.
Ma, per tornare a nostro,
Sai che cosa farei s'io fossi Tordo?

Tordo
E che cosa faresti? Dillo un poco.

Masino
Io vorrei congegnare
Di fare un occhialone
Ch'avessi il fondo, e sopra il sfogatoio;
E perché dici che sempre embriaco
Vuole stare il buffone,
Acciò ch'il vino non mi fessi male,
Di quel mi servirei per serviziale!
Così vacuerei
E se bevuto avessi il renderei.

Tordo
A fé, che tu non l'hai pensata male.
Oh che ti pigli il granchio!
Quel che serve per meglio veder lume
Vuoi che serva per l'occhio del lordume?

under the Uffizi?
I buy glasses from them
and then sell them as my own
to whoever takes them to be mine. Oh, what brutes!

Masino
Isn't that the truth!
Every trade has its tricks.
See how easily people are fooled!
Everyone thinks that when it comes to glasses
you're number one in the world.

Tordo
Reputation seals the deal,
and nowadays so it goes
that you're a fool if you can't lead another by the nose.

Masino
Let's move on.
Getting back to the subject at hand,
do you know what I'd do if I were Tordo?

Tordo
And what would you do? Let's hear a little.

Masino
I'd like to design a telescope[179]
that would have a bottom
and a vent on top.
And since you say that the buffoon
always wants to be sloshed,
I'd use it as an enema tube
so the wine wouldn't impair me!
This way I would void
and give back the drink I had enjoyed.

Tordo
I swear, you've really thought this through, haven't you?
You're fooling yourself!
The thing that serves to better see the light
you'd instead use as a shithole?

E poi, come vuoi tu ch'in medicina
Io operi se non ho mai medicato?

Masino
Ch'importa il medicar? Non sta al sapere!
Da medico puoi far senza paura,
S'il medicare è dato
A chi sa far morire un ammalato.

Tordo
A la ragion di stato, che dirai?

Masino
A la ragion di stato,
Come non vuoi sapere
Più di quel che ne sappia il Tedeschino,
Non t'affannar di rimesciar le carte;
Anzi, quanto più asino sarai
Tanto più 'l Tedeschin somiglierai!

Tordo
Masino, fallo tu, ch'a fé ti giuro,
Ch'hai viso di buffone,
Bocca di Baldassarre,
Vita del Tedeschino,
E senza tua fatica
Par sempre che t'agranchi e facci smorfie.
Credi a Tordo, Masino,
Piglia il lor posto in corte,
E poi di' che ti passi
Lo Spagnol con le smorfie
E con ragion di stato il Tedeschino.

Masino
Tu vuoi la burla, Tordo:
Come vuoi tu ch'io faccia da buffone?
Bisogna aver gran ciarle, ed io la lingua
Non ho staccata ancora dal filello.

Tordo
Orsù, lasciamo il posto a chi lo vuole,
Facciam l'officio nostro, e già che s'usa

And anyway, how do you think I could work in medicine
if I've never even played doctor?

Masino

What does doctoring matter? There's nothing to know.
You can be a doctor without fear,
since doling out medicine is the schtick
of he who knows how to kill the sick.

Tordo

As for the reason of state, what say you?

Masino

As for the reason of state,
since you don't care to know
more about it than Tedeschino does,
don't bother reshuffling the cards.
To the contrary, the more you act the ass,
the more for Tedeschino you shall pass!

Tordo

Masino, you do it, for in truth I swear,
that you have a buffoon's face,
Baldassarre's mouth,
Tedeschino's bearing,
and without any effort
you are always contorting and grimacing.
Masino, listen to Tordo,
snatch up their place at court,
and then announce that you surpass
the Spaniard in grimaces
and the Little German[180] in the reason of state.

Masino

You're teasing me, Tordo.
How do you expect me to play the buffoon?
One needs a loose tongue,
and mine has yet to detach from the frenulum.[181]

Tordo

Come, let's leave the position to someone wants it.
Let's do our job, and since it's in vogue

Il far l'omo faceto, ancora noi
Facciam ridere altrui.
Andianne a ritrovar la principessa
Per dirle quel che disse Baldassarre.

Scena terza

Ancroia, Gobbo del violino detto Trafedi

Ancroia
Or ora ne la regia
Andar me n' voglio a ritrovare il prence
Ma la mi par pur dura.
L'aver a far con prenci
È fuor del mio mestiero.
Infatti son baiate,
Chi nacque per l'aratro
Malamente s'adatta al cavaliero.
Ma ve', ecco il Trafedi!

Gobbo del violino
Ancroia, dove vai così allindata?

Ancroia
Ne la regia da Meo a merendare.

Gobbo del violino
A merendar da Meo? Che non sai nulla?
Quell'impertinenton del Tedeschino
Con le tue proprie vesti in vece tua
V'andò poco anzi, ed è di già scoperta
La mal tessuta tela al'altrui danno.
Tutti non son Trafedi.
Com'io non v'ho le mani,
Ogni cosa a la peggio, tu lo vedi.

Ancroia
E come il Tedeschino? Oh, buffonaccio!
Che non gli basta di mal contrafare
Il gentilomo in corte,

to play the witty fellow,
we too can make others laugh.
Let's go find the princess
to tell her what Baldassarre said. [*they exit*]

Scene Three

Ancroia and Gobbo of the Violin, also known as Trafedi

Ancroia
I'd like to go to the palace
straightaway to find the prince,
though I bet it will be tough.
Dealing with princes
is not my area of expertise.
In fact it's such a joke:
one born for the plow
is poorly suited for a cavalier.
But look, here's Trafedi!

Gobbo of the Violin [*enters*]
Ancroia, where are you headed so dolled up?

Ancroia
To Meo's palace to have a little snack.

Gobbo of the Violin
To snack at Meo's? Haven't you heard?
A little while ago that insolent twerp Tedeschino
went there in your place and dressed in your clothes,
and the tangled web he spun to trap another
has now been unraveled.
Not everyone is like Trafedi.
Since I haven't a hand in this,
everything's gone from bad to worse, as you can see.

Ancroia
What's this about Tedeschino? Oh, that clown!
It's not enough for him to poorly impersonate[182]
a gentleman at court,

Ch'anco me vuol scimiare?
Ma chi l'abito mio li poté dare?

Gobbo del violino
La Filippetta al certo.
Vuoi ch'io ti dica, Ancroia?
Levatela da torno.
Tu sai per prova omai
Negli affari d'amor chi sia Trafedi?
Nel portare ambasciate
Il saper di Cillenio tengo a vile,
E più d'un può far fede
S'aggiustar so tre ova in un bacile.
Tu mi fai torto, a fé, questa è arte mia,
E di già in altro posto,
Ancroia, mi vedreste
Se si desse scoperta
D'amor l'imbascieria.

Ancroia
Vuò far quel che tu dici.
Dammi il braccio, vien qua, andianne in casa.
Or sì ch'io più non temo
Di perder le giornate;
S'il Trafedi s'è fatto
Il mio porta ambasciate.

Gobbo del violino
Andianne, e ognun di noi
Faccia le prove sue,
E al paragon si veda
Chi meglio sa spacciare
Per vitella di latte, anco del bue.

Scena quarta

Bertuccia, Marmotta

Bertuccia
Principessa, e che fia?
Sù, sù, non più sospiri!

now he even wants to ape me?
But who could have given him my clothing?

Gobbo of the Violin
It was Filippetta for sure.
Do you want my advice, Ancroia?
Send her packing.
Now do you understand
just who Trafedi is in the affairs of the heart?
In delivering messages
I have no use for Cyllenius's wisdom,[183]
and more than one can attest
that I can balance three eggs in a pail.[184]
You do me wrong, I swear, this is my art,
and you'd soon find me
in a tight spot, Ancroia,
if my embassies of love
were ever to come to light.

Ancroia
I'll do as you say.
Give me your arm, come here, let's go home.
Now I really don't fear
wasting my time any more
since Trafedi's become
my very own messenger.

Gobbo of the Violin
Let's go, and let's each
put ourselves to the test.
Let's compare and see
who can best pass off
an ox as a suckling calf. [*they exit*]

Scene Four

Bertuccia, Marmotta

Bertuccia
Princess, what are you doing?
Come now, no more sighs!

Raffrenate gli affanni!
Voi pur solei talvolta
Con il canto passar la fantasia.
Via, via, cantate un poco,
Rattempra il canto l'amoroso foco.

Marmotta
Ah quanto il ver m'aditi,
Mentr'a cantar m'inviti.
Suol talor sul Meandro augel canoro
Già vicino al morire
Cantando palesare il suo martoro.
Dunque cantar debb'io
E con voci dolenti
Accompagnar col canto il morir mio. [*Qui comincia il recitativo cantato in musica*]
Ahi lassa, e pur partire
Dovrò senza morire!
Pur lasciar devo, Amore,
La mia fede, il mio soglio,
La mia vita, il mio bene, anima e core.
Ah proterva Fortuna, ahi Fato indegno,
A che farmi di Meo real consorte?
A che portarmi su codeste arene
Se pure alfin dovevo
Delusa ritornar nel patrio regno?
Misera, e dove il piede
Volgerò forsennata?
Dove, dove smarrita
N'andrò di Fessa disprezzata erede?
Ah prence, ah crudo, e pure,
Pure potrai soffrire
Di vedermi partire?
Pur da te lunge, oh Cielo,
Ne debbo andar schernita?
Ohimè, ch'io cado, io moro, ardo, e m'aggelo.
Portentosa beltade, infausti vanti,
Se solo alfine io sono
Esca infelice di sospiri e pianti?
Oh padre, e con qual ciglio
Mi raccorrai nel seno?
Con quai braccia dolente

Bridle your sorrows!
You used to distract yourself
from time to time with song.
Sing a bit, go on, go on,
the flames of love are cooled with song.

Marmotta
Ah, you point to just the thing
by inviting me to sing.
The songbird on the river Meander[185]
when close to death
at times reveals his agony in song.
So sing I must,
and with pained voice
with song accompany my death: [*Here begins the recitative sung to music*]
And so depart I must,
alas, without dying!
Leave I must, Love,
my vows,[186] *my throne,*
my life, my beloved, heart and soul.
Oh cursed Fortune, oh base Fate,
why make me Meo's royal consort?
Why bring me to these sands,
only to return in the end
deceived to my native lands?
Where will I, wretched and crazed,
next turn my foot?
Adrift, oh where, where will I go,
the spurned heir of Fessa?
Oh Prince, oh cruel man,
will you really suffer
to see me go?
Must I really, oh Heaven above,
go far from you thus scorned?
Woe is me, for I fall, I die, I burn, and I freeze.
Is this beauty ominous, this pride ill-fated,
if in the end I am only
the unhappy bait for sobs and sighs?
Oh father, with what a troubled brow
will you draw me to your breast?
With what pained arms

Accorrai la tua prole
Se tra l'ombre son io
Ombra, ch'a forza fuggo il mio bel sole?
O stanza, ove il mio nido
Già sì lieto godei,
Fortunato ricetto, albergo caro
Or per me fatto amaro.
Prence, prence, e pur fia
Ch'altra più fortunata
Nel tuo bel seno ad onta mia superba
Riposerassi altera?
Altra fra dolci scherzi
Lieta godrà la miseria mia?
Ed io fra tante pene
Lunge da' tuoi bei lumi
N'andrò misera amante,
Né permetter mi vuoi, perfido e rio,
Che nel partire almeno
Possa dirti: spietato, io parto, a Dio. [*Qui finisce il recitativo in musica*]
Ma che vaneggio? Ahi che la donna suole
Sempre appigliarsi al peggio.
Io più qui non ne voglio! In Fessa, in Fessa
E stia in Marocco chi ci vuole stare.
Più tosto ivi zagnotta
Che con Meo principessa.

Bertuccia
Deh, per grazia, non più! Voi v'affligete,
Che parete una cagna arsa di sete.

Scena quinta

Marmotta, Bertuccia, Masino, Tordo

Marmotta
Ecco a punto qui Tordo con Masino.
Che v'è di novo, Tordo?
Trovaste Baldassarre? E vuole andare?

will you receive your scion
if I am a shade amid the shadows,
forced to flee my beautiful sun?
Oh chamber, where I had enjoyed
my once so happy nest,
lucky refuge, dear shelter,
now for me made bitter.
Prince, Prince, and shall another
more fortunate than I,
to my supreme disgrace,
haughtily repose in your fine breast?
Shall another, amid sweet jests,
happily enjoy my misery?
I, the forlorn lover,
amid so many sorrows
shall take leave of your fair lights,
and you, so treacherous and wicked,
will not even permit me to say as I go:
merciless man, I depart, adieu. [*Here ends the musical recitative*]
But why rave so?
Alas, a woman is always wont to cling to the worst.
I no longer wish to be here! To Fessa, to Fessa,
and let he who wishes stay in Morocco.
Better to be a trollop over there
than Meo's princess right here.

Bertuccia
For the love of God, no more! In grief you're so immersed
you look like a bitch parched with thirst.

Scene Five

Marmotta, Bertuccia, Masino, Tordo

Marmotta
Here comes Tordo with Masino.
What news have you, Tordo?
Did you find Baldassarre? Does he wish to go?

Tordo
Eccellentissima sì. Egli ci disse
Che quanto tu comandi, egli vuol fare.

Masino
Certo che Baldassarre
Si mostrò così pronto ed ubbidiente,
Che s'io l'avea per nulla, or l'ho per niente.

Tordo
Quando intese che voi
Volevi ambasciador mandarlo in Fessa,
Disse: «Son uomo de la principessa,
Farò prima i mie fatti, e poi gli suoi.
Andate, e dite ch'io
Anderò in Fessa capitan de l'armi,
E se non basta al padre, il farò al zio».
Infine gli è un fantoccio
Da tenerne più conto ne la corte,
E' sa torre la vita a chi vuol morte.

Marmotta
È pratico di Fessa, che vi disse?
Ch'ei farebbe il servizio come va?
Saprà far l'ambasciata?

Masino
Sì, sì, credete certo, principessa,
Ch'egli sia vero ambasciador di Fessa.

Marmotta
Orsù, che si spediscano le lettre,
Masino, ben formate
Lettre di condoglienze al padre mio.
Scrivete ch'in Marocco
La sua unica figlia
È mula senza striglia,
Che di Fessa l'erede
È fatta una pianella senza piede,
E che l'investitura
Non le tocca più giù de la cintura,

Tordo
Indeed, Your Excellency.
He said your wish is his command.

Masino
I must say that Baldassarre
proved himself so ready and willing
that if before I thought nothing of him, now I think nil.

Tordo
When he understood that you wished
to send him to Fessa as your ambassador,[187]
he said, "I'm the princess's man.
First I'll take care of my business, then hers.
Go, and tell her that I shall go to Fessa
as her master-at-arms,
and if I can't work it out with her father, I'll deal with her uncle."[188]
In short, he is a puppet
who should be more highly regarded at court,
for he knows how to cut a man's life short.

Marmotta
He is familiar with Fessa, what did he tell you?
That he would perform the service as needed?
Will he know how to get the job done?

Masino
Yes, yes, rest assured, *principessa*,
that he is a true ambassador of Fessa.

Marmotta
Come on, Masino,
let's send out those letters,
some well-written letters of condolence to my father.
Write that in Morocco
his only daughter
is a mule without a groom,
that Fessa's heir
has been become a slipper without a foot,[189]
and that her title
does not extend below the waist,

Ch'Ancroia è de le carte il sette e l'asso,
Io con cinquantacinque faccio passo.
Mi dice il cor che per aver io sia
Da Baldassarre ogni allegrezza mia.

Tordo
Veramente gli è forte
Ch'ogni ora cambiar Meo vogli consorte?

Marmotta
Gli è forte, e non si può più sopportare,
Ch'egli de l'altrui case sia pontello,
Mentre la sua sta quasi per cascare.

Tordo
Signora, io vi consiglio
Che voi più tosto Meo facciate bue,
Ch'egli Marmotta debba far coniglio.

Masino
Ed io vi dico che s'egli vi cozza,
Voi la cozziate seco, e se giumenta
Di lui già foste, or d'altro siate rozza.

Marmotta
Di ritornare in Fessa è la mia meta
E abbandonar marito così fatto
Che sol la patria mia mi può far lieta.

Tordo
Oh così vadan tutti, e chi non vuole
L'eclisse de la luna in casa sua
Rimiri i rai d'un eclissato sole.

Bertuccia
Facciam che con il sol perda la luna.
Cambiar cielo talor porta fortuna.

Marmotta
Farò quel che la sorte
Vorrà di me. Tu intanto,

that Ancroia has been dealt the seven and the ace
while even with a stacked deck I come in last place.[190]
But my heart tells me that with Baldassarre's help
I shall soon find happiness.

Tordo
Is Meo really cruel enough
to swap out consorts every hour?

Marmotta
He is, and I will no longer stand
for him to be the pillar propping up another's home
while his own is ready to fall down.

Tordo
Madam, I instead suggest that
you ought to make an ox out of Meo
since he should be making a rabbit out of Marmotta.[191]

Masino
And I say that if he locks horns with you,
take that bull by the horns,
and if once you were his mare, now be another's old nag.

Marmotta
My goal is to return back to Fessa
and to abandon a husband such as this,
for only my homeland can bring me happiness.

Tordo
Everyone should do the same,
and whoever doesn't want a lunar eclipse in their home
should gaze upon the rays of an eclipsed sun.

Bertuccia
Let's have it so that along with the sun, he loses the moon.
New horizons sometimes bring good fortune.

Marmotta
I'll do whatever fortune has in store for me.
Meanwhile you, Bertuccia,

Bertuccia, vanne a trovar Baldassare
E di' che venga, che li vuò parlare
Di cosa che mi preme, ed egli ha a fare.

Bertuccia
Io me ne vado; or ora
Qui Baldassar conduco a la malora.

Marmotta
Meo, Meo, ben fia che tosto
Marmotta di te faccia aspra vendetta.
Ben di mio padre la debil potenza
Farà quel che non mai potei far io.
Bestia senza ragione,
Animal senza senno,
Prence ignorante, senza discrezione,
Così, così dovevi
Condur me, che ti fui
Disturbo ne' contenti,
Digiuno nel mangiare,
Arsione nella sete,
Esca ne l'appetenza,
Cibo fuori di pasto,
Male ne la salute,
Dispetto ne' piaceri,
Salsa senza appetito,
Moglie senza marito!
Così, così Marmotta,
Dee veder crudo Meo?
Ma ve', questo è d'Ancroia il cibo amato:
Ecco Grasso, che viene
Con la vivanda cotta, e Michelino
Guardiano è fatto de' miei mal bocconi.

Scena sesta

Michelino, Grasso e li medesimi

Michelino
Oh Grasse, buone odore di cucine!

go find Baldassarre and tell him to come,
for I wish to speak with him
about a pressing matter to which he must attend.

Bertuccia
Off I go, right away,
I'll lead Baldassarre back to his ruin.

Marmotta
Meo, Meo, and so Marmotta
shall soon take her bitter revenge on you.
Despite my father's weakened power
he'll do what I never could do.
Beast without reason,
animal without judgment,
ignorant prince without discretion,
like this, did you have to
treat me like this?
I, who was the sorrow in your joys,
the fast in your feast,
the burn in your thirst,
the lure of your greed,
the food when it's not time to feed,
the displeasure in your delight,
the sauce without an appetite,
the wife without a spouse!
Alas, must this be
how cruel Meo sees Marmotta?
But look, here comes Grasso
with the cooked viands,
that food loved by Ancroia,
along with Michelino,
the guardian of my bitter fruits.

Scene Six

Michelino, Grasso and the same

Michelino
Oh Grasso, good smell of cooking!

Oh che robbe ben fatte,
Mi va in giù per le gole quelle gatte.

Grasso
E a questa cutta sdrucciola l'unto
Più che non fa il sedere a' pescatori.

Michelino
Oh ecco principesse!
Oh Grasse, Grasse, che le dirai tu?

Grasso
Corpo, non so che dirle!
Ella vorrà sapere
Chi del mio cucinato avrà a godere.

Michelino
Sempre il malsciorne a le vostre escellenze.
Portate pesce crude, e carne cotte,
Il prenscie a la sua bella Ancroie.

Grasso
Che diavolo dirai, razza di boia?

Marmotta
Chi? Che? Che Ancroia? Che?

Michelino
Quelle Ancroie bellissime,
Di Baldassarre scrofole
Fa con il prenscie a rozzole.
Filippette dulcissime
Con gatte, scimie, e topole
Pasturar vuole il ventrule
Ventraglie ne le pentole.

Grasso
Che ti venga il morbo ranocchione!
E forse, che non parla per isdrucciolo?

Oh *v*at tasty stuff!!
Zat cat slides right down *zee z*roat.

Grasso
This greasy wagtail drips more
than a fisherman's backside.

Michelino
Oh here is *zee* princess.
Oh Grasso, Grasso, *v*at *v*ill you tell her?

Grasso
Crap! I don't know what to tell her!
She'll want to know who gets to sup
on all the things that I've cooked up.

Michelino
A very bad day[192] to Your Excellency!
Zee prince has brought rare fish *und* cooked meat
to his beautiful Ancroia.

Grasso
What the hell are you saying, you damn snitch?

Marmotta
Who? What? Ancroia what? Huh?

Michelino
Zat most beautiful Ancroia,
zat sow of Baldassarre,
plays *zee* old nag *vis zee* prince.
Vis cats, monkeys, *und* rats
sweetest Filippetta
*v*ants to fodder her gut-*o-la*
vis entrails in her pot-*o-la*.[193]

Grasso
I hope you croak, you old toad!
Could he be speaking in *sdrucciolo*?

Marmotta
Che diavolo di' tu? Parla ch'intenda!
Che cosa porti qui con Grasso a Meo?

Michelino
Civette, gatte, cornacchione, e cutte,
Tope fritte in guazzette, e grille arroste,
Con une brave zuppe a la fransciese
Tarantan, trà, trà.

Marmotta
Bestia, rispondi a tono!
Che cosa è quel che porti? È crudo o cotto?

Michelino
Crude, cotte, e non è cuscinate;
Grasse coche l'ha fatte, sciagurate.

Grasso
Il malan che ti pigli, bestiaccione!

Marmotta
Mostra qua, mostra qua! Che non so io
Ch'è roba cucinata per Ancroia!

Grasso
Piano, piano, signora, ella non è.
Egli è un certo liquore
Che voglion coltivare,
E pria del fiore il frutto saporare.

Marmotta
Tu non mi vuoi dir nulla? Michelino,
Mostra qua! Che cosa è dentro quel piatto?

Michelino
Queste è un fiasche di Greche di cantine.

Marmotta
Oh, to', va' e porta la vivanda, mo'!
E tu Grassaccio, coco del mal tempo,

Marmotta
What the devil are you saying? Speak so I can understand!
What are you and Grasso bringing Meo?

Michelino
Owls, cats, crows, *und v*agtails,
Fried rats in gravy *und* grilled grasshoppers,
vis a good soup *à la française,*
Tra-la-la, tra-la-la-lay.

Marmotta
Beast! Give me a straight answer.
What is that you're carrying there? Is it raw or cooked?

Michelino
Raw, cooked, *und* cured,
he made big, fat eggs, *zat* devil.

Grasso
Damn you, you brute!

Marmotta
Show me, show me! As if I didn't know
that this stuff was cooked for Ancroia?

Grasso
Calm down, ma'am, calm down, it's not that.
It's a special kind of liquor
that they want to refine
and taste its fruit before it's flowered.

Marmotta
You don't want to tell me anything?
Show me, Michelino! What's on that tray?

Michelino
Zis is a flask of Greco from *zee* cellar.

Marmotta
Here, go on, take the food, move it! [*knocks over the serving tray*]
And you, fat-ass Grasso, chef of misfortune,

Cucina per Ancroia, e pe'l tuo Meo
Quel ch'in terra cadéo!
La robba, che qui ascosa si tenea,
È per me diventata fracassea.

Michelino
Adascie, adascie, briccono.
So ch'il prenscie ed Ancroie pranserà
Tarantan, tarantan, tarantan, tà, tà, tà.

Marmotta
Oh ve' se gli l'ho fatta!
Portate da mangiare nel giardino,
Razza di portapolli!
A le forche con Grasso, Michelino.

Scena settima

Meo, Tedeschino, Mantuano e li medesimi

Tedeschino
Che rumore è cotesto? Oh, quanta roba!
Era pur meglio in vece di gettarla
Darla al mio cannarone a trangugiarla.

Michelino
A soscellenze, a soscellenze, adesse
Vuoglie dirle ogni cose.
Scellentissime,
Tutte gatte, tope, e le scivette,
Le cornacchie, le cutte tutte in terre.
Il buon fiasche di Greche Micheline
Ha salvate ne le sue maghezzine.

Meo
Chi, chi gettò per terra
Quel ch'io volea mangiar? Che lo risappia,
E poi se la vendetta
Non fo del prence Meo,
Mi si strappi la stringa a la brachetta.

cook up for Ancroia and for your Meo
whatever fell onto the dirt below!
This grub, which was kept hidden from me,
I have now turned into a fracas fricassee.

Michelino
Settle down, you minx.
I know *zee* prince *v*ill dine *vis* Ancroia.
Taran-tan, taran-tan, taran-tan, ta-ta-ta.

Marmotta
Oh, now I've got them!
Go bring their food to the garden,
you damn weasels.
Off to the gallows with Grasso, Michelino!

Scene Seven

Meo, Tedeschino, Mantuano and the same

Tedeschino
What's all this racket? Oh, look at all this stuff!
Instead of throwing it all away
you could have shoved it down my guzzler.

Michelino
Your Excellency, Your Excellency,
now I'll tell you everything.
Your Most Excellency,
all of *zee* cats, rats, *und* owlets,
zee crows *und v*agtails are all on *zee* ground.
Zee good flask of Greco
Michelino has saved in his larder.

Meo
Who did this? Who threw the stuff I wanted to eat
down in the dirt?
I'll find out who did it,
and if I don't exact revenge for Prince Meo,
may I be yanked up by the strings of my codpiece.

Marmotta
Io, io, io son quella
Ch'ho rovesciato al piano
Quel che doveva empirti le budella.
Or ch'hai mangiato, lavati la mano.

Meo
Dunque cotanto ardire avete avuto
Di mal trattar la roba e chi mi serve?

Marmotta
Mi duole ch'io non gli ho rotto il mostaccio,
Ma quel che non ho fatto, adesso il faccio.

Michelino
Adascie, adascie, queste son picchiate!

Meo
Oh bestia da bastone,
To', piglia 'sto sgrugnone.

Marmotta
E tu pigliati questa,
Vedi s'anch'io nel dar la mano ho lesta.

Tedeschino
Olà, olà signori
Fermatevi, non fate;
Marmotta, ecco per te il Tedeschino.

Michelino
E per Meo, Michelino.

Meo
Che dici, ombra di notte?
Ti piacciano le botte?

Marmotta
E tu ombra di giorno,
Ben va quel che t'ho fatto
In su la fronte, rilevato corno?

Marmotta
It was me, me, me! I am she
who threw down to the ground
what should have filled up your belly.
Now that you've had your fill, wash your hands of it all.

Meo
So you had the nerve to mistreat
my servants and my goods?

Marmotta
I'm only sorry that I didn't punch his lights out.
But what I didn't do then, now I'll bring about. [*she beats Michelino*]

Michelino
Settle down, settle down, zese are real blows!

Meo
Oh you beast best for beating,
here, take this thrashing. [*he beats Marmotta*]

Marmotta
And you take this one. [*she beats Meo*]
I'll show you I'm as quick on the draw.

Tedeschino
Hey, hey, Masters,
stop, don't do this.
Marmotta, Tedeschino is here for you.

Michelino
Und Michelino for Meo.

Meo
What are you saying, you shadow of night?
Do you enjoy these blows?

Marmotta
And you, shade of day,
do you like the lump
I've exposed on your brow?

Tedeschino
Marmotta, io son qui teco:
Se ti dà più, l'avrà da finir meco.

Michelino
Oh belle bricconascie, ignorantascie.
Fa', fa' quel che ti tocca, forfantono,
L'arte tua è del buffono,
E non di far lo brave e 'l bel mustascie.

Mantuano
Oh ve' se la va bene?
Un buffone vuol far d'innamorate?
Che ti venga mostaccie d'appiccate!

Michelino
Vedete belle in piasce, oh Tedeschine,
Io meglio faria te, te Michelino.

Marmotta
Bisogna ch'imbriaca la fortuna
Fosse, quando ti diede a comandare.
Oh ve' faccia di prence! Che ti venga
Nel meglio de l'urina la renella,
La lebra ne le scarpe,
La tosse ne le mani,
La podagra ne' denti,
La rogna a la francese, e pelarella.

Meo
E a te possa venire
Il sonno senza voglia di dormire.

Tedeschino
Ed a me venga or ora
Marmotta mia signora.

Michelino
E al mio buon cacciator Micheline
Venga piscione arroste, e del buon vine.

Tedeschino
Marmotta, I'm here for you.
If he keeps it up, he'll have to answer to me.

Michelino
Oh you scoundrel, you numbskull.
Stick to *v*at you do best, you hooligan,
yours is *zee* art of *zee* buffoon,
not of putting on a tough, handsome mug.

Mantuano
Oh look, isn't this something?
A buffoon wants to play the lover?
May you end up with a dead man's mug.

Michelino
Oh how suave, Tedeschino,
I'd be a better you, *und* you a Michelino.[194]

Marmotta
Fortuna must have been sauced
when she gave you your command.
Look here, you royal pain in the butt![195]
May you get a kidney stone in your fine urine,
leprosy in your shoes,
a cough in your hands,
the gout in your teeth,
the French pox, and ringworm.

Meo
And may you instead succumb
to a sleepless slumber.

Tedeschino
And may Marmotta my lady
come to me without delay.

Michelino
Und to *zee* good hunter Michelino
let *z*ere come roast pigeons *und* some good vino.

Grasso
E a Grasso, coco a modo,
Venga da leccar piatti e scolar brodo.

Tedeschino
E il Tedeschine Amore
Faccia del suo giardin l'innaffiatore.

Michelino
E al Tedeschine fascie
Meo, che Michelin rompa la fascie.

Mantuano
E a Mantuan die segne
Che le rompa la schiena con un legne.

Grasso
E a Grasso dia licenza
Che gli dia d'una trippa in sua presenza.

Tordo
E a Tordo con Masino …

Masino
Su l'asino scopare il Tedeschino.

Scena ottava

Baldassarre, Croatto, Filippetta e i medesimi

Filippetta
Padrona, eccovi qua
Condotto Baldassarre!

Croatto
E 'l serva sua Croatta
Che sempre a bresso va
Com'al larda solir andar la gatta.

Marmotta
Baldassar, benvenuto. Io ho bisogno

Grasso
And may Grasso, a cook who's first rate,
get to slurp the sauces and lick the plate.

Tedeschino
And may Love upon Tedeschino confer
the chance to be his garden sprinkler!

Michelino
Und may Meo allow Michelino
to smash in *zee* face of Tedeschino.

Mantuano
Und may Mantuano be given the nod
to break*en* his back with a wooden club.

Grasso
And may Grasso be granted the liberty
to give him a good kick in the belly.

Tordo
And may Tordo and Masino …

Masino
Flog Tedeschino.[196]

Scene Eight

Baldassarre, Croatto, Filippetta, and the same

Filippetta
Mistress, here you go,
I have brought Baldassarre to you.

Croatto
And his servant Croatto,
who always chases after him
like a dog its bone.[197]

Marmotta
Baldassarre, welcome.

Da te d'un gran piacere;
E con un certo affetto,
Che non so da che nasce,
Di te mi fido assai: me lo vuoi fare?

Baldassarre
De mui buona gana, sennora, es mi servitio,
Che los espagnolos
Tenemos mas opras che palavras.
Mandamie in che soi buene
Che sarà servida.

Marmotta
Voglio mandarti in Fessa;
E già ch'io sola sono
Erede de lo stato,
Io voglio nel mio regno comandare.

Baldassarre
In huera buena, sennora.

Marmotta
Così questo cervel da far lunari
Per piede servirà de l'arcolaio
Ad Ancroia, ch'è fatta il suo vivaio.
Or senti Baldassarre,
Racconta al padre mio
Quel che da Meo sopporto.
Digli ch'il vedovile
Egli m'ha dato prima d'esser morto,
E digli ancora che d'Ancroia affatto
È diventato matto.
Infin digli ch'andare
Io voglio in Fessa, e più con Meo non stare.

Baldassarre
Biene, dieme la cifra,
Y con l'ordin che mi dares,
Seghiremo, che son plattico en la tierra
Essendo nassido in eglia,
Y entiendo la lingua.

I have a great favor to ask.
I have a certain fondness for you,
though I know not why,
and trust you completely. Can you do this for me?

Baldassarre
Gladly, *señora*, I am at your service,
for we *españoles*
are better in deeds than in words.
Ask what you wish of me,
and you shall be served.

Marmotta
I want to send you into Fessa.
And since I alone
am the heir to the state,
in my own kingdom I wish to command.

Baldassarre
Congratulations, *señora*.

Marmotta
This way, that numskull
can pump Ancroia's spinning wheel,[198]
she who's become his hatchery.
Now listen up, Baldassarre.
Tell my father
what I've had to abide.
Tell him that Meo has made me a widow
before he's even died,
and also tell him that for Ancroia
he has gone utterly mad.
And lastly, tell him that I would prefer
to go to Fessa and stay with Meo no longer.

Baldassarre
Bien, give me the missive,
and I shall follow your orders.
Let's proceed, I know that *tierra*,
since I was born there,
and I understand the tongue.

Che sagnale me derà paraque sia
Conossido da eglio?

Marmotta
Solo per contrasegno,
Come s'usa fra noi mentre vogliamo
Mandar certe ambasciate,
Digli che ciò gli dice chi nel braccio
Destro tien una perla, per segnale,
Che Natura l'impresse nel natale.

Baldassarre
Me scuse, creo che vostra istié me burle,
Y che la mas collera
Le haz salir de ghuditio.

Marmotta
Io non ebbi altro segno con mio padre
Di quello ch'io ti dico.

Baldassarre
Ia non es menester, che mas me burle,
Che iá l'ho entendido.

Croatto
Oh star bella! Marmotta
Giocar con Baldassarre a la bilotta.

Marmotta
Che forse non lo credi?
Ecco, ostinato, il segno.

Baldassarre
Es possibiles tal cosas?
Y achí sta el mio.

Marmotta
Ohimè, che veggio? Io sento
Scotermi tutta l'alma. Oh Cielo, è forse
Questo il fratello mio che già perdei?
Or in Fessa (oh che provo!)
Perdo il marito ed il fratello trovo.

What sign will you give me
so that I may be recognized by him?

Marmotta
Only the countersign
that the two of us use
when we wish to send certain messages:
tell him this is coming from she
who on her right arm has a pearl—
a sign which Nature imprinted on the newborn girl.

Baldassarre
Excuse me? Surely you mock me
and an excess of *cólera*[199]
has made you lose your mind.

Marmotta
I've never used any other sign with my father
than the one I am describing.

Baldassarre
You need no longer mock me,
I see how it is.

Croatto
Oh, isn't this nice!
Marmotta is *b*laying ball with Baldassarre.

Marmotta
Perhaps you don't believe me?
Look, obstinate man, here is the sign. [*shows her arm*]

Baldassarre
Are such things *posibles*?
And here is mine. [*shows his arm*]

Marmotta
Oh, what's this I see?
I feel my whole soul tremble.
Oh Heaven, could this be my long-lost brother?
Now in Fessa (oh, what a feeling!)
I lose my husband and find my brother.

Baldassarre
Oh mi ermana ermosa,
Ermana de mi occhos,
Mi alma, mi corazon, mi vida,
Dames sto brazzos.
Iá, iá me pares ch'il sole y la luna
Stien in coniunzion, mi alma,
Donde potrà dar lus a nostras tierras,
Y gustos a nostros padres.

Marmotta
Sempre con Baldassarre
Ho avuto simpatia.
Oh come i miei tormenti
Ora cangio in contenti!
Oh fratello bramato, ecco ch'è giunto
L'ora ch'insiem faremo del pan unto.

Meo
Oh quel ch'io vedo e sento!
Oh quel ch'appresso miro!
Di star meco del pari,
O Baldassarr, vi sia
Autorità concessa:
Principe io di Marocco, e voi di Fessa.
Signor cognato caro,
Del principato mio vero contento,
Io ho tant'allegrezza
Che non ebbi già mai maggior tormento.
E fra tanti disturbi
A nova così cara
Mi congratol con voi, oh principessa,
Prole accoppiata del regno di Fessa.
Spesso vien che si veda
Ch'il male nasce, perché il ben succeda.

Baldassarre
Y io m'aliegro mas de vos, cognado,
Mi parentes costumbrados,
Puor puoder meghiorar lo estado vuostro,
Che vuestro beneficios mereces muccio,

Baldassarre
Oh my beautiful sister,
sister of my eyes,
mi alma, mi corazón, mi vida,[200]
give me those arms.
It is as if the sun and the moon
are in conjunction,[201] *mi alma,*
and will be able to bring light to our *tierras*
and joy to our parents.

Marmotta
I've always felt
an affinity for Baldassarre.
Oh, how my miseries
now change to felicities!
Oh, my longed-for brother, the time has come
for us to break bread together.

Meo
Oh, what's this I see and hear?
Oh, what's this I behold here?
May you be granted the authority,
oh Baldassarre,
to stand with me on par,
I prince of Morocco and you of Fessa.
My dearest brother-in-law,
the true joy of my principality,
my happiness is so great
that it surpasses my prior torment.
And for this wonderful news
after so many troubles,
I congratulate you, oh Princess,
coupled issue of the kingdom of Fess.
It is often true
that evil is born so that good may ensue.

Baldassarre
And I am even happier than you, brother-in-law,
my courteous kin,
to be able to improve your estate,
since you deserve *mucho* for your generosity,

Y io desio pagarlos;
Voiste puede mandar de quel reinos
Puor secundas personas.
Sarà vuestro servitio conossido,
Y como buen cognado
Mi obligacion pagada.

Croatto
Oh paesa più grada de pan unta,
Ova comu star funga
Solir nascer i brincipo in un punta!

Marmotta
Principe, in giorno di sì gran contento
Vorrei mi compiacessi d'un piacere.

Baldassarre
L'aghas lo ch'ella chiere.

Meo
Comanda pur, Marmotta,
Ch'io farò quanto vuoi
Né piu sian differenze qui fra noi!

Baldassarre
Garbato cavagliero, puor mi vida!

Marmotta
Voglio che Filippetta
Facci bandir dal regno di Marocco
Per ricompensa di quel che mi fece
Quando ch'Ancroia a te diede in mia vece.

Meo
Ora che Baldassarre
Si scopre erede del regno di Fessa,
E sì grand'uomo è fatto mio cognato,
Si faccia quanto vuoi; fate bandire
Filippetta dal nostro circuito
Ed abbia questo per suo ben servito.
Ed io per tanta gioia

which I intend to repay.
You may send me to that kingdom
as your second-in-command.
Your *servicio* shall be celebrated,
and, as I am a *buen* brother-in-law,
my *obligación* shall be repaid.

Croatto
Oh, what a land,
better than sliced bread,
where *b*rinces seem to *b*op up like mushrooms!

Marmotta
Prince, on such a joyful day,
I'd like you to grant me a favor.

Baldassarre
Do as she asks.

Meo
Marmotta, command away,
for I shall do as you wish,
let this be the end of our fray!

Baldassarre
Upon my life, what a courteous *caballero*!

Marmotta
I want you to banish Filippetta
from the kingdom of Morocco
as payback for the trouble she bred
when she gave you Ancroia in my stead.

Meo
Now that Baldassarre
is revealed to be the heir to the kingdom of Fessa,
and so great a man has become my brother-in-law,
may your every wish be granted:
banish Filippetta from our territories
in payment for services rendered.
And so great is my joy

E l'osterie rinunzio, ed i buffoni,
E con Marmotta mia,
Ch'è capo di marmotte,
Io fedelmente voglio
Passar il giorno e consumar la notte.

Scena nona

Catorchia e li medesimi

Catorchia
Oh ve' qua quanta gente radunata.
Bertuccia, ci è di novo qualche cosa?

Bertuccia
Purtroppo ci è di novo: si è scoperto
Baldassarre fratello di Marmotta.

Catorchia
Don Baldassarre, mi rallegro assai;
Dopo i stenti talor vengono i guai.

Baldassarre
E io di vostra isté senor Catorchio.

Marmotta
Principe, se ti piace,
Vuò mandar per Ancroia, e 'n una gabbia
La vuò metter per cutta a cinguettare,
E poi porre in un'altra
Il Tedeschino per un pappagallo,
E con occasione de la nuova
Di Baldassarre in Fessa
Mandarle tutte duoi al padre mio.

Baldassarre
Oh bueno, oh bueno, oh bueno,
Che si mandeno in Fessa a nostros padres.

Meo
In dì sì lieto grazia non si nieghi.

that I renounce both taverns and buffoons,
and with my Marmotta,
who is the best of all marmots,
I shall faithfully delight
to spend the day and consume the night.

Scene Nine

Catorchia and the same

Catorchia
Oh look how many people have assembled here.
Bertuccia, has there been some news?

Bertuccia
I'll say there's been some news!
It turns out that Baldassarre is Marmotta's brother.

Catorchia
Don Baldassarre, I'm so filled with joy:
sometimes after trials come tribulations.

Baldassarre
As I am for you, *señor* Catorchio.

Marmotta
Prince, if you so please,
I want to send for Ancroia
and put her in a cage to chirp like a wagtail,
and then stick Tedeschino
in another like a parrot.
And along with the news about Baldassarre,
I want to send them both
to my father in Fessa.

Baldassarre
O bueno, bueno, bueno.
Let them be sent off to Fessa to our parents.

Meo
On this happy day such favors shall not be denied.

Lo scoprimento, ch'ora
Di Baldassar s'è fatto,
Promettere mi puote
Del principe di Spagna anco l'amore.
Sì che per lui già veggio
Le provincie del mondo esser unite
E contra ogni ribello
Fessa, Spagna, e Marocco,
Esser l'arco, esser l'asta, esser lo stocco.

Marmotta
A Bertuccia si dia in ricompensa
Del piacer che mi fe' con Baldassarre,
Sposo Catorchia con vostra licenza.

Meo
Se gli dia: mi rallegro con Bertuccia.

Bertuccia
Vi ringrazio signore. Oh Catorchino,
S'eri un Marte, ti vuò fare un Martino.

Catorchia
Io ringrazio la vostra signoria.
Catorchia sposo? Oh Bertuccia mia!

Baldassarre
Y io al mi Croatto agho
Magherdomo de todas la mis casas.

Croatto
Lec, salem ber ti, e ber mi badrona.
Mi magerdoma?
Or sì che volir fare il gentiloma.

Meo
Che si portin le gabbie.

Ancroia
Che diavolo sarà? Io che la gabbia
Fui di tanti uccelli, or ingabbiata
Sarò da Meo. Oh ve' beneficiata!

This discovery which has now
been made about Baldassarre
ensures that I shall have
the love of the Spanish prince.
And so because of him I already see
the provinces of the world unite,
and against any rebellion,
Fessa, Spain, and Morocco
together shall be the bow, the spear, and the sword.

Marmotta
As a reward for her help with Baldassarre,
let Bertuccia be given
Catorchia as a groom, with your permission.

Meo
May it be so granted. My congratulations to Bertuccia.

Bertuccia
I thank you sir. Oh my dear Catorchin,
if once you were a Mars, now I'll make you a Martin.[202]

Catorchia
My thanks to your lordship.
Catorchia a groom? Oh, my Bertuccia!

Baldassarre
And I my Croatto do make
majordomo of all of my *casas*.

Croatto
Lec salem to you and to my master.[203]
Me, a majordomo?
Now I do want to be a gentleman.

Meo
Bring out the cages.

Ancroia
What the devil is this?
Am I, who was the cage to so many birdies,
now to be encaged by Meo? What a fine reward.

Meo
Che 'l Tedeschin s'arresti, e non si parta.

Tedeschino
Che sarà di novo anco per me?

Meo
Il Tedeschin, per troppo cicalare,
Sia messo in una gabbia a svolazzare.

Marmotta
E ne l'altra si metta, olà, l'Ancroia,
E sia una cutta, se già fu 'na troia.

Ancroia
Temevo il boccalone,
E m'han dato una gabbia.

Tedeschino
Ed io temea una fune,
E m'han dato per grazia una prigione.

Meo
A tutto il resto de la nostra corte
Cresco la provisione, ed un banchetto
Per segno d'allegrezza a la reale
Le vuò dar domatina a un ospedale.
Tra tanto a questi belli animaletti
Se li balli davanti una ciaccona,
E poi si manderanno al re di Fessa,
Per spassatempo de la sua persona.
E in questa festa mia
Marocco e Fessa riunita sia.

Il fine

Meo
Detain Tedeschino and don't let him leave.

Tedeschino
And now what will become of me?

Meo
For his excessive prattling, Tedeschino
shall be placed in a cage to flutter to and fro.

Marmotta
Oh yes, and in the other have Ancroia jailed.
Since she had been a strumpet, now let her be a wagtail.

Ancroia
I feared the vultures,[204]
and they gave me a cage.

Tedeschino
And I feared the rope,
and mercifully they gave me a prison.

Meo
And as for the rest of our court,
I shall increase their allowances,
and tomorrow morning as a sign of our joy
I'll throw them a royal banquet at a hospital.
In the meantime we shall dance a *ciaccona*[205]
before these pretty little beasts,
and then they will be sent off to Fessa,
for the amusement of the king.
And through this, my celebration,
Morocco and Fessa shall unite as one.

The end

Canzonetta da cantarsi e ballarsi in ciaccona intorno l'ingabbiati personaggi in scorno della cutta e pappagallo nella fine terzo ed ultimo atto

Scenda qua, posi qui
Strepitando il cornacchione,
Ed al suon del nottolone.
Ecco faccia il chichirichì.
Ogni razza buscaina
D'animali pennacchiuti
Degli uccelli la regina,
Delle bestie il re saluti.
Oh che scherzo, oh che gioia.

In gabbia è 'l Tedeschin portabrachiero,
E gioca a la balorda con l'Ancroia.
Questa a bianco ed a nero,
E quegli veste a verde, a rosso, e giallo,
E l'una è cutta, e l'altro è pappagallo.

Che fai tu? Che di' tu?
Oh statista Tedeschino,
Tu non vali un raperino
E sei peggio d'un cucù.
Oh ritratto de' bagei
Così mutulo che fai?
Canta mò ch'in gabbia sei
La canzona del cucai.
Oh che scherzo, oh che gioia.

E tu omai lungi va',
Da stivali robba frusta;
Più di te l'Affrica adusta
Brutta scimia non avrà.
Ed a te questa canzone
Cantar s'oda, oh vecchia Ancroia;
Il disciogliersi in carbone,
È fin degno d'una troia.
Oh che scherzo, oh che gioia.

Canzonette

Canzonetta *to be sung and danced as a* ciaccona *around the encaged characters in mockery of the wagtail and parrot at the end of the third and final act.*[206]

Come on down,
place that cackling crow over here,
and at the cry of the owl
have it sound the cock-a-doodle-doo.
May every wild breed
of feathered brute
the queen of birds
and the king of beasts salute.
Oh what a lark, oh what joy.

That trussed-up[207] Tedeschino is in a cage
and playing the fool with Ancroia.
She's in black and white,
and he's dressed in green, red, and yellow.
One is a wagtail, the other a parrot.

What's that you're you doing? What's that you're saying?
Oh, you statesman Tedeschino,
you're not worth a finch
and you're worse than a cuckoo.
Oh, you spitting image of a dodo,
why so tongue-tied?
Sing, now that you're in a cage,
the song of the cuckoo.
Oh what a lark, oh what joy.

Let's finally be off with you,
you leathery old boot;
not even sun-scorched Africa
has an ape uglier than you.
Let's hear this canzone
sung for you, Ancroia, you old hag.
It is a fitting end for such a whore
to turn to ash.
Oh what a lark, oh what joy.

Così suole avvenir
A chi senno in sè non abbia
In catena, o ver in gabbia,
Di sua vita i dì finir.
Per pastura, per bevanda
A tai mostri, ed a tai belve
Serva l'esca de la ghianda,
Si dia il suco de le selve,
Oh che scherzo, oh che gioia.

In gabbia è 'l Tedeschin portabrachiero,
E gioca a la balorda con l'Ancroia.
Questi a bianco ed a nero,
E quegli veste a verde, a rosso, a giallo.
E l'una è cutta, e l'altro è pappagallo.

Questa sottoscritta canzonetta si canterà nella fine del primo atto.

Le coppe in bastoni
Cangiato ha Cupido.
Fuggite buffoni,
Fuggite l'infido.
Ha tolto il pennuto
A' vostri ardor vani
Invece de l'arco la sferza de' cani.

La qui sotto canzonetta da cantarsi nel fine del secondo atto.

Piangete, o folli amanti,
La forsennata spene,
Ch'Amor è dio di pene,
E son esca le gioie a' duoli e pianti.
Nostra fede
Per mercede
Ha tocco altro che bolzoni;
Ahi,[xxxix] ch'ei l'arco vi mostra, e dà bastoni.

Fuggite, oh stolti, omai,
D'un orbo che v'offende,

And so this is what often happens
to those without a lick of sense:
in chains, or rather, a cage
they pass their livelong days.
For the fodder, for the drink
of such monsters and such brutes,
let the bait of acorns suffice,
let them have the nectar of the forests.
Oh what a lark, oh what joy.

That trussed-up Tedeschino is in a cage,
and playing the fool with Ancroia.
She's in black and white,
and he's dressed in green, red, and yellow.
One is a wagtail, the other a parrot.

The following canzonetta *is to be sung at the end of the first act.*

Cupid has swapped out
cups for clubs.[208]
Flee, buffoons,
flee the treacherous one.
He plucked the plume
from your vain passions,
not with his bow but with his dogs' lashings.

The following canzonetta *is to be sung at the end of the second act.*

Weep, oh mad lovers,
for irrational hope,
since Love is the god of pain
and joy is the bait for agony and tears.
Our faith
is rewarded
with a strike different from the sword's.
Alas, he shows you his bow but hits you with blows!

Flee, oh fools, at long last
from the blind one who wounds you

E sol busse vi rende,
Il mentito gioir gli acerbi guai.
Vi darà,
Picchierà,
Nè saranno più sferzate,
Ma colpi di bastone, e piattonate.

and repays you in beatings alone,
illusory joys and bitter woes.
He'll get you,
he'll pound you,
and next time it won't be lashes
but blows of his club and the flat of his sword.

Notes to the Italian Edition

i. The Magliabechiano edition (hereafter referred to as M) is missing this page. The text picks up again at ln. 39.

ii. *E non ti diede il regno in una gabbia.*

iii. M changes the punctuation to an exclamation mark.

iv. *Starò su la parata.*

v. *io sempre pronto | Lo stromento terrò per simil caso*

vi. *se ciò può stare | Oh sciocca.*

vii. *stessi a pestar*

viii. *che tutte le fantesche | Soglion portare in mano quando piove.*

ix. Lines cut in M.

x. The character's name is erroneously left off the page.

xi. *Di, dimmi il vero. | Tu vai a cacciar gatte?* M corrects the final punctuation, which in the other editions was left as a comma.

xii. *trude*

xiii. Lines cut in M.

xiv. *sdegni*

xv. M has a comma.

xvi. M here inserts a line. The full text reads: *Quel naso di Braccaccio a la francese, | Quella bocca piccina spalancata, | Che si tien Baldassarre a le sue spese.*

xvii. Lines cut in M.

xviii. *men lieta*

xix. *cotanto grato, | Che non vi è forestiero, o cittadino, | Che non resti da lor preso e legato.*

xx. *Di dare al buio dentro un passatoio.*

xxi. *e son sì grandi, | Ch'accor vi si potrebbe | De l'Ibera nazione i pellegrini.*

xxii. *d'assai, o casareccie?*

xxiii. Lines cut in M.

xxiv. *patria.*

xxv. Lines cut in M.

xxvi. *che lasci, che per lei arda d'Amore, | E che fra tante pene | Le permetta pietosa aura di spene; | E ciò perché si suole | Sperar anco fra l'ombre i rai del sole.*

xxvii. *Nel nostro stato è proprio il regalare.*

xxviii. Lines cut in M.

xxix. Lines cut in M.

xxx. *zampogna.*

xxxi. *Da noi fin ne' villani | È la virtude eretta; | E di sonare ognuno si diletta.*

xxxii. Lines cut in M.

xxxiii. *dello strascico,*

xxxiv. *Or lo portan*

xxxv. Lines cut in M.

xxxvi. *E qual paese | È più fertil del nostro in latticini?*

xxxvii. *casciaggioni.*

xxxviii. All editions misnumber this and subsequent scenes in this act; correct numbering has been restored.

xxxix. The editors share Ferrone's assessment that the text's *hai* here is likely a typographical error.

Notes to the English Translation

1. The parodic use of a title such as *cavaliere* for a buffoon was not uncommon in sixteenth- and seventeenth-century Italy. Several comic performers were known to have been addressed using mock aristocratic, military, and ecclesiastical honorifics. See Ricci, *Il Tedeschino* (1995), 16–18.

2. "Il Tedeschino," meaning "the little German." On the historical identity of Bernardino Ricci, "il Tedeschino," see the Introduction, 42–43. The character explains the origins of this moniker in I.x.63–73.

3. While in this instance the adjective *politico* conveys Tedeschino's astuteness, other subsequent uses of *politico/politica* refer to his self-identification as a statesman.

4. As noted in the Introduction, Teresa Megale determined that most of Costa's characters, particularly the men, are clear or likely caricatures of historical figures connected to the Medicean court—hence Costa's stated desire to depict her figures *al naturale*, that is, as from life (an expression in fact used to describe portraits). The historical identifications that follow are based on Megale's work. For her archival sources, see Megale, "La commedia decifrata," 66–70.

5. Meo, here Costa's prince, was historically a notorious local madman who received financial support from the Medici household.

6. Masino was a servant in the household of Giovan Carlo de' Medici whose physical deformity made him the object of court jokes and hijinks.

7. Michelino was the name of one of Ferdinando's German mercenary bodyguards.

8. Mantuano was another member of the grand duke's German guard.

9. The buffoon Baldassarre is modeled on Ricci's historical rival at court, the Spanish buffoon Don Baldassarre Biguria.

10. "Pawn," one of the dwarfs at Ferdinando's court.

11. "Hunchback," one of the dwarfs in Ferdinando's court.

12. "Fatty," a cook in the Medici kitchen.

13. Megale hypothesizes that the figure of Croatto may have been based on a member of a band of Turkish musicians that resided and performed in Florence during this period, though the evidence is less clear in this case.

14. A dwarf in Giovan Carlo's household.

15. A dwarf in Leopoldo de' Medici's household.

16. "Hunchback of the Violin" refers to the famous buffoon Tommaso Trafedi employed in the household of Ferdinando's uncle Lorenzo. At several points (II.x.41, 75 and in III.iii), other characters and the stage directions refer to him as Trafedi. For this identification, see Crimi, *Nanerie del Rinascimento,* 310n.

17. A name meaning marmot, a rodent akin to a groundhog. Given Meo's complaints about Marmotta's nagging, it is also worth noting that the word derives from the French *marmotte*, which may have roots in the verb *marmotter*, meaning to mutter.

18. The name Fessa alludes to both the Kingdom and the principal city of Fez, located in the north of present-day Morocco. However, the word *fessa* is also a lewd reference to the female genitalia, meaning "slit," and can additionally refer to a foolish woman. For more on Costa's use of Fessa, see the Introduction, 36–37. As a resource on Italian sexual euphemisms, see especially Valter Boggione and Giovanni Casalegno, eds., *Dizionario letterario del lessico amoroso: Metafore, eufemismi, trivialismi* (Turin: UTET, 2000).

19. Also meaning monkey or ape, the word *bertuccia* describes an ugly woman known for being a busybody. Megale also suggests that Costa may have in mind a certain servant Bertuccia who was in the employ of Ferdinando's brother Mattias.

20. Numerous references to Tordo's activities making and selling lenses allows for a clear identification of the character with one Ippolito, also known as Tordo (meaning "thrush," a small songbird), who worked at the Uffizi as Ferdinando's lens crafter.

21. The name Ancroia perhaps derives from the Neapolitan expression *faccia d'Ancroia* (face of Ancroia), which disparagingly refers to an old, deformed woman. See the glossary to Mariti's *Commedia ridicolosa*, 328.

22. In Massi and Landi's original edition of the *Buffoni*, the opening lines of the Prologue are not explicitly assigned to any character, though they are clearly delivered by Ancient Comedy. We have added the character name in brackets for clarity.

23. Ancient Comedy's razor and shears can be seen hanging from the waist of the crooked female figure standing stage right in Stefano della Bella's frontispiece. They are the tools of Ancient Comedy's trade—the physical equivalents of the cutting words which she then uses to chastise the various classes of men in attendance.

24. The *canario* and *spezzata* were courtly dances and step sequences popular in seventeenth-century Italy. Distinguished by its exotic stamping of the feet, the "canary" is thought to have been named after the Canary Islands and to have made its way from Spain to Italy in the sixteenth century. Fabritio Caroso's dance manual *Nobiltà di dame* describes a variation of the "canary" known as the *seguito spezzato schisciato al canario*, or "Sliding Broken Sequence in the Canary" (LVIII). For more on these steps, see Fabritio Caroso, *Courtly Dance of the Renaissance: A New Translation and Edition of the* Nobiltà di dame *(1600) by Fabritio Caroso*, ed. and trans. Julia Sutton and F. Marian Walker (New York: Dover, 1995).

25. [*Fare come*] *la gatta di Masino*, a proverbial phrase meaning to pretend not to see what is going on in order to avoid taking action.

26. Narcissus and Ganymede are both mythological figures associated with beauty and sexual longing. The goddess Nemesis punished Narcissus for his rejection of the nymph Echo by causing him to fall in love with his own reflection and, unable to consummate such a love, to end his life. Ganymede was a beautiful young boy whom Zeus desired and, assuming the form an eagle, abducted to Mount Olympus.

27. *Ghiande* can also be a euphemism for testicles.

28. Costa frequently employs bird and fowling imagery as sexual euphemisms; see Introduction, 58–60. Here the two kinds of owls are euphemisms for pimps (*allocchi*) and loose women or prostitutes (*civette*). *The Buffoons* makes frequent reference to eroticized women as *civette*. In fowling, a live decoy bird (*zimbello*) is tied to a rope and manipulated by hunters to bait other birds. Also see I.i.161 and I.iv.86.

29. "Dried laurel" (bay leaf) translates *lauro secco*, the title of one of two printed anthologies of musical works assembled for the *virtuosa* Laura Peverara by Torquato Tasso; see Vittorio Baldini and Luca Marenzio, *Il lauro secco: Libro primo di madrigali a cinque voci di diversi autori* (Ferrara: Baldini, 1582; republished 1584 and 1596). As a singer herself, Costa may have known the work and be referring to it here.

30. *Nottola* commonly refers to a bat but can also mean an owl. Given the preponderance of bird imagery in the comedy, particularly in the context of the *canzonetta* for Act III when Costa again uses the word (ln. 3), we have opted to translate it as owl.

31. *Greco* was a variety of white wine reported to have been introduced to Italy by the Greeks.

32. Like many before her, Costa puns on the meaning of *medico* as physician.

33. "Medicean stars" was the name given to Jupiter's four moons by Galileo in his 1610 *Sidereus nuncius*, dedicated to Cosimo II de' Medici. This imagery became a commonly used means of honoring the

ducal family in Florence. It also plays a prominent role in the manuscript edition of Costa's equestrian ballet *Festa reale*, written in the same period as the *Buffoni*, in which the characters are lifted into the sky in order to form the Medicean Stars. See Goethals, "The Patronage Politics of Equestrian Ballet."

34. Costa is presumably referring to Ferdinando II de' Medici.

35. Beginning especially with Cosimo I, Medici image campaigns associated the grand dukes with Augustus, first emperor of ancient Rome.

36. Florence.

37. The brothers Tiberius and Gaius Gracchus were Roman tribunes of the second century BCE. They were respected as orators of fine Latin, earning high praise from Cicero as being "of all the men I have heard … the most eloquent"; Cicero, *On the Ideal Orator*, trans. James M. May and Jakob Wisse (Oxford: Oxford University Press, 2001), I.38. However, their proposed agrarian reforms provoked the anger and hostility of the senatorial elite, resulting in Tiberius's assassination and Gaius's suicide. Costa unfavorably contrasts their lofty style but unpopular message with the antics of the ancient mimes, low-status actors known for their crude imitations, gestures, and other forms of physical comedy. For more on mimes and ancient buffoonery, see Ruth Webb, *Demons and Dancers: Performance in Late Antiquity* (Cambridge, MA: Harvard University Press, 2008), 95–138.

38. The Italian states that the scene is *sciocca*, a word that means both foolish and, in Tuscan idiom, flavorless.

39. The Italian *zuppa* (soup) was a euphemism for coitus and the production of ejaculate or vaginal secretions. For example, Antonfrancesco Grazzini (1505–1584), called "Il Lasca," composed a burlesque poem entitled *In lode della zuppa* in which he praises it as "of all delicate dishes, by far the best and tastiest one which satisfies and succors the young and the old, the healthy and the sick" (cibo tra tutt' i cibi delicati | più che bel, più che buon, che piaci e giovi | a' putti, a' vecchi, a' sani e agli ammalati). Grazzini, *Le rime burlesche, edite e inedite*, ed. Carlo Verzone (Florence: Sansoni, 1882), 622.

40. As a punishment for having committed a murder, the mythological hero Hercules was forced into the servitude of the Lydian queen Omphale, who obliged him to wear women's attire and to weave. Omphale was in turn often represented wearing Hercules' lion skin and carrying his club. Hercules was similarly convinced by his mistress Iole to swap attire. On this trio, also see II.xi.56–61.

41. The Italian *frugnolare* refers to hunting with a *frugnolo*, a night lantern used to stun fish and fowl. Both terms have strong sexual overtones. Also see II.vi.8.

42. The Italian *bertuccia* also recalls the name of Marmotta's lady-in-waiting.

43. The Italian *corno* can refer to both the musical instrument and the cuckold's horns. Costa employs this play on words throughout the comedy.

44. Cf. Prologue, ln. 63.

45. In addition to its sexually suggestive use here, the Italian idiom *pestare l'acqua nel mortaio* refers to the performance of a futile act, akin to "flogging a dead horse" in English.

46. The Italian *calepino* became a common means of referring to a dictionary after the 1502 publication of lexicographer Ambrogio Calepino's magisterial and multilingual one, republished more than 200 times over the next two and a half centuries.

47. Sunken or hollow cheeks are a symptom of Hippocrates' "cadaverous face." Giovanni Battista della Porta associates these *gote cadute* with people who are "ugly in appearance" in the 1610 translation and expanded edition of his 1586 *De humana physiognomonia libri*; Della Porta, *Della fisionomia dell'huomo* (Naples: Giovan Giacomo Carlino and Costantino Vitale, 1610), 279.

48. Here and immediately below, the answers to Meo's riddle allude to male and female genitalia: Filippetta guesses that the gift is a *sporta* (a basket, or vagina), and Meo states that it is instead a *cappello* (headgear, or the foreskin or head of the phallus). For a similar use of *cappello*, see II.viii.110.

49. The Italian *campan da botta* seems to be an intentionally nonsensical statement.

50. Venus, goddess of love and beauty, is also known by the name Ciprigna or Cypris after her cult in that location. Also see ln 61 in this act and II.iii.189. Gabrina, in contrast, is an ugly and perfidious old woman in the *Orlando furioso* whom the female warrior Marisa encounters in Canto XX and, bound by the rules of chivalry, must twice defend as beautiful when her appearance is mocked by the characters Pinabello and Zerbino: see Ludovico Ariosto, *Orlando furioso*, ed. Lanfranco Caretti (Turin: Einaudi, 1992).

51. The mineral cinnabar was used to make lipsticks. It could also serve as a euphemism for female genitalia.

52. Here and elsewhere Costa's characters blend staple Petrarchan amorous language (including antithesis and oxymoron) with baroque stylistics.

53. *Lumi* (literally, "lights") is a conventional image for eyes.

54. The *pagliaio*, or haystack, could allude to the female genitalia (in as much as it was held up by a metal "stack pole"), or describe an old or ugly woman, particularly in satirical poetry.

55. The popular *moresca*, or "Moorish dance," typically staged a battle between two parties, often between Christians and Muslims (represented by dancers in blackface), or celebrated a victory. The dance was at time performed by buffoons who incorporated burlesque and pantomimic gestures while shaking bells attached to their bodies. The rhythmic, frenzied dance lent itself to sexual allusions as well.

56. The Italian *cappio* is a slipknot, including the kind used to ensnare birds.

57. The *ranocchio*, or frog, is a sexual position described by Aretino in which the woman pulls her legs up to her buttocks: see Pietro Aretino, *Il piacevol ragionamento de l'Aretino: Dialogo di Giulia e di Madalena*, ed. Claudio Galderisi (Rome: Salerno, 1987), 100–104.

58. See Act III, Scene ix, in which the characters Tedeschino and Ancroia are locked inside two cages. These cages are also depicted in the *canzonetta* for Act III and Stefano della Bella's frontispiece. Also see the reference to cages in I.i.37.

59. Though Costa's meaning here is not entirely clear, the foot is a historically common euphemism for the phallus. Cf. similar uses in I.ix.91, 100; I.xi.47, and III.v.31, for example.

60. At its literal level, the *gioco della civetta* was a game in which two children tried to knock a hat off of a third, who bobbed his head up and down in a manner that recalled a bird. For different uses, see also II.x.79 and III.i.26.

61. The Uffizi, now one of Italy's most important art museums, were constructed as the offices (here *Offici*) of the Medici. As discussed in the Introduction, the character Tordo is based on a historical figure who fashioned and sold telescopes and other optical devices at the Uffizi. Also see Act III, Scene ii.

62. The expression *mandare al bordello* is an idiom for sending someone to hell or the devil.

63. Costa's *perdee* seems to be Michelino's German pronunciation of Verdea, a white wine.

64. A fried liver dish.

65. Costa plays with two different kinds of pillows: the *guanciali* upon which one rests one's head and the long cylindrical bolsters, *capezzali*, that are placed below them.

66. Ottoman pirate ships that in this period terrorized the Christian world with their kidnappings throughout the Mediterranean. On the corsairs and their relation to Italy, see Robert C. Davis, *Christian Slaves, Muslim Masters: White Slavery in the Mediterranean, the Barbary Coast and Italy, 1500–1800* (New York: Palgrave Macmillan, 2003).

67. The *cingulum* was part of a Roman bride's wedding costume and was meant to be untied by the groom when consummating the marriage. For associations of the *cingulum* with virginity and chastity belts, see Karen Hersch, *The Roman Wedding: Ritual and Meaning in Antiquity* (Cambridge: Cambridge University Press, 2010), 109–11. This belt, or *cingolo* in Italian, was similarly associated with the restraint or release of female sexuality in the Middle Ages and early modern period. For example, Boccaccio notes that "Venus had a girdle [*cingulum*] which [the Greeks] called a *cestos*: this had not at all been given to her by nature, nor would it have been given to her by the poets unless it had been appropriate for her according to the most sacred and venerable authority of laws, its purpose being to provide some kind of restraint to bridle her excessive wantonness" ("Cingulum Veneri quod vocavere ceston insuper esse dixere, quod illi minime a natura datum fuerat, nec a poetis fuisset ni santissima atque veneranda legum autoritate illi fuisset appositum, ut aliqua li coertione vaga nimis lascivia frenaretu"). He adds that Venus wore this belt only when occupied with "legitimate marriages" (*legitimis … nuptiis and honestas nuptias*) and removed it when engaged in other erotic affairs. Giovanni Boccaccio, *A Genealogy of the Pagan Gods*, ed. and trans. Jon Solomon, vol. 1 (Cambridge MA: Harvard University Press, 2011), 380–81, 386–89.

68. The *bracco francese*, or *Braque français*, is a French hunting dog prized for its ability to point and flush game.

69. Marmotta alludes to *primiera*, a card game comparable to poker in which the key hands were a four of a kind (*primiera*) and a flush (*flusso*). Both the game itself and these two hands also acted as euphemisms for coitus. Francesco Berni highlighted these sexual connotations in his 1526 *Capitolo del gioco della primiera* (Rome: Calvo, 1526). Tasso also treated the game, looking specifically at its relation to women, in *Romeo, ovvero del gioco* and its revised version, *Il Gonzaga secondo, overo del gioco*; a modern edition of the latter is available in Torquato Tasso, *Dialoghi*, ed. Ezio Raimondi, 3 vols. (Florence: Sansoni, 1958), 1:449–97. See George W. McClure, *Parlour Games and the Public Life of Women in Renaissance Italy* (Toronto: University of Toronto Press, 2013). Also see III.v.34–35.

70. While this originally read *più lieto* (happier), Costa or her editors corrected it in the Magliabechiano version to *meno lieto* (less happy).

71. From this point forward, the scene becomes an extended series of risqué jokes that play on Fessa's double meaning as both a city and female genitalia.

72. A *guardadonna* was a woman who tended to a pregnant woman during and after her labor, alongside a midwife. The term could also refer to the female chaperone or nurse for a young lady. Costa's use of the masculine form of the adjective *bello* (attractive, fine) suggests a pun, a man who looks (*guarda*) at women (*donne*).

73. The adjective *bizzarro* in this period referred especially to someone capricious and spirited, while in the Middle Ages it described someone of irascible temperament; the association with strangeness developed later.

74. Literally meaning "little gourd," the *zucchetto* is also a hemispherical skullcap typically worn in ecclesiastical functions.

75. That is, *motu proprio*, "of one's own volition." The term refers specifically to documents personally signed by the pope on his own initiative.

76. The *piva* is an Italian bagpipe, commonly used as a phallic euphemism.

77. Bertuccia misunderstands Marmotta's use of the word *ortolano*, which can mean both a gardener or an ortolan bunting, a small bird in the passerine family and a culinary delicacy when roasted and eaten whole. Like many other avian terms, *ortolano* is also a euphemism for male genitalia.

78. Apparently coining the term *cercastabbio*, Costa refers to peddlers of manure (*stabbio*) for fertilizer. As Ferrone suggests, this may be intended as a reference to panderers. See the notes to his edition of *Li buffoni*, 279n49.

79. The Genovese in this period were famous for their rich and often heavily ornamented fabrics, though the practice of inserting padding and wearing skirts stretched over a hoop (*falda*) that Marmotta goes on to describe was widespread. In contrast to Costa's assessment, Cesare Vecellio praised Genovese women in his famed costume book *Habiti antichi et moderni* for their modesty, though he does single out the noble women for their ability to buy and sell in the marketplace without any harm to their reputation and represents women across classes with small purses for "spending money and other small things necessary to women." See Vecellio, *The Clothing of the Renaissance World: Europe, Asia, Africa, The Americas: Cesare Vecellio's* Habiti Antichi et Moderni, ed. and trans. Margaret F. Rosenthal and Ann Rosalind Jones (London: Thames and Hudson, 2008), 258–61.

80. A long and open-fronted outer gown.

81. Costa perhaps has in mind a statue in Rome called *Il Facchino* (The Porter). One of the city's famous "talking statues" upon which were posted anonymous satirical poems, it depicts a man carrying a round, protruding barrel at his waist from which bubbles a small fountain of water. More generally, porters could be seen around Renaissance cities carrying bundles at their hips or on their shoulders.

82. Harlequin (Arlecchino), one of the most recognizable *commedia dell'arte* characters, was a masked servant often wearing a colorful checkered costume.

83. In a continuation of the running sexual joke, Bertuccia inquires about green produce (*erbaggio*, a euphemism for female genitalia, in contrast to the root vegetables, *radiche*, eaten below) and dairy products (*latticini*, a euphemism for seminal fluid).

84. *Grossi* were silver coins minted in Florence since the Middle Ages that euphemistically referred to male genitalia due to their size and association with power.

85. Despite the line's upbeat tone, Saturn is associated with melancholy and cruelty as well as power and authority.

86. I.e, Cupid.

87. Tedeschino's narrative here is closely modeled on Bernardino Ricci's account of how he earned the name "Tedeschino," or "little German," in the treatise he authored, *Il Tedeschino* (1995), 78–79. For a comparison of the two passages, and for more on buffoons, musicians, and other performers jumping out of cakes, see Megale's introduction to the work (40–42).

88. The *gagliarda*, or galliard, was a vigorous dance composed of hops and kicks.

89. The expression *appoggiare l'alabarda* ("to rest one's halberd," a military weapon consisting of a spiked axe blade on a long pole) means to eat at another's expense.

90. A *doblone* was gold coin minted in Spain and in the New World. Like "doubloon," the word derives from the Spanish *doblón*. Cf. note 104.

91. While the terms *scopacorte* and *frustacavalcate* do not appear to be used widely, if at all, they parody forms of punishment in the early modern period. The "horse" (*cavallo*), for example, involved a teacher whipping the bare buttocks of a wayward student placed astride the back of a peer. See Beecher, *Renaissance Comedy*, 2:462n193.

92. In the lines that follow, Tedeschino employs a series of sexually suggestive images drawn from the art of goldsmithing and metalworking.

93. In gilding, gold leaf can be applied by breathing onto the surface to create moisture and then pressing the leaf into place with brushes.

94. Tedeschino adaptively employs the technical term *tempra* (quenching), the tempering of a hot metal by plunging it into a cooler liquid. Unsurprisingly, the term has a strong sexual connotation, though the plural tempre also has a more literary meaning of timbre or harmony.

95. Here, as in other instances, the foot may also allude to male genitalia. Cf. note 59.

96. Tedeschino makes a pun on "galley slave" and "scribe," conflating oars and pens.

97. *Bastonare il pesce* is an idiomatic expression meaning "to be sent to the galleys."

98. Baldassarre's line recalls Tedeschino's self-assigned epithet, the "cavalier of pleasure."

99. Costa's word *escamberada* is of uncertain meaning but may be an attempt to use or refer to the Spanish *ciambellano* (chamberlain).

100. As noted in the Introduction, buffoons were often associated with medical quackery. Also see III.iii.117–23.

101. A world map.

102. The *moriscos* were Iberian Muslims compeled to convert to Christianity. Like *marranos* (Iberian Jews similarly forced to convert, seen below at I.xii.133 and II.xiii.42), the term was used pejoratively to imply that someone had heretical beliefs. This is one of numerous moments in which other characters assail Baldassarre's Christian orthodoxy.

103. The French House of Condé was the cadet branch of the royal House of Bourbon. Baldassarre perhaps refers to Henri II de Bourbon, Prince of Condé (1588–1646). What follows is a seemingly haphazard list of aristocratic families and figures, which Baldassarre recites in order to burnish his image of international success and influence.

104. The *dobla* was a Spanish gold coin, as was the *ducado* (v. 95).

105. The dukedom of Buckingham was recreated in 1623 after a century of disuse by James I for George Villiers (1592–1628), a highly influential royal favorite whose corruption and botched military and political records nevertheless made him unpopular.

106. The Spinolas were a noble Genovese family. Baldassarre likely refers to Ambrogio Spinola (1569–1630), a celebrated general of the Spanish army to whom Costa dedicates a lament poem in *La selva dei cipressi.*

107. The "great duke of Osuna" in Andalusia, Pedro Téllez-Girón (1574–1624), who also served as the Viceroy of Sicily and Naples. The historical Ricci served at his court in Naples for a period in the 1610s. See the introduction to Ricci, *Il Tedeschino* (1995), 61.

108. Tedeschino alludes to the Catholic ritual prohibition against eating meat on Friday and Saturday. Here, as in the lines that follow, he contrasts Muslim and Jewish dietary laws with Christian practices in order to characterize Baldassarre as a Spanish infidel.

109. I.e., pork products, prohibited for both Muslims and Jews.

110. As noted above, *marrano* is a pejorative term for Iberian Jews forced to convert to Christianity.

111. Here and in the lines that follow, Tedeschino alludes to bandages which come undone during their brawl. In the next act (II.iii.199–224) it becomes clearer that he has these bandages in order to treat a hernia.

112. Costa may have in mind the Roman and Neapolitan proverb *chi sparte c'ha la mejo parte*, meaning that whoever divides something into shares keeps the better part for himself.

113. Mars and Cupid, the son he conceived with Venus.

114. The shield of Heracles (also known as Alcides) was the subject of an eponymous poem by Hesiod. The shield, described at length, shows the face of Fear: "In the centre was Fear worked in adamant, unspeakable, staring backwards with eyes that glowed with fire. His mouth was full of teeth in a white row, fearful and daunting, and upon his grim brow hovered frightful Strife who arrays the throng of men: pitiless she, for she took away the mind and senses of poor wretches who made war against the son of Zeus. Their souls passed beneath the earth and went down into the house of Hades; but their bones, when the skin is rotted about them, crumble away on the dark earth under parching Sirius." *Hesiod, The Homeric Hymns and Homerica*, trans. Hugh G. Evelyn-White (London: W. Heinemann; New York: Macmillan, 1914), 231.

115. Civet is a strong, musky substance produced in the glands of an eponymous cat-like mammal and used to make some perfumes.

116. The sun is in Aquarius during the winter, specifically between January 21st and February 21st.

117. The Italian *cancellare dal calendario*, here used metaphorically, refers to the removal of feast days from the calendar of saints.

118. In the *Orlando furioso* the knight Zerbino is separated from his love, Isabella. Shortly after they are finally reunited, however, he is killed and their happy ending is thwarted. It should be noted that another Zerbino figure surfaces periodically in Costa's letters and poetry, there a dandy mocked and scorned by women.

119. Tedeschino specifically announces his intention to recite *sdrucciolo* ("slippery") verse, in which the stress falls on the antepenultimate syllable of the final word of each line. While figures like Giambattista Giraldi Cinthio would criticize the introduction of *sdruccioli* to drama as being utterly unfitting to the genre, it gained more traction in opera. On the latter, see Rosand, *Opera in Seventeenth-Century Venice*, 344. *Sdrucciolo* appears again in III.vi.17–24. For the sake of readability, we have opted not to replicate the trisyllabic rhyme but have set off Tedeschino's poem in italics.

120. *Alfana*, originally of Arabic origins, describes a large and spirited mare. Cf. the *Orlando furioso*'s description of Gradasso's horse as "una alfana, la più bella | e la miglior che mai portasse sella" (the best and most beautiful that ever wore a saddle, II.li.7–8). The allusion sets up the long series of equestrian images that follow.

121. The *ciaccona*, or chaconne, was a baroque dance with Latin American and Spanish roots often accompanied by guitars, castanets, and tambourines. The dance played a key role in performative representations of foreign spaces, including northern Africa, as well as the celebration of a sexual union; see Rose A. Pruiksma, "Music, Sex, and Ethnicity: Signification in Lully's Theatrical Chaconnes" in *Gender, Sexuality, and Early Music*, ed. Todd M. Borgerding, 227–48 (New York: Routledge, 2002), 227.

122. The distinction Tedeschino makes between comportment of the true and distinguished buffoon and the antics of his more ignoble peers echoes those put forth in Bernardino Ricci's dialogue on the art of buffoonery.

123. With the phrase *cucù de le minchiate*, Tedeschino alludes to two decks of cards and the eponymous games with which they were played. The game of Cuckoo is named after its trump card; upon revealing this card to another player hoping to exchange his lowest card for a higher one, the holder calls out "cucù."

124. The courbette is one of the challenging dressage moves known as "airs above the ground." To perform it, the horse rears up on its hindquarters, tucks in its front legs, and executes a series of hops. The lines that follow refer repeatedly to the increasingly popular art of dressage and equestrian ballet, which became a key element of baroque state spectacle, particularly in Florence. While in her *Festa reale* Costa envisions a grandiose equestrian ballet, this scene satirizes such performances by presenting a buffoon riding astride a hobbyhorse.

125. Apollo.

126. In the *Orlando furioso*, Astolfo uses the terrible sound of his magical horn to frighten and scatter his enemies.

127. One of the most difficult "airs above the ground." In order to perform a capriole, the horse jumps from a raised position with its forelegs tucked in, kicks out its hind legs when horizontal to the ground, and lands back in the same spot. The term can also refer to a somersault.

128. A small Renaissance guitar.

129. The *manège*, or riding academy, emerged in the sixteenth century. Schools in Ferrara, Rome, and Naples became particularly illustrious and served as models for subsequent French and English institutions.

130. The rambade was an elevated platform above the artillery at the prow of a ship. Given that Tedeschino is straddling the pole, Costa might have in mind the bowsprit, the projecting beam.

131. A half-turn to the right or left. When done alternately, this dressage maneuver results in a zigzag movement.

132. A Circassian character from Torquato Tasso's *Gerusalemme liberata*; see the modern edition by Lanfranco Caretti (Turin: Einaudi, 1971).

133. Costa may be making a pun here, as *crepacciate* can refer to both tumbles and a disease causing cracks to develop in horse hooves.

134. The *saltarello* was a frolicsome dance similar to the galliard (cf. I.x.76), incorporating hops and kicks.

135. In addition to being an augmentative word for "moth," the Italian *farfallone* also refers to a tall tale or a blunder.

136. A reference to Hermes, born on Mount Cyllene (Kyllini), who, like his Roman equivalent Mercury, is associated with trickery.

137. A handsome youth, from the mythological story of the beautiful boy loved by Aphrodite/Venus.

138. Venus betrays her consort Vulcan with the more comely Mars. While the *stidione*, a metal spit used to roast and turn meats, has a clear sexual connotation, a turnspit (*voltastidione*) referred not only to the device itself but also the dog that at times powered it by running in a wheel.

139. Marmotta spots Tedeschino's loosened hernia bandages, which become the subject of the joke exchange that follows.

140. A girth (*cigna*) is the band that holds a horse's saddle in place, while the halter (*fune*) is the headpiece that allows one to guide and control a horse by means of an attached lead rope.

141. The Italian *rottura*, used here as a pun on *rotto* (hurt), is a common name for hernia.

142. A *double entendre* also referring to the testicles.

143. Likely a reference to a truss, a medical device used to hold a hernia in place. During this period, trusses could at times consist of a belt and a metal plate rather than a softer pad.

144. Allusions to the male and female genitalia, respectively.

145. Like much of the bird and hunting imagery, wagtail (*cutta*) is a sexual euphemism, in this case referring to a woman. This hunt scene offers a continual string of innuendos as well as slapstick comedy.

146. The Italian *banchetto* (banquet, feast) and verb *banchettare* (to banquet) allude to the sexual act inasmuch as feasting satisfies a hunger. Costa employs this pun frequently throughout the remainder of the comedy.

147. The odd lines that follow are rich in culinary-based sexual euphemisms. The cheese *cascio* became a euphemism based on its linguistic similarities with *cazzo*, a vulgar term for the male genitalia. Terms like *gelatina* (gelatin), *arrostire* (to roast), and *guazzetto* (meat sauce) had similar sexual connotations. Cf. I.i.12 on *zuppa* (soup) as coitus.

148. A very soft, fresh cheese produced in Tuscany and surrounding regions.

149. Venus and Cupid. Costa's language here recalls Petrarch's *Rerum vulgarium fragmenta* 64, which imagines an angered Laura unable to free herself from her lover's breast "where Love from that first laurel grafts many branches" (*del petto ove dal primo lauro innesta Amor più rami*), 6–7; from Francesco Petrarca, *Canzoniere*, ed. Marco Santagata (Milan: Mondadori, 1996); translation by Mark Musa: *The Canzoniere, or Rerum vulgarium fragmenta* (Bloomington: Indiana University Press, 1996), 101.

150. Costa's *grattar con l'altrui la propria rogna* echoes an example of Dante's low, comic style from *Paradiso* XVII.129, where Cacciaguida instructs the pilgrim to speak truthfully about what he has seen and, should those truths prove upsetting to others, "lascia pur grattar dov'è la rogna" (let them scratch where it itches). More broadly, the expression *grattare una rogna* means both to offend or to assail another and, as in English, to satisfy one's sexual urges. Dante Alighieri, *La Commedia secondo l'antica vulgata. Paradiso*, ed. Giorgio Petrocchi. Milan: Mondadori Editore, 1967

151. With the Italian *cornicione*, Tedeschino plays on the word *corna*, or horns, signaling adultery.

152. In Italian, as in English, getting or giving one's greens alludes to copulation.

153. A small red or purplish blotch caused by a small hemorrhage in the skin resulting from excessive coughing, vomiting, or crying.

154. A pus-filled abscess in the tonsils.

155. Here, and in the jokes that follow in this scene, Costa plays with the paradoxical identification of Catorchia as both a bravo and a dwarf.

156. While Catorchia is also a dwarf, Scatapocchio is an especially small one.

157. An almond cookie originating in Prato and typically consumed with the dessert wine Vin Santo.

158. That is, Gobbo of the Violin. Costa's use of this nickname, which becomes more regular in III. iii, indicates that she models the character on the historical and famous musician-buffoon Tommaso Trafedi. See the Introduction, 42.

159. The Italian *portare polli* is an idiomatic expression for whore-mongering.

160. Meaning "between the strands," *Trafila* is a play on Trafedi, Gobbo of the Violin's nickname.

161. The *cornetto*, meaning "little horn," was a woodwind instrument popular during the baroque period and referred euphemistically to male genitalia and cuckolding.

162. The expression *gioco della civetta*, already encountered in I.vii.42, could also be used to refer to frivolous activities, while the association of the *civetta* with sexually promiscuous women also opens this act of play up to more bawdy interpretations. Also cf. III.i.25–26.

163. The Italian *donato* was an eponym for any primer after the Roman grammarian Aelius Donatus.

164. I.e., Cupid

165. In order to prevent her son from fighting and dying at Troy, Achilles' mother Thetis disguised him as a maiden at the court of King Lycomedes. Odysseus successfully identified him by presenting all of the king's daughters with an assortment of gifts, including a sword and shield; Achilles revealed himself by reaching for the weapons of war instead of jewels or finery.

166. On Hercules' donning of Iole and Omphale's clothing, see I.i.17–18 and note.

167. One of Hercules' twelve labors was to fetch golden apples from the garden of the Hesperides nymphs. Hercules enlisted the help of the nymphs' father, Altas, who had been condemned to hold up the heavens in punishment for his rebellion against the gods, by offering to take his place. Once Altas returned with the apples, however, Hercules tricked him into reassuming his heavy load.

168. Costa's Spanish in this line is unclear. We have provided our best estimate of her meaning based on context.

169. The double meaning of the Italian *Troia* as both the ancient city of Troy and a whore plays off of the comparable *double entendre* of Fessa as both Fez and female genitalia.

170. The renowned Muslim doctor and philosopher Avicenna (c. 980–1037), alluded to in order to derisively question Baldassarre's religious identity.

171. Likely a reference to the punishment and torture of prisoners by hanging them by their hands bound behind their backs; cf. II.xiv.12–13.

172. In addition to being a punishment for traitors, as memorialized in defamation paintings (*pittura infamante*) showing prisoners strung upside-down, hanging by the feet or a foot—often above savage dogs—was associated with infidels as the so-called "Jewish execution."

173. Croatto's meaning is not clear, but the phrase *per man d'un gatta* may be his misconstruction of the expression *con la zampa del gatto*, meaning "to make a cat's paw of" (that is, to trick) someone.

174. Costa plays off a line from Petrarch's *RVF* 206: "un bel morir tutta la vita onora" (a good death honors one's whole life, ln. 65).

175. Cf I.vii.42 and II.x.79.

176. The Italian *piccardia* alludes to the gallows, or "land of the hanged," through a play on the linguistic similarities between the French region of Picardy and *impiccati*, those condemned to die by the noose.

177. Giovanni Botero's political treatise *Della ragion di stato* was published in 1589.

178. Cf. I.vii.48–51.

179. The telescope was invented in 1608. Galileo's technological improvements on it allowed him to publish the *Sidereus Nuncius* two years later. Ferdinando II de' Medici dedicated substantial resources to the development and improvement of lenses at the Florentine court. Masino here pokes fun at the instrument by imagining it being used as a chamber pot. The telescope reappears in Stefano della Bella's frontispiece in the hands of one of the players.

180. I.e., Tedeschino

181. The lingual frenulum is the tissue that connects the tongue to the floor of the mouth. As the tongue continues to elongate after a child's birth, the frenulum appears to retract. When this does not happen fully, one has the appearance of being "tongue-tied."

182. Buffoons themselves used the term *contraffare* to describe the improvisation of character impressions. See Henke, *Performance and Literature*, 52–54.

183. Cf. II.iii.85.

184. The Tuscan expression *sapere conciare tre uova in un bacile* refers to the execution of a facile task and here also alludes to Gobbo of the Violin's ability to arrange adulterous relationships.

185. The Meander River in present-day Turkey, known for its tortuous course. According to myth, the river takes its name from King Maeander, who, after having to kill his son, mother, and sister in order to fulfill a vow, threw himself into its waters.

186. The Italian *fede* may refer to faith, fidelity, and, as a symbol of the latter, a wedding band.

187. As in the case of Ancroia's exchange with Gobbo of the Violin in III.iii, lns. 30 and 44, the jokes that follow play on the double meaning of *ambasciatore* (lns. 10, 23) and *fare ambasciata* (ln. 21), referring to both the delivery of messages and the completion of sexual acts, the latter highlighted by the repeated references to Fessa.

188. This is perhaps an adaptation of the expression *cadere in grembo allo zio* (literally, to fall into your uncle's lap), meaning to negotiate with someone amenable to one's own cause.

189. Cf. the similar set of images given by Tordo and Bertuccia in I.ix.91–102.

190. Marmotta once again alludes to the card game *primiera*. Marmotta has been dealt one of the strongest possible hands (a *cinquantacinque*, 55, composed of an ace, a six, and a seven of the same suit) while that of Ancroia is weaker (containing merely the ace and seven). Nevertheless, Marmotta fails to win at the game. On this game and its sexual connotations, see I.viii.24.

191. Costa perhaps has in mind the Florentine expression *fare bue fiesolano* (literally, to be a Fiesolan bull), describing someone unable to attain something he desires. It might also suggest giving the horns to a partner, to make him a cuckold. The reference to rabbits suggests prolific sexual activity.

192. Michelino confounds *buon giorno* (good day) with *mal giorno* (bad day).

193. As Grasso will note immediately below, Michelino begins speaking in *sdrucciolo* (trisyllabic) verse beginning with line 17. In a manner that recalls but surpasses Tedeschino's earlier recitation of *sdrucciolo* poetry to Marmotta (II.iii.12–28), Michelino invents nonsensical trisyllabic rhymes by appending "-ole" to shorter words. In order to give readers a taste of this farcical passage without compromising clarity, we have opted to replicate Michelino's style in the final two lines.

194. Michelino's language and meaning here is unclear.

195. Costa's original *faccia da prence* may pun on similar expressions such as *faccia da culo* (a brazen and odious person, literally an ass-face).

196. The original Italian phrase *su l'asino scopare il Tedeschino* refers to a form of charivari punishment in which the accused was made to ride backwards on a donkey while being beaten and insulted.

197. Croatto's macaronic Italian phrase *com'al larda solir andar la gatta* (literally, as the cat usually goes to the lard) adapts the Tuscan expression *come il gatto al lardo* (like a cat to lard). We have opted for a comparable English equivalent.

198. The spinning wheel (*arcolaio*), a euphemism for female genitalia, is set in motion by the foot (*piede*), a euphemism for male genitalia.

199. According to the classical theory of bodily humors, an excess of choler (yellow bile) resulted in an irascible temperament.

200. "My soul, my heart, my life."

201. The conjunction of the sun and moon produces the New Moon, the start of the lunar cycle.

202. Bertuccia's pun contrasts Mars, the god of war, with Saint Martin, the protector of cuckolded husbands.

203. This expression is clearly intended to underscore Croatto's Turkish origins. It may be Costa's approximation of the Arabic greeting *alaikum as-salaam* (may peace be upon you too).

204. The Italian *boccalone* can refer both to a gossip or slanderer and to a type of bird identifiable by its large beak.

205. This dance, along with two other *canzonette*, follows below. For other references to the dance, see Marmotta's performance instructions to Tedeschino in II.iii.42.

206. For a discussion of this *canzonetta* as an example of polyphonic music within the comedic tradition, see Thomas F. Heck, "Incidental Music in Commedia dell'Arte Performances," in *The Routledge Companion to Commedia dell'Arte*, ed. Judith Chaffee and Olly Crick (New York: Routledge, 2015), 257.

207. A further allusion to Tedeschino's hernia bandages akin to those seen at I.xiii.24 and II.iii.199–224.

208. Cups (*coppe*) and clubs (*bastoni*) are two of the suits in traditional Italian card decks.

Bibliography

Works by Margherita Costa

Manuscripts and Archival Materials

Archivio Doria Pamphilj, Rome

Le sette giornate, o vero Il viaggio di Loreto della Signora Margarita Costa al S[ignor] C[onte]. Fondo Archiviolo, XX, busta 122, fols. 268r–297v.

Biblioteca Apostolica Vaticana, Rome (BAV)

All'ecc. principe di Palestrina per la festa a cavallo fatta da sua Eccell. alla maestà di Cristina Regina di Svezia. Arch. Barb. Indice I, fasc. 1088.

Cecilia martire. Barb. lat. 4069.

Letter to Mario Chigi and poem *Gran prence, a te, che di Quirino al trono.* Chigi I.VII.273, fols. 125r–126r.

Oh Dio, voi che mi dite. Musical scores by Marco Marrazoli. Chigi Q.VIII.177.9, fols. 15v–18r.

Codices Ferrajoli 125, cc. 53–118. Nineteenth-century transcriptions from Margherita Costa, *La tromba di Parnaso.*

Codices Ferrajoli 128, cc. 247–431. Nineteenth-century transcriptions from Margherita Costa, *La tromba di Parnaso.*

Biblioteca Nazionale Centrale di Firenze, Florence (BNCF)

Festa reale per ballo de' cavalli. 1640. MS II II 371.

Printed Works (chronologically by date of publication)

Istoria del viaggio d'Alemagna del serenissimo Gran Duca di Toscana Ferdinando Secondo. Venice: n.p., n.d. [after 1628].

Per l'incendio di Pitti. Florence: Stamperia nuova, 1638.

La chitarra, canzoniere amoroso. [Frankfurt: Daniel Wastch], 1638.

Il violino. [Frankfurt: Daniel Wastch], 1638.

Lettere amorose. Venice: n.p., 1639. Reprints: Venice: Li Turini, 1643; Venice: Giacomo Turini, 1674.

Lo stipo. Venice: n.p., 1639.

Flora feconda, poema. Florence: Massi e Landi, 1640.

La Flora feconda, drama. Florence: Massi e Landi, 1640.
La selva di cipressi, opera lugubre. Florence: Massi e Landi, 1640.
Li buffoni, commedia ridicola. Florence: Massi e Landi, 1641.
Cecilia martire, poema sacro. Rome: Mascardi, 1644.
Festa reale per balletto a cavallo, opera. Paris: Cramoisy, 1647.
La selva di Diana. Paris: Cramoisy, 1647.
La tromba di Parnaso. Paris: Cramoisy, 1647.
Gl'amori della luna. Venice: Giuliani, 1654.
Al Serenissimo Ferdinando II, Gran Duca di Toscana, per la Festa di San Gio. Batista. Venice: n.p., n.d.
Alla Serenissima Vittoria della Rovere, Gran Duchessa di Toscana, per la Festa di San Gio. Batista. Venice: n.p., n.d.
Alla Serenissima Margherita de Medici, Duchessa di Parma, per l'arrivo in Fiorenza. Venice: n.p., n.d.
Al Serenissimo Principe Gio. Carlo di Toscana, per la carica di generaliss. del mare conferitagli dalla M. Cattolica. Florence: Massi e Landi, n.d.
All'Altezza Serenissima di Ferdinando Secondo Gran Duca di Toscana nel giorno della sua nascita. Florence: Stamperia de' Landi, 1655.
Li buffoni. In *Commedie dell'arte*, edited by Siro Ferrone, 2:234–359. Milan: Mursia, 1985–1986.
Voice of a Virtuosa and Courtesan: Selected Poems of Margherita Costa. Edited by Natalia Costa-Zalessow. Translated by Joan E. Borrelli. New York: Bordighera Press, 2015.

Other Primary Sources

Manuscripts

Archivio di Stato di Venezia

Faustini papers, Scuola Grande San Marco, b. 112.

Biblioteca Apostolica Vaticana (BAV)

Barb. lat. 4059, fols. 131v–137v. "*L'Orfeo* / Personaggi dell'opera."

Biblioteca Nazionale Centrale di Firenze (BNCF)

Magliabechi, Antonio. MS Magl. IX 14 fol. 7r.
Marmi, Antonfrancesco. *Miscellanea di diverse notizie letterarie e storiche raccolte per lo più dagli eruditissimi discorsi del Signor Antonio Magliabechi tenuti col Cavalier Antonfrancesco Marmi*. MS Magl. VIII 15, fol. 39r.

———. *Miscellanea di diverse notizie letterarie e storiche*. MS Magl. VIII 16, fols. 51r– 51v.

Biblioteca Statale di Lucca

"Raccolta di varie composizioni della signora Isabetta Coreglia." MS 205.

Printed Sources

Abriani, Paolo. *Poesie*. Venice: Francesco Valvasense, 1663.

Adimari, Alessandro. *La Tersicore, o vero scherzi, e paradossi poetici sopra la beltà delle donne fra difetti ancora ammirabili, e vaghe*. Florence: Massi e Landi, 1637.

Alighieri, Dante. *La Commedia secondo l'antica vulgata*. Edited by Giorgio Petrocchi. Milan: Mondadori Editore, 1967.

Andreini, Isabella. *La Mirtilla*. Edited by Maria Luisa Doglio. Lucca: Pacini Fazzi, 1995.

———. *Lettere di Isabella Andreini padovana, comica gelosa e academica intenta nominata l'Accesa*. Venice: Marc'Antonio Zaltieri, 1607.

Aretino, Pietro. *Cortigiana; Opera nova; Pronostico; Il testamento dell'elefante; Farza*. Edited by Angelo Romano. Milan: BUR, 1989.

———. *Il piacevol ragionamento de l'Aretino: Dialogo di Giulia e di Madalena*. Edited by Claudio Galderisi. Rome: Salerno, 1987.

Ariosto, Ludovico. *Orlando furioso*. Edited by Lanfranco Caretti. Turin: Einaudi, 1992.

Baldini, Vittorio, and Luca Marenzio. *Il lauro secco: Libro primo di madrigali a cinque voci di diversi autori*. Ferrara: Baldini, 1582.

Baldinucci, Filippo. *Notizie de' professori del disegno da Cimabue in qua*. 6 vols. in 5. Florence: Santi Franchi, 1681–1728.

Barbieri, Nicolò. *La supplica, discorso famigliare a quelli che trattano de' comici*. Edited by Ferdinando Taviani. Milan: Il Polifilo, 1971.

Bardi, Ferdinando. *Dcescrizione delle feste fatte in Firenze per le reali nozze de' serenissimi sposi Ferdinando II, Gran Duca di Toscana, e Vittoria, Principessa d'Urbino*. Florence: Zanobi Pignoni, 1637.

Beecher, Donald, ed. *Renaissance Comedy: The Italian Masters*. 2 vols. Toronto: University of Toronto Press, 2008–2010.

Bergalli, Luisa, ed. *Componimenti poetici delle più illustri rimatrici d'ogni secolo*. Venice: Antonio Mora, 1726.

Berni, Francesco. *Capitolo del gioco della primiera col comento di messer Pietropaulo da San Chirico*. Rome: Calvo, 1526.

Boccaccio, Giovanni. *A Genealogy of the Pagan Gods*, vol. 1. Edited and translated by Jon Solomon. Cambridge, MA: Harvard University Press, 2011.

Cantatas by Marco Marazzoli. Edited by Wolfgang Witzenmann. In *The Italian Cantata in the Seventeenth Century*, vol. 4. New York: Garland, 1986.

Caroso, Fabritio. *Courtly Dance of the Renaissance: A New Translation and Edition of the* Nobiltà di dame *(1600) by Fabritio Caroso*. Edited and translated by Julia Sutton and F. Marian Walker. 2nd. ed. New York: Dover, 1995.

Cavalli, Francesco. *La Calisto.* Edited by Jennifer Williams Brown. Middleton, WI: A-R Editions, 2007.

Cecchini, Pier Maria. *Frutti delle moderne comedie, et avisi a chi le recita.* Padua: Guaresco Guareschi, 1628.

Cicero. *On the Ideal Orator.* Translated and edited by James M. May and Jakob Wisse. Oxford: Oxford University Press, 2001.

Costa-Zalessow, Natalia, ed. *Scrittrici italiane dal XIII al XX secolo: Testi e critica.* Ravenna: Longo, 1982.

Crescimbeni, Giovanni Mario. *Comentari intorno alla sua istoria della volgar poesia*. 5 vols. Rome: Lorenzo Basegio, 1730–1731.

De Blasi, Jolanda, ed. *Antologia delle scrittrici italiane dalle origini al 1800.* Florence: Nemi, 1930.

Della Porta, Giovanni Battista. *Della fisionomia dell'huomo*. Naples: Giovanni Giacomo Carlino and Costantino Vitale, 1610.

Erythraeus, Janus Nicius [ps. Giovanni Vittorio Rossi]. *Eudemiae libri decem.* Amsterdam: Iodocum Kalcovium et socios, 1645.

———. *Pinacotheca imaginum illustrium doctrinae vel ingenii laude virorum.* 3 vols. Amsterdam: Iodocum Kalcovium et socios, 1643–1648.

Facezie, motti, buffonerie et burle, del Piovano Arlotto, del Gonnella, et del Barlacchia. Florence: Giunti, 1565.

Ferrone, Siro, ed. *Commedie dell'arte.* 2 vols. Milan: Mursia, 1985–1986.

Franco, Veronica. *Poems and Selected Letters.* Edited and translated by Ann Rosalind Jones and Margaret F. Rosenthal. Chicago: University of Chicago Press, 1998.

Galilei, Galileo. *Dialogo sopra i due massimi sistemi del mondo, tolemaico e copernicano*. Florence: Gio. Batista Landini, 1632.

———. *Opere di Galileo Galilei.* 2 vols. Bologna: per gli heredi del Dozza, 1656.

———. *Sidereus nuncius, magna longeque admirabilia spectacula pandens.* Venice: Baglioni, 1610.

Garzoni, Tommaso. *La piazza universale di tutte le professioni del mondo.* Venice: Giovanni Battista Somascho, 1585.

Gianni, Angelo, ed. *Anch'esse "quasi simili a Dio": Le donne nella storia della letteratura italiana, in gran parte ignote o misconosciute: Dalle origini alla fine dell'Ottocento.* Viareggio [Lucca]: M. Baroni, 1997.

Grazzini, Antonfrancesco [Il Lasca]. *Le rime burlesche, edite e inedite.* Edited by Carlo Verzone. Florence: Sansoni, 1882.

Hesiod. *Hesiod, the Homeric Hymns, and Homerica*. Translated by Hugh G. Evelyn-White. London: W. Heinemann; New York: Macmillan, 1914.

Le incisioni di Jacques Callot nelle collezioni italiane. Exhibition Catalogue. Milan: Mazzotta, 1992.

Kaborycha, Lisa, ed. and trans. *A Corresponding Renaissance: Letters Written by Italian Women, 1375–1650*. Oxford: Oxford University Press, 2015.

Mandosio, Prospero. *Bibliotheca romana, seu Romanorum scriptorum centuriae*, 2 vols. Rome: Ignati de Lazzaris, 1682–1692.

Marinella, Lucrezia. *Exhortations to Women and to Others If They Please*. Edited and translated by Laura Benedetti. Toronto: Centre for Reformation and Renaissance Studies, 2012.

Marinelli, Elvira, ed. *Poesia: Antologia illustrata*. Florence: Giunti, 2002.

Marino, Giambattista. *Egloghe boscherecce del cavalier Marino, cioè, Tirsi, Aminta, Dafne, Siringa, Pan, Elcippo, et i Sospiri d'Ergasto, con cinque canzoni … et il Camerone d'istesso*. Milan: G. B. Cerri, 1627.

———. *Lettere*. Edited by Marziano Guglielminetti. Turin: Einaudi, 1966.

Menestrier, Claude-François. *Des représentations en musique anciennes et modernes*. Paris: René Guignard, 1681.

Ottonelli, Giovanni Domenico. *Della christiana moderatione del theatro*. Florence: G. A. Bonardi, 1652.

Petrarca, Francesco. *Canzoniere*. Edited by Marco Santagata. Milan: Mondadori, 1996.

———. *The Canzoniere, or Rerum vulgarium fragmenta*. Translated and edited by Mark Musa. Bloomington: Indiana University Press, 1996.

Quadrio, Francesco Saverio. *Della storia e della ragione d'ogni poesia*. 5 vols. in 7. Milan: A. Agnelli, 1739–1752.

Ricci, Bernardino. *Il Tedeschino, overo Difesa dell'Arte del Cavalier del Piacere. Dialogo dal medesimo dedicato a tutti quelli principi che si dilettano tenere buffoni appresso di loro*. Venice: n.p., n.d.

———. *Il Tedeschino, overo Difesa dell'Arte del Cavalier del Piacere: Con l'epistolario e altri documenti*, ed. Teresa Megale (Florence: Le Lettere, 1995).

Ronna, Antoine, ed. *Parnaso italiano: Poeti italiani contemporanei, maggiori e minori*. 2 vols. Paris: Baudry, 1843.

Salvadori, Andrea. *La flora, overo Il natal de' fiori*. Florence: Pietro Cecconcelli, 1628.

Scala, Flaminio. *The Commedia dell'Arte of Flaminio Scala: A Translation and Analysis of Thirty Scenarios*. Edited and translated by Richard Andrews. Lanham, MD: Scarecrow Press, 2008.

———. *Il teatro delle favole rappresentative*. Edited by Ferruccio Marotti. 2 vols. Milan: Il Polifilo, 1976.

Scielta di lettere amorose di Ferrante Pallavicino, Luca Asserino, Margarita Costa Romana, Gerolamo Parabosco. Venice: Giacomo Bortoli, 1656.

Solerti, Angelo. *Musica, ballo e drammatica alla corte Medicea dal 1600 al 1637: Notizie tratte da un diario, con appendice di testi inediti e rari.* Florence: R. Bemporad e figlio, 1905.

Tasso, Torquato. *Dialoghi.* Edited by Ezio Raimondi. 3 vols. Florence: Sansoni, 1958.

———. *Gerusalemme liberata.* Edited by Lanfranco Caretti. Turin: Einaudi, 1971.

Vecellio, Cesare. *The Clothing of the Renaissance World: Europe, Asia, Africa, The Americas: Cesare Vecellio's* Habiti antichi et moderni. Edited and translated by Margaret F. Rosenthal and Ann Rosalind Jones. London: Thames and Hudson, 2008.

Verucci, Virgilio. *Li diversi linguaggi.* Venice: Spineda, 1627.

Villani, Filippo. *Liber de civitatis florentiae famosis civibus.* Edited by Gustavo Camillo Galletti. Florence: J. Mazzoni, 1847.

Secondary Sources

Acton, Harold. *The Last Medici.* New York: Thames and Hudson, 1980.

Ademollo, Alessandro. *I primi fasti della musica italiana a Parigi, 1645–1662.* Milan: Ricordi, 1884.

Albala, Ken. *The Banquet: Dining in the Great Courts of Late Renaissance Europe.* Urbana: University of Illinois Press, 2007.

———. *Eating Right in the Renaissance.* Berkeley: University of California Press, 2002.

Andrews, Richard. "Erudite Comedy." In *A History of Italian Theatre*, edited by Joseph Farrell and Paolo Puppa, 39–43. Cambridge: Cambridge University Press, 2006.

———. *Scripts and Scenarios: The Performance of Comedy in Renaissance Italy.* Cambridge: Cambridge University Press, 1993.

Arlia, C. "Un bandito e una cortigiana letterati." *Il bibliofilo,* nos. 8–9 (1881): 164–66.

Bakhtin, Mikhail. *Rabelais and His World.* Translated by Hélène Iswolsky. Bloomington: Indiana University Press, 1984.

Battistini, Andrea. *Il barocco: Cultura, miti, immagini.* Rome: Salerno, 2000.

Baudi de Vesme, Alexandre, and Phyllis Dearborn Massar, eds. *Stefano della Bella: Catalogue raisonné.* 2 vols. New York: Collectors Editions, 1906, 1971.

Beecher, Donald. "Introduction, From Italy to England: The Sources, Conventions and Influence of 'Erudite Comedy.'" In *Renaissance Comedy: The Italian Masters*, 2:3–20. Toronto: University of Toronto Press, 2009.

Benadusi, Giovanna. "The Gender Politics of Vittoria della Rovere." In *Medici Women: The Making of a Dynasty in Grand Ducal Tuscany*, edited by Giovanna Benadusi and Judith C. Brown, 265–301. Toronto: Centre for Reformation and Renaissance Studies, 2015.

Bettella, Patrizia. *The Ugly Woman: Transgressive Aesthetic Models in Italian Poetry from the Middle Ages to the Baroque*. Toronto: University of Toronto Press, 2005.

Biagioli, Mario. *Galileo, Courtier: The Practice of Science in the Culture of Absolutism*. Chicago: University of Chicago Press, 1993.

Bianchi, Dante. "Una cortigiana rimatrice del Seicento: Margherita Costa." *Rassegna critica della letteratura italiana* 29 (1924): 1–31 and 187–203.

———. "Una cortigiana rimatrice del Seicento: Margherita Costa." *Rassegna critica della letteratura italiana* 30 (1925): 158–211.

Bianconi, Lorenzo and Thomas Walker. "Production, Consumption, and Political Function of Seventeenth-Century Opera." *Early Music History* 4 (1984): 209–96.

Bisceglia, Anna, Matteo Ceriana, and Simona Mammana, eds. *Buffoni, villani e giocatori alla corte dei Medici*. Livorno: Sillabe, 2016.

Brosius, Amy. "'Il suon, lo sguardo, il canto': The Function of Portraits of Mid-Seventeenth-Century *Virtuose* in Rome." *Italian Studies* 63, no. 1 (2008): 17–39.

Brown, Pamela Allen. "The Mirror and the Cage: Queens and Dwarfs at the Early Modern Court." In *Historical Affects and the Early Modern Theater*, edited by Ronda Arab, Michelle Dowd, and Adam Zucker, 137–51. New York: Routledge, 2015.

Bruni, Roberto. "Editori e tipografi a Firenze nel Seicento." *Studi secenteschi* 45 (2004): 325–419.

Boggione, Valter, and Giovanni Casalegno, eds. *Dizionario letterario del lessico amoroso: Metafore, eufemismi, trivialismi*. Turin: UTET, 2000.

Bowers, Jane. "The Emergence of Women Composers in Italy, 1566–1700." In *Women Making Music: The Western Art Tradition, 1150–1950,* edited by Jane Bowers and Judith Tick, 116–67. Urbana: University of Illinois Press, 1987.

Campbell, Malcolm. "Medici Patronage and the Baroque: A Reappraisal." *Art Bulletin* 48, no. 2 (1966): 133–46.

———. *Pietro da Cortona at the Pitti Palace: A Study of the Planetary Rooms and Related Projects*. Princeton, NJ: Princeton University Press, 1977.

Camporesi, Piero. *Rustici e buffoni: Cultura popolare e cultura d'élite fra Medioevo ed età moderna*. Turin: Einaudi, 1991.

Capponi, Niccolò. "Le Palle di Marte: Military Strategy and Diplomacy in the Grand Duchy of Tuscany under Ferdinand II de' Medici (1621–1670)." *The Journal of Military History* 68, no. 4 (2004): 1105–1141.

Capucci, Martino. "Costa, Margherita." In *DBI* 30 (1984): 232–34. <http://www.treccani.it/ enciclopedia/margherita-costa_(Dizionario-Biografico)/>.

Cheng, Sandra. "Parodies of Life: Baccio del Bianco's Comic Drawings of Dwarfs." In *Parody and Festivity in Early Modern Art: Essays on Comedy as Social Vision*, edited by David R. Smith, 127–42. Burlington, VT: Ashgate, 2012.

Cherchi, Paolo. "Marino and the Meraviglia." In *Culture and Authority in the Baroque*, edited by Massimo Ciavolella and Patrick Coleman, 63–72. Toronto: University of Toronto Press, 2005.

———. *La metamorfosi dell'Adone*. Ravenna: Longo, 1996.

Ciavolella, Massimo. "Text as (Pre)text: Erudite Renaissance Comedy and the *commedia ridicolosa*: The Example of Gian Lorenzo Bernini's *L'impresario*." *Rivista di studi italiani* 10 (1992): 22–34.

Claretta, Gaudenzio. *Storia della reggenza di Cristina di Francia, Duchessa di Savoia: Con annotazioni e documenti inediti*. Vol. 3. Turin: Civelli, 1868–1869.

Clubb, Louise George. *Italian Drama in Shakespeare's Time*. New Haven: Yale University Press, 1989.

Coelho, Victor. "The Baroque Guitar: Players, Paintings, Patrons, and the Public." In *The World of Baroque Music: New Perspectives*, edited by George B. Stauffer, 169–84. Bloomington: Indiana University Press, 2006.

Coller, Alexandra. *Women, Rhetoric, and Drama in Early Modern Italy*. New York: Routledge, 2017.

Cope, Jackson. "Bernini and Roman *Commedie Ridicolose*." *PMLA* 102, no. 2 (1987): 177–86.

Costa-Zalessow, Natalia. "Margherita Costa." In *Seventeenth-Century Italian Poets and Dramatists*, edited by Albert N. Mancini and Glenn Palen Pierce, 113–18. Detroit: Gale Cengage Learning, 2008.

———. "Una poesia femminista del 1672 anonima e dimenticata, da attribuire a Margherita Costa." *Esperienze letterarie* 35 no. 4 (2010): 79–85.

Cotta Stumpo, Irene. "Ferdinando II de' Medici, granduca di Toscana." *DBI* 46 (1996), 278–83. <http://www.treccani.it/enciclopedia/ferdinando-ii-de-medici-granduca-di-toscana_(Dizionario-Biografico)/>.

Cox, Virginia. *Women's Writing in Italy, 1400–1650*. Baltimore: Johns Hopkins University Press, 2008.

Crimi, Giuseppe. *Nanerie del Rinascimento: "La nanea" di Michelangelo Serafini e altri versi di corte e d'accademia*. Manziana [Rome]: Vecchiarelli, 2006.

Croce, Benedetto. *Nuovi saggi sulla letteratura italiana del Seicento*. Bari: Laterza, 1931.

———. *Storia della età barocca in Italia: Pensiero-poesia e letteratura vita morale*. Bari: Laterza, 1929.

Croce, Franco, et al. eds., *I capricci di Proteo: Percorsi e linguaggi del Barocco; Atti del convegno di Lecce, 23–26 ottobre 2000*. Rome: Salerno, 2002.

Cummings, Anthony M. *The Maecenas and the Madrigalist: Patrons, Patronage, and the Origins of the Italian Madrigal.* Philadelphia: American Philosophical Society, 2004.

———. *The Politicized Muse: Music for Medici Festivals, 1512–1537.* Princeton, NJ: Princeton University Press, 1992.

Cusick, Suzanne. *Francesca Caccini at the Medici Court: Music and the Circulation of Power.* Chicago: University of Chicago Press, 2009.

D'Accone, Frank A., et al. "Florence." *Grove Music Online.* Oxford University Press. <http://www.oxfordmusiconline.com.libdb.fairfield.edu/subscriber/article/grove/music/09847 >.

Davis, Robert C. *Christian Slaves, Muslim Masters: White Slavery in the Mediterranean, the Barbary Coast, and Italy, 1500–1800.* London: Palgrave Macmillan, 2003.

Dizionario biografico degli italiani. Rome: Istituto della Enciclopedia italiana, 1960–. Abbreviated as *DBI.* Online: <http://www.treccani.it/catalogo/catalogo_prodotti/la_biografia_italiana/dizionario_biografico_degli_italiani.html >.

Favaro, Antonio. *La libreria di Galileo Galilei descritta ed illustrata.* Rome: Tipografia delle matematiche e fisiche, 1887. Extract from the *Bullettino di bibliografia e di storia delle scienze matematiche e fisiche*, anno 19 (1886), 219–94.

Forlani Tempesti, Anna. *Mostra di incisioni di Stefano della Bella.* Florence: Olschki, 1973.

Frantz, David O. *Festum Voluptatis: A Study of Renaissance Erotica.* Columbus, OH: Ohio State University Press, 1989.

Freitas, Roger. *Portrait of a Castrato: Politics, Patronage, and Music in the Life of Atto Melani.* Cambridge: Cambridge University Press, 2009.

Gerboni, Luigi. *Un umanista nel Seicento, Giano Nicio Eritreo: studio biografico critico.* Città di Castello: S. Lapi, 1899.

Ghadessi, Touba. "Lords and Monsters: Visible Emblems of Rule." *I Tatti Studies in the Italian Renaissance* 16, no. 1/2 (2013): 491–523.

Ghislanzoni, Alberto. *Luigi Rossi (Aloysius de Rubeis): Biografia e analisi delle composizioni.* Milan: Fratelli Bocca, 1954.

Giachino, Luisella. "Cicero libertinus: La satira della Roma Barberiniana nell'*Eudemia* dell'Eritreo." *Studi secenteschi* 43 (2002): 185–215.

Giannetti, Laura. "Italian Renaissance Food-Fashioning, or The Triumph of Greens." *California Italian Studies* 1, no. 2 (2010): 1–16.

Glixon, Beth L., and Jonathan E. Glixon. *Inventing the Business of Opera: The Impresario and His World in Seventeenth-Century Venice.* Oxford: Oxford University Press, 2006.

Goethals, Jessica. "The Bizarre Muse: The Literary Persona of Margherita Costa." *Early Modern Women: An Interdisciplinary Journal*, 12, no. 1 (2017): 48–72.

———. "The Patronage Politics of Equestrian Ballet: Allegory, Allusion, and Satire in the Courts of Seventeenth-Century Italy and France." *Renaissance Quarterly* 70, no. 4 (Winter 2017): 1397–448.

Goggio, Emilio. "The Prologue in the *Commedie Erudite* of the Sixteenth Century." *Italica* 18, no. 3 (1941): 124–32.

Goldberg, Edward L. *Patterns in Late Medici Art Patronage.* Princeton, NJ: Princeton University Press, 1983.

Gordon, Bonnie. *Monteverdi's Unruly Women: The Power of Song in Early Modern Italy*. Cambridge: Cambridge University Press, 2004.

Gordon, Mel. "Lazzi." In *The Routledge Companion to Commedia dell'Arte*, edited by Judith Chaffee and Oliver Crick, 167–76. New York: Routledge, 2015.

Grieco, Allen J. "From Roosters to Cocks: Italian Renaissance Fowl and Sexuality." In *Erotic Cultures of Renaissance Italy,* edited by Sara F. Matthews-Grieco, 89–140. Burlington, VT: Ashgate, 2010.

Hale, John Rigby. *Florence and the Medici: The Pattern of Control.* London: Thames and Hudson, 1977.

Hammond, Frederick. *Music and Spectacle in Baroque Rome: Barberini Patronage under Urban VIII.* New Haven: Yale University Press, 1994.

———. *The Ruined Bridge: Studies in Barberini Patronage of Music and Spectacle, 1631–1679.* Sterling Heights, MI: Harmonie Park Press, 2010.

Harness, Kelley. *Echoes of Women's Voices: Music, Art, and Female Patronage in Early Modern Florence.* Chicago: University of Chicago Press, 2006.

———. "*La Flora* and the End of Female Rule in Tuscany." *Journal of the American Musicological Society* 51, no. 3 (1998): 437–76.

———. "Habsburgs, Heretics, and Horses: Equestrian Ballets and Other Staged Battles in Florence During the First Decade of the Thirty Years War." In *L'arme e gli amori: Ariosto, Tasso, and Guarini in Late Renaissance Florence: Acts of an International Conference, Florence, Villa I Tatti, June 27–29, 2001*, edited by Massimiliano Rossi and Fiorella Gioffredi Superbi, 2:255–83. Florence: Olschki, 2004.

Heck, Thomas F. "Incidental Music in Commedia dell'Arte Performances." In *The Routledge Companion to Commedia dell'Arte*, edited by Judith Chaffee and Olly Crick, 255–67. New York: Routledge, 2015.

Heilbron, J. L. *Galileo*. Oxford: Oxford University Press, 2010.

Heller, Wendy. *Emblems of Eloquence: Opera and Women's Voices in Seventeenth-Century Venice.* Berkeley: University of California Press, 2003.

Henke, Robert. *Performance and Literature in the Commedia dell'Arte.* Cambridge: Cambridge University Press, 2002.

Hersch, Karen. *The Roman Wedding: Ritual and Meaning in Antiquity.* Cambridge: Cambridge University Press, 2010.

Hill, John Walter. "Florence: Musical Spectacle and Drama, 1570–1650." In *The Early Baroque Era from the Late 16th Century to the 1660s*, edited by Curtis Price, 121–45. Englewood Cliffs: Prentice Hall, 1994.

Jaffe-Berg, Erith. *Commedia dell'Arte and the Mediterranean: Charting Journeys and Mapping "Others."* New York: Routledge, 2016.

———. "Language, Food and the Hierarchy of Values in the Commedia dell'Arte Performance from the Renaissance to the Eighteenth Century." *European Studies Journal* 17–18 (2000–2001): 115–30.

———. *The Multilingual Art of Commedia dell'Arte.* Toronto: Legas, 2009.

Jeanneret, Christine. "Gender Ambivalence and the Expression of Passions in the Performances of Early Roman Cantatas by Castrati and Female Singers." In *The Emotional Power of Music: Multidisciplinary Perspectives on Musical Arousal, Expression, and Social Control*, edited by Tom Cochrane, Bernardino Fantini, and Klaus R Scherer, 85–102. Oxford: Oxford University Press, 2013.

Johnson, Charles. *Stefano della Bella, Baroque Printmaker: The I. Webb Surratt, Jr. Print Collection.* Richmond, VA: Marsh Art Gallery, University of Richmond Museums, 2001.

Johnson, Christopher D. *Hyperboles: The Rhetoric of Excess in Baroque Literature and Thought.* Cambridge, MA: Harvard University Press, 2010

Katritzky, M. A. *The Art of Commedia: A Study in the Commedia dell'Arte 1560–1620 with Special Reference to the Visual Records.* Amsterdam: Rodopi, 2006.

Kerr, Rosalind. *The Rise of the Diva on the Sixteenth-Century Commedia dell'Arte Stage.* Toronto, University of Toronto Press, 2015.

Lazzeri, Alessandro. *Il principe e il diplomatico: Ferdinando II tra il destino e la storia.* Florence: Edizioni Medicea, 1996.

Lindenberger, Herbert. *Situating Opera: Period, Genre, Reception.* Cambridge: Cambridge University Press, 2010.

MacNeil, Anne. *Music and Women of the Commedia dell'Arte in the Late Sixteenth Century.* Oxford: Oxford University Press, 2003.

Mamone, Sara. "Accademie e opera in musica nella vita di Giovan Carlo, Mattias e Leopoldo de' Medici, fratelli del Granduca Ferdinando." In *Lo stupor dell'invenzione: Firenze e la nascita dell'opera: Atti del Convegno internazionale di studi, Firenze, 5–6 ottobre 2000*, edited by Piero Gargiulo, 119–38. Florence: Olschki, 2001.

———. "Most Serene Brothers-Princes-Impresarios: Theater in Florence under the Management and Protection of Mattias, Giovan Carlo, and Leopoldo de' Medici." *Journal of Seventeenth-Century Music* 9, no. 1 (2003). <http://sscm-jscm.org/v9/no1/mamone.html>.

———. *Serenissimi fratelli principi impresari: Notizie di spettacolo nei carteggi medicei: Carteggi di Giovan Carlo de' Medici e di Desiderio Montemagni suo segretario, 1628–1664.* Florence: Le Lettere, 2003.

———. "Tra tela e scena: vita d'accademia e vita di corte nel primo Seicento fiorentino." *Biblioteca teatrale* 37–38 (1996): 213–28.

Mariti, Luciano. *Commedia ridicolosa: Comici di professione, dilettanti, editoria teatrale nel Seicento: Storia e testi.* Rome: Bulzoni, 1979.

Massar, Phyllis Dearborn. "Presenting Stefano della Bella." *The Metropolitan Museum of Art Bulletin* 27, no. 3 (1968): 159–76.

———. *Presenting Stefano della Bella: Seventeenth-Century Printmaker.* New York: Metropolitan Museum of Art, distributed by New York Graphic Society, 1971.

McClary, Susan. *Desire and Pleasure in Seventeenth-Century Music.* Berkeley: University of California Press, 2012.

McClure, George W. *Parlour Games and the Public Life of Women in Renaissance Italy.* Toronto: University of Toronto Press, 2013.

Meads, Chris. "Narrative and Dramatic Sauces: Reflections upon Creativity, Cookery, and Culinary Metaphor in Some Early Seventeenth-Century Dramatic Prologues." In *Renaissance Food from Rabelais to Shakespeare: Culinary Readings and Culinary Histories*, edited by Joan Fitzpatrick, 145–66. Burlington, VT: Ashgate, 2010.

Megale, Teresa. "Altre novità su Anna Francesca Costa e sull'allestimento dell'*Ergirodo*." *Medioevo e Rinascimento* 7, no. 4 (1993): 137–42.

———. "La commedia decifrata: Metamorfosi e rispecchiamenti in *Li Buffoni* di Margherita Costa." *Il Castello di Elsinore* 2 (1988): 64–76.

———. "Il principe e la cantante: Riflessi impresariali di una protezione." *Medioevo e Rinascimento* 6 (1992): 211–33.

———. "Sproporzioni: Il teatro dell'assurdo buffonesco all'ombra dei Medici." In *Buffoni, villani e giocatori alla corte dei Medici*, edited by Anna Bisceglia, Matteo Ceriana, Simona Mammana, 69–71. Livorno: Sillabe, 2016.

Merrick, Jeffrey. "The Cardinal and the Queen: Sexual and Political Disorders in the *Mazarinades*." *French Historical Studies* 18, no. 3 (1994): 667–99.

Minor, Vernon Hyde. *The Death of the Baroque and the Rhetoric of Good Taste.* Cambridge: University of Cambridge Press, 2006.

Modesti, Adelina. "The Self-Fashioning of a Female 'Prince': The Cultural Matronage of Vittoria della Rovere." In *Representing Women's Authority in the Early Modern World: Struggles, Strategies, and Morality*, edited by Eavan O'Brien, 253–98. Rome: Aracne, 2013.

Monaldini, Sergio. *L'orto dell'Esperidi: Musici, attori e artisti nel patrocinio della famiglia Bentivoglio, 1646–1685.* Lucca: Libreria Musicale Italiana, 2000.

Morandini, Giuliana. *Sospiri e palpiti: Scrittrici italiane del Seicento.* Genoa: Marietti, 2001.

Nagler, A. M. *Theater Festivals of the Medici, 1539–1637.* New York: Da Capo Press, 1976.

Newcomb, Anthony. "Courtesans, Muses or Musicians? Professional Women Musicians in Sixteenth-Century Italy." In *Women Making Music: The Western Art Tradition, 1150–1950*, edited by Jane Bowers and Judith Tick, 90–115. Urbana: University of Illinois Press, 1987.

Nicoll, Allardyce. *The World of Harlequin: A Critical Study of the Commedia dell'Arte*. Cambridge: Cambridge University Press, 1963.

Norman, Larry F., ed. *The Theatrical Baroque*. Chicago: David and Alfred Smart Museum of Art, University of Chicago, 2001.

O'Bryan, Robin. "Grotesque Bodies, Princely Delight: Dwarfs in Italian Renaissance Court Imagery." *Preternature: Critical and Historical Studies on the Preternatural* 1, no. 2 (2012): 252–88.

Paoli, Maria Pia. "'Come se mi fosse sorella': Maria Selvaggia Borghini nella Repubblica delle lettere." In *Per lettera: La scrittura epistolare femminile, tra archivio e tipografia: secoli XV–XVII*, edited by Gabriella Zarri, 491–534. Rome: Viella, 1999.

Pietropaolo, Domenico, ed. *The Science of Buffoonery: Theory and History of the Commedia dell'Arte*. Ottawa, Canada: Dovehouse, 1989.

Pirrotta, Nino and Elena Povoledo. *Music and Theater from Poliziano to Monteverdi*. Translated by Karen Eales. Cambridge: Cambridge University Press, 1982.

Pollak, Martha D. *Turin, 1564–1680: Urban Design, Military Culture, and the Creation of the Absolutist Capital*. Chicago: University of Chicago Press, 1991.

The Princeton Encyclopedia of Poetry and Poetics. Edited by Alex Preminger. Princeton, NJ: Princeton University Press, 1965.

Pruiksma, Rose A. "Music, Sex, and Ethnicity: Signification in Lully's Theatrical Chaconnes." In *Gender, Sexuality, and Early Music*, edited by Todd M. Borgerding, 227–48. New York: Routledge, 2002.

Prunières, Henry. *L'opéra italien en France avant Lulli*. Paris: E. Champion, 1913.

Rasi, Luigi. *La caricatura e i comici italiani*. Florence: R. Bemporado e figlio, 1907.

Ray, Meredith. *Daughters of Alchemy: Women and Scientific Culture in Early Modern Italy*. Cambridge, MA: Harvard University Press, 2015.

———. "Letters and Lace. Arcangela Tarabotti and Convent Culture in Seicento Venice." In *Early Modern Women and Transnational Communities of Letters*, edited by Julie D. Campbell and Anne R. Larsen, 45–74. Burlington, VT: Ashgate, 2009.

———. *Margherita Sarrocchi's Letters to Galileo: Astronomy, Astrology, and Poetics in Seventeenth-Century Italy*. New York: Palgrave Macmillan, 2016.

———. *Writing Gender in Women's Letter Collections of the Italian Renaissance*. Toronto: University of Toronto Press, 2009.

Refini, Eugenio. "Prologhi figurati: Appunti sull'uso della prosopopea nel prologo teatrale del Cinquecento." *Italianistica* 35, no. 3 (2006): 61–86.

Rosand, Ellen. "Barbara Strozzi, 'virtuosissima cantatrice': The Composer's Voice." *Journal of the American Musicological Society* 31, no. 2 (1978): 241–81.

———. *Monteverdi's Last Operas: A Venetian Trilogy*. Berkeley: University of California Press, 2007.

———. *Opera in Seventeenth-Century Venice: The Creation of a Genre*. Berkeley: University of California Press, 1991.

Rosselli, John. *Singers of Italian Opera: The History of a Profession*. Cambridge: Cambridge University Press, 1992.

Rosenthal, Laura J. "'All injury's forgot': Restoration Sex Comedy and National Amnesia." *Comparative Drama* 42, no. 1 (2008): 7–28.

Rosow, Lois. "Power and Display: Music in Court Theater." In *The Cambridge History of Seventeenth-Century Music*, edited by Tim Carter and John Butt, 197–240. Cambridge: Cambridge University Press, 2005.

Rosselli, John. *Singers of Italian Opera: The History of a Profession*. Cambridge: Cambridge University Press, 1992.

Ruggiero, Guido. "Introduction: Hunting for Birds in the Italian Renaissance." In *Erotic Cultures of Renaissance Italy*, edited by Sara F. Matthews-Grieco, 1–18. Burlington, VT: Ashgate, 2010.

Rutgers, Jaco. "A Frontispiece for Galileo's *Opere*: Pietro Anichini and Stefano della Bella." *Print Quarterly* 29, no. 1 (2012): 3–12.

Salvi, Marcella. "'Il solito è sempre quello, l'insolito è più nuovo': *Li buffoni* e le prostitute di Margherita Costa fra tradizione e innovazione." *Forum italicum* 38, no. 2 (2004): 376–99.

Saslow, James M. *The Medici Wedding of 1589: Florentine Festival as Theatrum Mundi*. New Haven: Yale University Press, 1996.

Sica, Anna. *Eros nell'arte: Lo spettacolo delle maschere*. Palermo: L'epos, 1999.

Spera, Lucinda, ed. *Verso il moderno: Pubblico e immaginario nel Seicento italiano*. Rome: Carocci, 2008.

Stampino, Maria Galli. "A Regent and Her Court: Towards a Study of Maria Maddalena d'Austria's Patronage (Florence 1621–1628)." *Forum Italicum* 40, no. 1 (2006): 22–35.

Stein, Louise K. "How Opera Traveled." In *The Oxford Handbook of Opera*, edited by Helen M. Greenwald, 843–61. Oxford: Oxford University Press, 2014.

Strappini, Lucia, ed. *I luoghi dell'immaginario barocco: Atti del convegno di Siena, 21–23 ottobre 1999*. Naples: Liguori, 2001

———. *La tragedia del buffone: Percorsi del comico e del tragico nel teatro del XVII secolo*. Rome: Bulzoni, 2003.

Straussman-Pflanzer, Eve. *Court Culture in Seventeenth-Century Florence: The Art Patronage of Medici Grand-Duchess Vittoria della Rovere, 1622–1694*. PhD diss., New York University, Institute of Fine Arts, 2010.

Stoppato, Lisa Goldenberg. *The Grand Duke's Portraitist: Cosimo III de' Medici and his "Chamber of Paintings" by Giusto Suttermans*. Livorno: Sillabe, 2006.

Taviani, Ferdinando. "Cecchini, Pier Maria." In *DBI* 23 (1979): 274–80. <http://www.treccani.it/enciclopedia/pier-maria-cecchini_(Dizionario-Biografico)/>.

———, ed. *La commedia dell'arte e la società barocca.* 2 vols. Rome: Bulzoni, 1969, 1991.

Tessari, Roberto. *Commedia dell'arte: La maschera e l'ombra.* Milan: Mursia, 1981.

Thompson, Roger. *Unfit for Modest Ears: A Study of Pornographic, Obscene and Bawdy Works Written or Published in England in the Second Half of the Seventeenth Century*. London: Macmillan, 1979.

Treadwell, Nina. *Music and Wonder at the Medici Court: The 1589 Interludes for* La Pellegrina. Bloomington: Indiana University Press, 2008.

Treasure, Geoffrey. *Mazarin: The Crisis of Absolutism in France.* London: Routledge, 1995.

Ugolini, Paola. "Paradoxical Virtues: Intellectuals Between the Court and the Academy in Agostino Mascardi's *Che la corte è vera scuola non solamente della prudenza ma delle virtù morali* (1624)." *The Italianist* 34, no. 1 (2014): 54–72.

Varriano, John. "Fruits and Vegetables as Sexual Metaphor in Late Renaissance Rome." *Gastronomica: The Journal of Food and Culture* 5, no. 4 (2005): 8–14.

Vianello, Daniele. *L'arte del buffone: Maschere e spettacolo tra Italia e Baviera nel XVI secolo.* Rome: Bulzoni, 2005.

———. "Tra inferno e paradiso: Il 'limbo' dei buffoni," *Biblioteca teatrale* 49–51 (1999): 13–80.

Viatte, Françoise. "Allegorical and Burlesque Subjects by Stefano della Bella." *Master Drawings* 15, no. 4 (1977): 347–65 and 425–44.

Warrack, John. *German Opera: From the Beginnings to Wagner.* Cambridge: Cambridge University Press, 2001.

Watanabe-O'Kelly, Helen. "The Equestrian Ballet in Seventeenth-Century Europe — Origin, Description, Development." *German Life and Letters* 36, no. 3 (1983): 198–212.

Webb, Ruth. *Demons and Dancers: Performance in Late Antiquity.* Cambridge, MA: Harvard University Press, 2008.

Westwater, Lynn. *The Disquieting Voice: Women's Writing and Antifeminism in Seventeenth-Century Venice.* PhD diss., University of Chicago, 2003.

Wilbourne, Emily. *Seventeenth-Century Opera and the Sound of the Commedia dell'Arte.* Chicago: University of Chicago Press, 2016.

Wind, Barry. *"A Foul and Pestilent Congregation": Images of "Freaks" in Baroque Art.* Burlington, VT: Ashgate, 1998.

Wootton, David. *Galileo: Watcher of the Skies.* New Haven: Yale University Press, 2010.

Index

Page numbers in italics indicate illustrations.